HOUSEHOLD AND STATE IN UPPER MESOPOTAMIA

SMITHSONIAN SERIES IN ARCHAEOLOGICAL INQUIRY

Bruce D. Smith and Robert McC. Adams, Series Editors

The Smithsonian Series in Archaeological Inquiry presents original case studies that address important general research problems and demonstrate the values of particular theoretical or methodological approaches. Titles include well-focused collections as well as works by individual authors. The series is open to all subject areas, geographical regions, and theoretical modes.

PATRICIA WATTENMAKER

HOUSEHOLD AND STATE IN UPPER MESOPOTAMIA

SPECIALIZED ECONOMY AND THE SOCIAL USES OF GOODS IN AN EARLY COMPLEX SOCIETY

SMITHSONIAN INSTITUTION PRESS
WASHINGTON AND LONDON

COPY EDITOR: Debbie K. Hardin
PRODUCTION EDITOR: Jack Kirshbaum

Library of Congress Cataloging-in-Publication Data

Wattenmaker, Patricia.
Household and state in upper Mesopotamia : specialized economy and the social uses of goods in an early complex society / Patricia Wattenmaker
p. cm.
Includes bibliographical references and index.
ISBN 1-56098-782-0 (alk. paper)
1. Kurban Höyük Site (Turkey) 2. Copper age—Turkey—Karbaba Basin. 3. Bronze age—Turkey—Karbaba Basin. 4. Industries, Prehistoric—Turkey—Karbaba Basin. 5. Economics, Prehistoric—Turkey—Karbaba Basin. 6. Excavations (Archaeology)—Turkey—Karbaba Basin. 7. Karbaba Basin (Turkey)—Antiquities. I. Title.
GN778.32.T9W37 1998
939.2—dc21 98-4881

British Library Cataloguing-in-Publication Data is available

Manufactured in the United States of America
04 03 02 01 00 99 98 5 4 3 2 1

♾ The paper used in this publication meets the minimum requirements of the American National Standard for Information Sciences—Permanence of Paper for Printed Library Materials ANSI Z39.48-1984.

TO MY PARENTS, EDITH AND BERNARD WATTENMAKER

CONTENTS

PREFACE

During a brief period in the history of Near Eastern archaeology, traces of an early urban society inhabiting the area known today as Turkish Euphrates Valley, Şanlıurfa Province, were exposed by archaeologists. The 1980s was an exciting time to be working in this region. Turkish government plans for the construction of the Karakaya and Ataturk Dams in the upper Euphrates Basin of southeast Turkey led to pioneering surveys of the area by Ümit Serdaroglŭ (1977) and Mehmet Özdoğan (1977). Prior to this work, little was known of the prehistory of the upper Euphrates area. These surveys helped launch an international salvage project sponsored by the Turkish Ministry of Culture to excavate numerous sites that would be flooded when the dams were to be filled just over a decade later. The first archaeological salvage expeditions in the Ataturk Dam area were initiated in 1979. By the time excavations connected with this international salvage project came to a close between 1984 and 1991, the various projects had together revised understanding of this part of southwest Asia.

This work would not have been possible without the support of the Turkish Ministry of Culture and Directorate of Monuments and Museums, then headed by Drs. Hikmet Gurcay and Nurettin Yardımcı.

It is with sorrow as well as gratitude that I must acknowledge Mr. Adnan Mısır, director of the Şanlıurfa Museum when I conducted this fieldwork. His untimely death in June 1997 represents a major loss to Middle Eastern archaeology. His dedication to the archaeology of Turkey and active support of numerous excavations have made Şanlıurfa Province one of the best documented areas of Syro-Anatolia for the period of early urbanism. Without his support and assistance throughout the course of my fieldwork, this project would not have been possible.

In 1980, when the first excavations at Kurban Höyük commenced, the complexity and scale of urbanism in upper Mesopotamia during the mid-third millennium B.C. was only beginning to be realized. Only two years earlier, Seyton Lloyd (1978) had published his book, *The Archaeology of Mesopotamia,* which included a chapter on the north titled, "Illiterate Peoples of Northern Mesopotamia." Yet, perceptions of third millennium B.C. northern Mesopotamian societies were beginning to change as work continued at known sites, and new centers were discovered. Chuera, an urban site between the Balikh and Khabur river valleys in north Syria, only approximately 150 km southeast of Kurban Höyük, grew to 100 ha. in the mid-third millennium B.C. (Kühne 1976; Moortgat and Moortgat-Correns 1975). Further to the east, urban centers such as Hamoukar (van Liere 1963, fig. 3b) and Tell Brak were already known from the upper Khabur region of northeast Syria. Tell Taya provided an example of an early city on the northern plains of Iraq (Reade 1968). Perhaps most significant, the 1975 discovery of more than 15,000 cuneiform tablets and fragments from Tell Mardikh (ancient Ebla) in northwest Syria provided incontrovertible evidence that at least this center had a sufficiently complex economic and political system to require the extensive use of written records by the administrative elites (Pettinato 1991).

Despite the growing realization that the degree of political centralization and scale of urbanism in upper Mesopotamia had been underestimated, researchers adhered to the assumption that societies in southeast Anatolia were simply organized and less complex than those on the upper Mesopotamian plain. In retrospect, there were numerous hints that societies in southeast Anatolia were part of the great upper Mesopotamian urban process of the mid-third millennium B.C. The Ebla texts provided clues that sites in southeast Anatolia were closely linked to the north Mesopotamian urban sites. Harran, approximately 90 km southeast of Kurban Höyük, was known to be a major political and economic center in the mid-third millennium B.C. Yet, no urban centers or public buildings were known from the Turkish Euphrates region prior to the Roman occupation at Samsat. The small sizes of the known sites in the Euphrates Basin, where most surveys and excavations took place, caused archaeologists to hold to the traditional view of this area as one that lacked a centralized political system.

Discoveries on several projects during the 1980s revealed that although settlements in the Euphrates Basin were indeed smaller than those on the Mesopotamian plain, they were nonetheless hierarchically organized and economically specialized. For example, Dr. Harold Hauptmann, director of excavations at Lidar Höyük, uncovered a large kiln workshop (Hauptmann 1983b, 255), providing clear evidence for specialized pottery production. Together with Mr. Mısır he excavated a series of tombs at Titriş Höyük. Differences between graves hinted at some degree of social stratification. Tony Wilkinson's survey (1990) of the Kurban Höyük hinterland traced the formation of a differentiated settlement system that included a center as well as large and smaller towns in the mid-third millennium B.C. Perhaps most significant for changing our understanding of the area, in 1983 Wilkinson (1990) found that Titris Höyük, located on a tributary of the Euphrates River just over 20 km from Kurban Höyük, was an urban-sized center in the mid-third millennium B.C. This altered our impressions of the scale of the system in the Upper Euphrates Basin and provided a likely candidate for a regional center. These discoveries, as well as those from excavation of neighborhoods at Kurban Höyük during the 1981–1983 seasons, caused me to question prevalent views about the organization of mid-third millennium societies of southeast Anatolia.

My interest in the ancient non-elite households that formed the backbone of this newly discovered urban society developed while I worked on the Oriental Institute excavations at Kurban Höyük in the capacity of zooarchaeologist. I owe the opportunity to join the Kurban project to both Robert McC. Adams and Leon Marfoe. The team had uncovered a series of building remains that varied in the scale and care with which they were constructed. In his analysis of ceramics from the site, Guillermo Algaze (1990b) observed that wheel-made ceramics were common across the site, raising the possibility that specialist-produced goods were widely distributed in this society. In the study of animal bones, I found that as early as the fourth millennium B.C., some neighborhoods appear to have been raising and exporting animals, possibly as tribute (Wattenmaker and Stein 1986). These findings led me to wonder (1) why people who apparently lived in modest structures and had few possessions chose to use highly standardized, well-made, and sometimes decorated ceramics produced in workshops and (2) how their increasing participation in the specialized economy related to factors such as the increasing political centralization, tribute demands, and differentiation between elites and commoners that took place during this time. I will return to these questions, which form the heart of this book, in Chapter 1.

Although the sites in the vicinity of Kurban are now flooded, work continues in adjacent areas (cf. Algaze et al 1992). In 1992 I began excavations of a mid-third millennium walled city at the site of Kazane, just 50 km southeast of Kurban Höyük, in collaboration with Mr. Mısır. In the first season of mapping, we determined that Kazane grew to 100 ha by approximately 2500 B.C. The realization that Kurban Höyük was just beyond, if not part of, an urban system of the scale found elsewhere in north Mesopotamia helped account for the high degree of economic specialization we found in the Euphrates Valley. It was the unexpected complexity of small settlements and modest houses from sites like Gritille Höyük (in Adiyaman Province), Kurban Höyük, and Lidar Höyük that led me to re-examine traditional assumptions regarding the nature of sociopolitical organization in this area. It is now clear that Şanlıurfa Province provides a new case study with which to examine urbanism in Upper Mesopotamia.

A project such as this, which draws on studies by a number of researchers and was conducted in a number of institutions, incurs many debts. It is a pleasure to finally be able to acknowledge the friends and colleagues who helped bring this work to fruition. The excavations for this project were conducted as part of the Oriental Institute, University of Chicago, excavations at Kurban Höyük, directed by Dr. Leon Marfoe. The fieldwork at Kurban Höyük was sponsored by the Oriental Institute and funded primarily through grants to the University of Chicago and Leon Marfoe from the National Endowment for the Humanities as well as private donors. I am indebted to the Oriental Institute, Marfoe, and Janet Johnson, director of the Oriental Institute at the time that I worked with the Kurban field records, for allowing me to conduct this study, as well as for logistical support and access to field records.

I first conceived of this book while I was a graduate student at the Museum of Anthropology, University of Michigan. This project has benefited from the advice and comments of several faculty members on proposals and manuscripts. Henry Wright encouraged me to pursue my research interests by extending the study of the Kurban faunal remains to other categories of data as well. Throughout the course of this research, he has provided invaluable suggestions, insights, and comments on manuscripts. Joyce Marcus too has been a source of encouragement since I was an undergraduate student. Her theoretical expertise on complex societies has had a major impact on my approach to the ancient Near East. From John Speth's accounts of his own research experiences and the complex relationship between hypotheses and data, I was inspired to develop the construct presented in this book. I first became aware of the rich historical record from my research area in a seminar on the Ebla archives offered by Piotr Michalowski. His enthusiasm for combining the fields of assyriology and archaeology encouraged me to make use of published epigraphic data and deal with questions that I could not have addressed with archaeology alone. Kent Flannery kindly gave me space in his laboratory, and I am grateful for his support of this project through the years. An earlier version of this manuscript also benefited from the careful comments of Jeffrey Parsons.

The staff members of the Oriental Institute excavations at Kurban Höyük contributed to this study in various ways. The excavations I conducted expanded on earlier work supervised by numerous members of the Kurban team. Without their careful work and detailed recording, this study would not have been possible. The first excavations of Areas B and G were initiated by Thomas McClellan and Leon Marfoe, respectively. Michael Ingraham, Naomi Miller, and Kathy Ataman assisted with the 1984 excavations in Areas B and G. Judy Wilkinson, photographer for the Kurban excavations, took many of the photographs of the excavations included in this book. Funding from the American Schools of Oriental Research, the University of Michigan Museum of Anthropology, and the Sigma Xi Foundation allowed me to conduct this study.

Following the excavations, I spent a year in Turkey completing the analysis of artifacts. This phase of the research was funded by a Fulbright Scholarship and a grant from the American Research Institute in Turkey. In addition, a grant awarded by the American Schools of Oriental Research to Gil Stein supported his work on chipped stone. A number of people throughout Turkey facilitated this research. I am grateful to Halet Çambel, Mehmet Özdoğan, Ilknur Özgen, and Engin Özgen for their help in many phases of this research. Toni Cross, director of the American Research Institute in Turkey, provided assistance throughout the course of this study. David French and Ann Murray, then director and assistant director of The British Institute of Archaeology at Ankara, generously allowed me to make use of the Institute's zoological comparative collection and library facilities. Gul Pulhan assisted with the Area B excavations, analyses of ceramics, and many logistical aspects of this study. Kathy Ataman assisted with analysis of chipped stone.

I am fortunate to have such generous and talented colleagues working in southeast Turkey. While working at Kurban Höyük, I benefited from numerous discussions with Guillermo Algaze, Naomi Miller, and Tony Wilkinson. From start to finish, Guillermo Algaze consistently offered his support, time, data, and expertise in complex societies of the Near East. He has helped in matters ranging from providing unpublished ceramic data, discussing ideas, and reading sections of manuscripts on short notice. Gil Stein also assisted with various aspects of this project, including analysis of chipped stone artifacts, comments on an earlier draft of this manuscript, and the completion of many of the illustrations. Researchers from nearby projects who helped in important ways include Richard Ellis, Charles Gates, Marie-Henriette Gates, Harold Hauptmann, Scott Redford, Glenn Schwartz, and Mary Voigt.

A fellowship from the Smithsonian Institution allowed me to complete the analysis of mid-third millennium animal bones from Kurban Höyük. I am grateful to Bruce Smith and Melinda Zeder for their support of this phase of the research. Mindy's support of my interest in zooarchaeology dates back to my undergraduate years, when she took time out of her own busy student schedule to train me in zooarchaeology. This work has benefited from numerous discussions with her since that time.

Many other colleagues and friends have contributed to the completion of this book in various ways. Though the list is much longer, some of these include Richard Handler, Jeffrey Hantman, Michelle Hegmon, Mary Hodge, Adria LaViolette, Susan McKinnon, Steve Plog, Richard Redding, Carla Sinopoli, and Bruce Verhaaren. Julie Perlmutter completed Figures 1, 2, and 39. Thanks also to Debbie Hardin for her editorial improvements to the manuscript, and to Robert Lockhart and Jack Kirshbaum of the Smithsonian Institution Press for their patience and advice in the editing and production stages of this project. This manuscript has benefited from the comments of an anonymous reviewer as well. I thank Alan Ash for his understanding and encouragement.

This volume is dedicated to my parents, Edith and Bernard Wattenmaker, who have always enthusiastically supported my interest in archaeology. Although my father did not live to see this book in its final form, he provided steadfast and thoughtful support for this project that dated from the first field season until the final manuscript was completed.

1 THE ECONOMICS AND SYMBOLISM OF SPECIALIZED PRODUCTION IN EARLY COMPLEX SOCIETIES

Well, if we're in the pottery business, we ought to have a place to be. The way we are, when people come to the pueblo to buy pottery, they come right to our house. I'm going to make a room for them to come to. Then, they won't be tracking dirt all over the floor, and seeing what I'm cooking for dinner.

Maria Martinez, master potter, about 1915. San Ildefonso Pueblo (as quoted in Marriott, 1948)

Why does economic specialization intensify as societies become more politically complex? Understanding the cultural context for why people want particular goods is central to explaining the growth of specialized economies. Although ethnographic studies reveal that many societies have resisted becoming involved in specialized economies, the archaeological record illustrates a general trend toward increasing specialization as complex societies developed (e.g., Clark and Parry 1990; Johnson and Earle 1987). Yet, there is no widely accepted explanation for why people of ancient societies increasingly desired goods produced by specialists as their societies grew and became more hierarchically organized.

Douglas and Isherwood stated the problem well: "It is extraordinary to discover that no one knows why people want goods" (1979, 15). Since this statement was made, there have been numerous anthropological works that examine the meaning and uses of goods (e.g., Appadurai 1986; McCracken 1988; Thomas 1991). Within the field of archaeology, efforts to understand demand for specialist-produced goods have focused largely on *political elites,* with relatively little consideration of consumption among *non-elites.* However, production and consumption are vital components of social process for all members of a society, and exclusion of non-elite consumption patterns from many archaeological studies has resulted in biased and incomplete understanding of how and why people produced and used goods in the past.

Reasons for increasing demand for specialist-produced goods are investigated in this study of economic change associated with political centralization at the site of Kurban Höyük (Mound of Sacrifice) in the Euphrates Valley of Upper Mesopotamia. Mid- to late-third millennium B.C. neighborhoods were excavated to determine why households increased their reliance on specialists as complex societies developed. To help understand why people increasingly wanted goods produced by specialists in one early state society, I will examine evidence for changes in food and craft production and consumption during an approximately 500-year period of increasing sociopolitical complexity. I will then use the findings to evaluate an explanation to account for increasing economic specialization in non-elite households. The proposed explanation links changes in production organization to the changing role of goods in communicating social information in complex societies. Results of the study call into question the widely held view that specialization in early state society served primarily to meet elite demands for prestige goods. They also question the assumption that when specialization did occur among the non-elites, it resulted primarily from the need for more efficient production. Based on findings, I propose a new construct for factors guiding production and consumption among both the elites and non-elites in early state societies. This construct addresses the basic question of why people want goods, and provides a social context for the increased demand for select categories of goods.

PERSPECTIVES ON ECONOMIC SPECIALIZATION IN EARLY COMPLEX SOCIETIES

As discussed in the introduction to this chapter, most efforts by archaeologists to understand economic specialization have focused on specialization that benefited the elite class. This may stem from the relatively greater visibility of specialist-produced goods in the elite sphere, as a consequence of the traditional emphasis in archaeology on the recovery of elite architecture, sumptuary goods, and texts. Specialized production by lower ranking households not working primarily for the state (in the capacity of low-level administrators, centrally sponsored craft specialists, etc.) has received little attention, in part because detecting specialization on this level requires careful recovery and detailed analysis of the ubiquitous but less spectacular categories of artifacts, such as pot sherds and flint debitage. Although specialization of goods at the non-elite level is not as conspicuous in the archaeological record, regional surveys and excavations in both the Old (Falconer 1994; Johnson 1973; Wright 1981) and New (Blanton et al. 1982; Marcus 1983, 217; Sheets 1992) Worlds have revealed that smaller sites of some early state systems did participate in specialized economies. Because of the lack of studies focusing on non-elite economies in the ancient Near East, basic questions remained unanswered. These include the proportion of households involved in specialized economy and the aspects of household economy that were transformed (e.g., subsistence production or craft production). These questions must be addressed before one can understand why specialized economies developed.

In order to clarify the role of specialized economy in early state societies, this study examines production on the non-elite, domestic level. I consider the degree to which members of households in an early state society produced their own goods and surpluses for exchange, the extent to which households procured specialist-produced goods, the changes in these patterns as the state society developed, and the reasons for these changes.

Specialization is defined as the production of either comestible or nonedible goods for consumption by social groups other than those that produced them. This definition emphasizes the productive context rather than the means of distribution, and intentionally includes not only exchange but also means of asymmetrical distribution, such as tribute sent to political elites. Production specialization was monitored at Kurban Höyük through the analysis of the spatial location and density of manufacturing implements and industrial by-products compared with the location and density of finished products found in residential areas. This approach permits assessment of the degree of specialization and does not depend on the chance recovery of workshops of specialists.

Specialization is viewed as a complex process with many facets, including the proportion of time invested in production, the way production is organized, and the categories of goods produced. Specialized production may range from occasional specialization by one person in less complex economies to specialized production of most goods in more complex societies. The goods produced by specialists may serve various subgroups of a society, including the political elites or low-status households. In complex societies, specialization takes on a multitude of forms, such as small-scale surplus production by households, surplus production by specialists in spatially segregated workshops that operate without intervention from the political elite, and administered production (Sinopoli 1988, 1994; see also Balfet 1965; Brumfiel and Earle 1987, 5; Costin 1991, 5; Peacock 1982, 8–9; van der Leeuw 1984, 720–24). It may be organized in various ways, such as on the extended family level, community level, or regional level.

This study distinguishes between three contexts of specialized production: *small-scale specialized production, nucleated production,* and *administered production.* The first two terms refer to the scale and locations of workshops. The distinction between small-scale specialized production and nucleated production is a relative one. *Small-scale specialized production* refers to surplus production (for exchange) in a relatively informal setting, such as a house or small workshop associated with a house. Specialized production in this context is more likely to be carried out relatively infrequently. *Nucleated production* refers to production in larger scale and spatially segregated workshops. Either form of production may be administered, or may operate independently of political intervention. Following Sinopoli (1988, 581), I use the term *administered production* to refer to production that is regulated by the political elite. In theory, production on any level (e.g., small-scale specialized production, nucleated production) may be administered, although administered production is most easily recognizable in an archaeological situation when workshops are nucleated and associated with administrative buildings or artifacts.

Productive specialization represents part of an integrated system of production, exchange, and consumption that cannot be fully understood without reference to the factors guiding consumption patterns. In this study, goods are viewed as part of cultural information systems, with the value of a good depending on its culturally assigned role within a specific information system (Appadurai 1986, 29; Douglas and Isherwood 1979; Veblen 1934, 84). The use of goods to convey social information stems from the fact that they make tangible and relatively stable statements about categories of culture (Douglas and Isherwood 1979, 4–5, 59, 67). A person's choice of goods contributes to his or her efforts to create and express a sense of social identity and order (Douglas and Isherwood 1979, 5).

In many economic studies, anthropologists distinguish between *sumptuary* and *utilitarian* goods. Although this dichotomy may be useful for some purposes, it has obscured the role of goods in other cases. Many goods have multiple functions, and a specific good may be viewed as both being a symbol of prestige and as having a useful, if not essential, function (e.g., a sports car in modern American society or a horse in ancient Mesopotamia). A good considered a prestige symbol in one segment of society may be neutral or even undesirable in another sector. When goods are viewed as an integral part of a cultural system—rather than as a reflection of culture—then all goods function to express and maintain, if not reproduce or change, aspects of that culture. Thus, prestige goods may have a utilitarian function (to communicate and maintain rank differences), and utilitarian goods, which also convey social information (e.g., cultural identity, geographic affiliation) have symbolic value. For these reasons this study avoids the conventional dichotomy between *prestige goods* and *utilitarian goods.* Some readers may be troubled by this treatment of household or utilitarian goods as laden with symbolic meaning. However, by virtue of being designed and constructed by members of a culture, it is inescapable that goods, however mundane their functions, bear social information. As Hodder (1982) has shown, it is the information embedded in widely used household goods that appeals to the consumers and accounts for why consumers may go to extra effort to obtain one kind of good over another.

THEORIES ON THE RISE OF SPECIALIZED ECONOMIES

Most explanations for specialization center around two key characteristics. The first is the potential for greater efficiency that specialization provides. Specialized production makes it possible to produce greater amounts with less effort, because supplies are delivered to fewer locations and workers develop greater speed and efficiency when tasks are repeated at greater frequencies (Blau 1977, 188). This attribute of specialized production has been emphasized by archaeologists in explanations of specialization on the non-elite level. Such explanations often implicitly assume that efficiency and effort minimization would have been major concerns in archaic state societies, assumptions that may be incorrect.

Second, explanations for specialized production often emphasize the potential to produce higher quality goods as a result of the greater skill that develops through practice or the natural talent of the specialist (Blau 1977, 188). This characteristic has been used to account for the use of specialists to produce sumptuary goods for the elite.

Compelling as these advantages of specialization may seem, there are also serious disadvantages to specialized production. Although specialization is more efficient than household production for creating large quantities of surplus or high quality goods, not all societies value surplus or the high quality products of specialists (Douglas and Isherwood 1979; Sahlins 1972, 41, 211–12). Even in instances in which opportunities exist for obtaining exotic goods through trade, groups have not always participated in such trade (e.g., Evans-Prichard 1974, 88; Gell 1986; see Thomas 1991, 1). The lack of interest in producing surpluses among some societies stems in part from the absence of an association between status and wealth. This reflects the fact that goods do not have an intrinsic value—that they in fact are valueless until endowed with meaning within a society's communication system (Douglas and Isherwood 1979, 12.)

In some societies, the display of exotic goods may be viewed as an act of rebellion and detract from, rather than enhance, the status of the owner (Gell 1986, 111). This suggests that in small-scale societies, in which cohesion and cooperation among all members of a group may be crucial to survival, goods that set members apart are viewed as leading to potential divisiveness. Consumption patterns in such cases have been characterized as "conspicuous parsimony" (Appadurai 1986, 30). Paradoxically, in large-scale complex societies, the formation of subgroups is essential to group cohesion (see Johnson 1982). In these societies, goods that serve to define and demarcate subgroups may actually promote, rather than detract from, social cohesion.

Another reason for a reluctance among consumers to rely on specialists for necessities, or perceived necessities, is that specialization effectively limits the flexibility of a society in times of stress (Sahlins 1972). In order for an economic unit that normally produces a certain essential item to rely on exchange, it must have confidence in the reliability of the exchange system. This is particularly true of agricultural products, which are essential but cannot be produced on short notice if the supply fails. Although the political elite would be partially protected from fluctuations in supplies—because in general they are better able to store surplus and can often obtain food through coercion—the non-elites would be in greater danger of being cut off from supplies. The Aztec economy illustrates the reluctance of people to rely on specialists for food supplies. A highly specialized market system co-existed with rural self-sufficiency in food production; even craft specialists were part-time agriculturalists (Brumfiel 1987, 110–11).

Specialized economies made households more vulnerable to intervention in the economy by the political elites. It is easier for governments to meddle with production and consumption when it occurs in a limited number of workshops than when it occurs on a household basis. Nucleated production paves the way for states to intervene with production through means such as extortion (see Brumfiel 1994, 2), taxation, or diverting supplies or products.

The opening quote provides an example of the intricate link between specialized production and the demand for specialist-produced goods. Martinez established a store, one hallmark of a specialized economy, in *response* to demand for her pots rather than in an effort to create that demand. Increasing specialization of the economy is intricately linked to the demand for specialist-produced goods. The fact that demand for surplus and specialist-produced goods is not culturally universal underscores the need to account for the development of *demand* for specialist-produced goods when attempting to explain the emergence of specialized economies. Therefore, the following discussion of explanations proposed for the development of specialized economies focuses on reasons offered for an increased *demand* for goods produced by specialists.

EXPLANATIONS FOR SPECIALIZATION ON THE ELITE LEVEL

When scholars discuss *elites* in early state societies, they are generally referring to a small percentage of the population enjoying both prestige and comparatively greater access to highly valued resources, such as land. As used in this book, this category includes, but is not restricted to, members of the society who held high-level administrative positions. I use the term *political elites* to refer to members of the society involved in higher order administrative activities.

In accounting for the elite demand for specialist-produced goods in complex societies, scholars have emphasized the symbolic value of goods. In most views, the demand for specialist-produced goods on the elite level was a by-product of the hierarchization of social roles, with specialized economies serving to provide elites with goods of limited availability. The ability of specialists to produce higher quality goods plays a prominent role in explanations of elite demand for specialist-produced craft goods.

It is generally recognized that the display of goods made of scarce materials is a key elite strategy for symbolizing the gulf between themselves and other members of society. Specialized production also plays a crucial role in this process of controlling access to symbols of power (Brumfiel 1994, 3;

Costin 1991, 11; Peregrine 1991, 2; Pollock 1983b, 19; Rowlands 1973, 594). By specifically supporting craft specialists who produce goods of a quality other members of the society are not able to acquire, the elites can control access to those goods, thereby creating symbols of status and power. This strategy is particularly effective when the craft specialists work with scarce raw materials, such as precious metals.

Ownership and display of goods not available to other members of the society provides tangible evidence of power, thereby facilitating the use of authority (Johnson 1982, 409). This may contribute to the demand for prestige symbols in hierarchical societies.

The display of goods that differ from those used by other members of society may be crucial in interactions between the political elite of different polities, because the goods provide foreign elites with verification of prestige. They also serve as items for trade in the formation or maintenance of political alliances. The procurement of foreign trade goods in turn serves as verification of status internally by demonstrating access to foreign goods and knowledge (Flannery 1968, 102; Helms 1988, 263–4). Trade items, like goods of scarce materials or those produced by skilled specialists, are well-suited for use as prestige goods, because they are of limited availability.

In societies in which talented artisans are believed to be gifted by deities, the products of specialists may also be considered to have connections with the supernatural (Davenport 1986, 105; Helms 1988, 117–18). In such cases, possession of goods made by the specialists symbolizes proximity of the owner to the gods. This sacred quality of the goods makes them particularly effective political symbols. By supporting craft specialists and controlling access to their products, the elite of complex societies would effectively be controlling a symbol of proximity to sacred powers and providing proof of their own access to such powers, important verification of their elite standing and authority.

These explanations consider the reasons for the specialized production of limited quantities of sumptuary goods on the elite level; archaeological and ethnohistoric literature show that the political elite were also supplied with subsistence goods in a wide range of complex societies (e.g., Archi 1981, 3; Brumfiel 1976, 247; Peebles and Kus 1977, 425). Elite demand for subsistence products may be met simply through surplus production by households, but in state societies may also involve more structured systems of production or procurement, distribution, and processing of subsistence goods by state-supported specialists. Specialization designed to provide the political elites with food may have arisen to relieve the elites and their dependents (for example, military personnel, craft specialists) from involvement in farming and herding so that they could effectively carry out other responsibilities (e.g., Galvin 1987, 128). Zeder (1988, 5; 1991, 15–16) considered this factor in arguing that specialization will occur when scheduling conflicts arise between different production activities or when nonspecialized modes of production fail to meet demand for a product, presumably because of the greater potential for efficiency with specialized production. She suggested that specialized production and indirect distribution (in which producers and consumers do not come in contact) will be most pronounced in high-status administrative and craft production areas (Zeder 1988, 5, 18, 22; 1991).

Most explanations for specialization on the elite level have focused on the production of prestige goods, rather than utilitarian or subsistence goods; the potentially greater efficiency of specialization was considered only by Zeder (1991), in an effort to account for the provisioning of the elites with subsistence goods. Motives for specialized craft production center on the elite demand for goods of restricted distribution; the obvious inefficiency of production of prestige goods may have enhanced their value (Brumfiel 1994, 8). In contrast, most considerations of specialization on the non-elite level emphasize the potentially greater efficiency in the production of utilitarian goods and comestibles (e.g., Brumfiel 1980, 466).

EXPLANATIONS FOR SPECIALIZATION AMONG THE NON-ELITE

The term *non-elite* is used in a relative sense to refer to those members of a society not involved in political administration and having comparatively modest resources. The identification of the remains of elites and non-elites in the archaeological record is discussed further in Chapter 4. There are few explanations for specialization among the non-elites, perhaps because the existence of such specialization in prehistoric and early historic societies is not widely acknowledged.

Two explanations that have been offered for household productive specialization emphasize the greater efficiency of specialized economies and attempt to identify the stresses that created the need for more efficient economic organization. Focusing on food production systems and the rise of specialized nomadic pastoralism in Mesopotamia, Lees and Bates (1974, 189–90) suggested that conflicts in household labor allocation for agricultural activities and pastoralism led to household specialization in either agricultural or animal production. Because this hypothesis focuses on irrigation agriculture and the time-consuming activities it involves, it is not directly applicable to Upper Mesopotamia, where irrigation was probably not used in the third millennium B.C. (Wilkinson 1990, 1994). However, the essential component of this construct, the emergence of scheduling conflicts on the household level, is of general utility.

A second model focuses on the political centralization, consequent increased surplus production (see Sahlins 1972, 140), and household production reorganization. Blanton et al. (1982, 22–3) suggested that household scheduling conflicts in production activities may have led to the development of specialized regional economies in the Valley of Oaxaca, Mexico. They propose that increased demands on households to provision the capital may have led to agricultural intensification, which, in turn, resulted in less time for the production of utilitarian craft goods. Producers experienced a scheduling crisis whereby they faced difficulty meeting surplus demands imposed by the political elites as well as their own needs for food and craft goods. This scheduling crisis created a demand for the products of specialists, ultimately leading to decreased household self-sufficiency. This model for specialized economy in the Valley of Oaxaca is of interest because it proposes a relationship between increased political centralization and increased economic specialization (increased tribute demands), and addresses the underlying question of why the demand for specialist-produced goods increases (time constraints).

This book follows the example of Blanton et al. (1982) in considering reasons for increasing *demand* for specialized goods in complex societies. The construct presented views household productive specialization as a result of changes in the use of goods to communicate social information as state societies developed.

SOCIAL SCALE AND THE USE OF GOODS FOR COMMUNICATING INFORMATION: AN ALTERNATIVE EXPLANATION FOR HOUSEHOLD ECONOMIC SPECIALIZATION

The construct to be evaluated considers specialization to result from changes in the way goods are used in "communication systems" of complex societies, and emphasizes two attributes of specialized production: the potentially greater standardization in products and the enhanced ability to restrict access to goods when they are made by specialists. Changes in the uses of goods are linked to increased social scale and complexity.

It is proposed that two distinct but closely related factors contributed to the shift to specialized production in complex societies, in both the non-elite and elite sectors of society. These include (1) the increased importance of goods to signal social identity, consequent efforts to control access to goods expressing prestige, as well as attempts to gain access to, or imitate, them; and (2) the need for greater standardization within the categories of goods used to convey information as sociopolitical complexity increased. The need for standardization resulted from greater social scale and complexity and the consequent need for more distinctions in social identities to be made by goods (used as communicators). The greater efforts to control access to goods stemmed from increased status differentiation in hierarchical societies and the increased role and effectiveness of materials in signaling status in large-scale societies (see Binford 1972, 29).

The following overview of how goods function in communication systems and why they are used this way is background to the explanation proposed in this chapter for specialization among non-elite households. Archaeologists have tended to treat material aspects of culture as by-products of society, rather than active components of a cultural system. However, goods may play an integral role in maintaining cultural order or in contributing to cultural change.

One aspect of society in which goods play a dynamic role is the communication system. There are a number of reasons why societies use goods to communicate information. Messages conveyed through artifacts provide participants in social interactions with the information needed to guide behavior, such as whether an individual is from a friendly or hostile group (Wobst 1977, 327). Artifacts can also be used to deliberately create specific emotional reactions. For example, the visual impact of monumental art depicting military conquests may inspire fear among the populace or enemies (e.g., Marcus 1973, 90; Winter 1985, 25). Wobst (1977) pointed out that artifacts effectively convey certain social messages, such as ethnic affiliation or status, for several reasons. A message can be produced without the receiver being present, and it can be received without the sender being present. Moreover, messages delivered on material goods may have high visibility because of their portability (e.g., clothes), size (e.g., sculptures), or context of use (e.g., serving vessels used in a public feast). A message can be monopolized by specifying scarce raw materials or costly energy. The visual dimension is relatively easy to manipulate. The fact that certain messages transmitted on artifacts may require the use of specific materials or craft practices, combined with their longevity, facilitates standardization in communication systems. For these reasons, materialistic culture plays a key role in processes of social integration and social differentiation (Wobst 1977, 322).

Wobst (1977, 330) argued that the goods most likely to bear social information are those that are highly visible, come into contact with a large number of individuals, and are present when information is exchanged. For example, a tool used by an individual working alone would be an unlikely candidate for transmitting a message to a large group of people, whereas a headdress would be highly appropriate (Wobst 1977, 328, 334). The delivered messages serve to signal appropriate behavior and minimize stress or ambiguity of social identity in interactions (1977, 327). Within groups, the use of goods symbolizing affiliation serves to reinforce group identity (Hodder 1982, 45; Wobst 1977, 327) and promote group cohesion. Information conveyed by material objects includes membership in ethnic, religious, or social groups; status; motives such as intent to fight; and the nature of specific occasions (Barber 1994, 128; Wobst 1977, 323). While the high social visibility of some goods facilitates their role as communicators of certain kinds of information, such as rank, even goods of relatively low visibility used within the household bear messages for family members about their social identity (e.g., Hodder 1982).

If goods were used to signal group affiliation and status, it is reasonable to expect that increased complexity in sociopolitical organization would result in increased complexity in the message system (see Pollock 1983a, 35). I argue that specialization, and the attendant increased standardization of goods, was an effective response to increased horizontal and vertical complexity that characterized the process of state formation, because it enhanced the ability to convey unambiguously social information through materials in a larger and more diverse society.

SOCIAL COMPLEXITY AND THE ROLE OF GOODS

Increasing scale and social differentiation are critical to the process of increasing specialization among both the elites and non-elites. As discussed previously, in nonhierarchical societies goods function to convey information primarily about ethnicity, group affiliation, age, and gender, or the social significance of a particular occasion. There is relatively little concern with ownership. Goods do not function to convey (hierarchical) social status of individuals.

In large-scale state societies, characterized by both vertical and horizontal complexity, competition for control and access to information and goods is more intense than in less complex societies. Because there is more variability in identity, status, and wealth, there is a greater need for symbols of social identity, and use of goods becomes more important as a means of conveying social information.

State formation, characterized by increased hierarchicization (Wright 1977, 383), is generally associated with increasing demographic scale, although the relationship between these two variables is not clear (Wright and Johnson 1975, 284). Increased vertical complexity in state societies permits an exponential increase in both organizational and demographic scale (Johnson 1982, 408–9). The higher potential for integration resulting from increased hierarchicization (Johnson 1982, 414–15) would make it possible for state societies to absorb larger and more diverse populations, and archaeological evidence suggests that state societies often did so. Once state societies emerge, populations often increase, perhaps partially in response to the need for labor for agricultural activities, military purposes, and so on. Increased sociopolitical complexity and demographic scale in state societies will affect how goods are used because of the greater effectiveness of goods in conveying information as social diversity and social distance between individuals (within a society) increase, as is discussed next.

A close relationship exists between the scale of a society, its organizational complexity, and the use of goods. Ethnographic data indicate a positive correlation between population and organizational complexity (Carneiro 1967), as well as between population size and the degree of craft specialization (Naroll 1956). Increased social scale and diversity result in a greater number of potential social interactions in which the individuals have little or no information about one another. This, in turn, increases the role of goods in conveying information, because the utility of goods to deliver social messages increases with social distance (Wobst 1977, 323). In general, people have more direct contact and know more about one another in smaller societies than in larger ones. The more information one has about another person, the less need there is to receive information through goods, and the less successful will be efforts to manipulate information through display of materials.

The use of goods to make statements about identity serves not only to inform socially distant individuals but also to reinforce intragroup identity

(Hodder 1982, 56–7). The need to strengthen group identity may increase as social scale and complexity increase as a result of the potential threat of losing members to other groups or of conflict between groups. This might also result in greater importance being placed on goods signifying group identity.

As with all communication systems, however, there is a danger of miscommunication (see Blanton 1994, 14) The greater the amount of information to be conveyed, the greater the potential for confusion and the greater the need for clarity in delivering messages. When the number of sociopolitical units increase, the amount of potential information regarding affiliation increases, particularly in complex societies in which status varies both between and within different segments of society (e.g., lineage, ethnic group, occupational category, geographic location). This social variability increases the likelihood of miscommunication.

Whereas in small-scale societies there may be only one publicly recognized scheme of valuation for goods and services, in complex societies various subsets of the society will have different value schemes that conflict with one another (Kopytoff 1986, 79–80). This ambiguity, combined with an overall increase in the possible content of messages conveyed, would tend to encourage greater standardization within the categories of goods used to convey information in a complex society, because standardization makes it possible to fine-tune messages.

Specialization generally increases standardization within categories of goods (Rice 1981, 223), in part because of the proportionately smaller number of producers (relative to items produced), the technological skill developed through repetition, and the fact that goods are generally not produced with individual needs or preferences in mind. Specialization permits greater control over the information conveyed as a result of the greater skill of specialists and elimination of irrelevant information such as individual variability in manufacturing skill and techniques. Therefore, specialization would serve to standardize the messages conveyed through materials. For this reason, I suggest that specialization, and concomitant standardization, arose partially in response to a need to enhance the effectiveness of the material component of the communication system. The clarity of information conveyed by specialist-produced goods may have been part of their appeal to all consumers.

Specialization would increase not only as a result of scale, but also as a result of increased vertical complexity. When pronounced differences in status exist, resources that mark status and symbolize access to information, such as trade goods that signify participation of the owner in a widespread social network, may in fact help people in positions of authority effectively carry out responsibilities by providing visible proof of their power or knowledge (Helms 1988, 148–49; Johnson, 1982, 409). As discussed previously, this may be accomplished by using rare or imported raw materials, imported craft goods, or specialist-produced craft goods as prestige symbols. Sumptuary laws that prohibit lower status social groups from displaying high-status goods (Anawalt 1980) may be established to control consumption patterns. By erecting such material barriers, access to information may be further limited. For example, a certain expected level of hospitality would prevent commoners from socializing with more powerful and well-informed members of a society. The demand for goods in state societies can be partially explained in terms of strategies by some to verify their affiliation and exclude others and efforts by those excluded to gain affiliation (Douglas and Isherwood 1979, 89).

The elites may have sponsored craft specialists and imported goods in an effort to control access to goods denoting rank. However, use of specialist-produced goods among the non-elite may have followed when lower ranking members of society tried to elevate their status by displaying goods similar to those of the elite (see Pollock 1983b). In describing this process of emulation, Appadurai has emphasized the dynamic nature of the emulation process in terms of the relationships between different status groups: "Elite tastes, in general, have this 'turnstile' function, selecting from exogenous possibilities and then providing models, as well as direct political controls, for internal tastes and production" (1986, 31). Sumptuary laws in some societies must have arisen in response to attempts by the non-elite to imitate the consumption patterns of the elites. In addition to shifting to specialized production, the non-elite may have used substitute materials when status goods were made of scarce materials.

The use of goods to communicate status is especially important in large-scale societies or in interaction with foreigners, when the attributes of individuals are not readily known, as they might be to members of a smaller society. In smaller scale societies, goods cannot be used as effectively to convey information within one's group, because the attributes of each person, such as his or her degree of influence within the group, are widely known. However, because of the greater anonymity in larger scale societies, a person can, for example, appear wealthier or more powerful by displaying certain categories of goods. This capacity for deception through the display of goods (see Blanton 1994, 14) is one of the risks to the recipient of relying on goods for information, but it is also one of the driving forces underlying the demand for goods. By controlling production and distribution of goods, elites may have been able to deceive members of their society by exaggerating their power and may have attempted to prevent deception among others (by restricting access).

Standardization in the goods used to convey specific messages serves to make clear-cut statements about the unacceptability of substitutes. Douglas and Isherwood (1979, 145) have argued that in instances in which competition is intense, careful comparison of values are made, and homogeneity in goods is greater. This does not imply greater homogeneity in the overall material culture, but only in the *set of goods* used to convey a specific message. Homogeneity would be high both within a category of goods (e.g., imported ceramic serving bowls signaling high status) and within a set of goods used to convey a particular message (e.g., imported serving vessels, lamb meat, and wine signaling a celebratory occasion hosted by elites). Greater standardization probably results from the higher social risk of deviating from conventions, the importance of clarity in conveying the intended messages, and the close attention paid to the messages. Although homogeneity within categories of goods might be greatest among the elite (among whom competition would be great and more careful attention might be placed on delivery of messages), one would expect emulation of elite consumption patterns to result in greater homogeneity within categories of goods used by the non-elites as well.

Finally, specialized production facilitates rapid changes in the styles of material objects. In state societies, the material culture tends to change relatively rapidly, although reasons for this are not widely known. Presumably, the relatively fast pace of change in material culture relates to the accelerated rate of change in sociopolitical organization of state societies (see Johnson 1982). Factors such as shifting leadership, centers of power and political boundaries, and large-scale movements of populations may have contributed to rapidly changing social identities as members of the society tried to define their own identities in relation to other members of the society as well as outsiders. One process contributing to this fast pace of change in material culture may be that of innovation on the part of the elites and emulation by the non-elites (see Pollock 1983b). The elites may continuously develop new styles in order to set themselves apart and stay a step ahead of the non-elites imitating these styles. If standardization in the appearance of goods was important to consumers (because of the information conveyed through the artifact), and if styles changed rapidly, then it may have been difficult for household producers to learn new styles quickly and produce goods that were sufficiently similar to the "model" to convey the intended social information. Production in a few locations by specialists with the time to practice new techniques and styles would have facilitated the rapid and clear transmission of information on new styles as well as the production of goods according to new standards. Moreover, complex societies change quickly, and rapid changes in scale and sociopolitical organization would have resulted in rapid changes in social identities of individuals relative to others in their society. By allowing more rapid changes in the appearance of goods, specialized production would have facilitated the use of goods as social markers.

SUMMARY

I have suggested that specialization among the non-elite in early state societies may have developed as a result of (1) increased sociopolitical complexity and the resulting increased number of social units within society, (2) the increased role of goods in the information system as social scale and diversity increased, (3) emulation of higher status groups using specialist-produced goods to signify status as a result of greater opportunities to use goods to promote one's own status in large-scale societies, and (4) the greater need for standardization in the physical attributes of goods used to convey social information to counter the greater potential for confusion. Although homogeneity within categories of goods may have been more pronounced on the elite level, it would have been relatively high on the non-elite level as well as a result of efforts to convey specific messages about social identity, as well as to imitate the standardized prestige goods used by the elite. Goods would have been used to communicate not only rank but also other aspects of social identity, such as geographic affiliation, age, gender, and marital status. The implications of this model for increasing specialization in complex societies are as follows:

1. Coincident with or following an increase in scale of the society, consumption of specialist-produced goods should have increased among the non-elite.
2. Non-elite households would have continued to be self-sufficient in production of food and goods generally not viewed by people outside the household (utilitarian crafts, such as cooking pots and storage jars).
3. There should be increased consumption among the non-elite of specialist-produced goods that fall into the category of items likely to

> be seen by a socially distant group (Wobst 1977, 325–7). These include items such as serving vessels (Pollock 1983a, 360), textiles (Barber 1994), and ornaments.

In summary, the previous explanation presents specialization within the context of increasing sociopolitical complexity and the need for greater standardization in goods used to communicate social information, as well as new opportunities to promote status as demographic scale increases. We now turn to a description of the research design and fieldwork that investigates changing patterns of domestic production and consumption at Kurban Höyük.

2 NORTH MESOPOTAMIAN URBANISM AND EXCAVATIONS AT KURBAN HÖYÜK

The formation of cities on the fertile plains of north Mesopotamian approximately 2500 B.C. represents one of the earliest known cases of urbanism. Despite the knowledge of several large centers in north Mesopotamia, such as Tell Brak and Carchemish, scholars have traditionally emphasized the simplicity of the relatively small-scale dry-farming-based settlements in the north, compared with those of the irrigation-based southern Mesopotamian societies. However, when the attention of researchers shifted northward in the 1970s, in part as a result of numerous salvage projects connected to dam construction, it became clear that the scale and complexity of societies in the north had been underestimated. Surveys and excavations have since documented the emergence of a series of urban-sized (50–100 ha.) centers (such as Tell Taya, Tell Leilan, Kazane, and Tell Mardikh) and satellite communities throughout the steppe of northern Syria and northern Iraq (hereafter Syro-Mesopotamia), and more recently, Southeastern Turkey, during the mid-late third millennium B.C. (Plate 1). The archives from the palace of Tell Mardikh (ancient Ebla) provided unexpected documentation of the existence of a highly integrated and hierarchically organized regional economic system in the neighboring area of northwest Syria at this time (Archi 1982, 216–20). Tablets from Tell Beydar illustrate that Ebla was not an isolated case (see Bretschneider and Dietrich 1994) and that writing may have played

Plate 1. Kazane, an early Bronze Age center to the southeast of Kurban Höyük. High mound and city wall that surrounds the lower town. Photograph courtesy of Henry Wright.

an important role in the administration of urban systems in upper Mesopotamia during this time.

The dry-farming societies of northern Mesopotamia represent an alternative urban pattern to that of irrigation farming societies in southern Mesopotamia. Ecological constraints may have contributed to a more dispersed settlement pattern in the north, whereby centers were smaller but spaced over an extensive area (see Weiss 1983).

For several reasons, Syro-Mesopotamia provides an excellent setting for a study of the linkages among political centralization and increasing economic specialization. In many archaeological settings, the study of production poses a particular challenge because of the difficulty of locating workshops. Moreover, some types of goods, such as textiles, do not preserve well, whereas others, such as metal objects, may have been recycled rather than discarded. Numerous surveys (e.g., Algaze et al. 1994; Wilkinson 1990) and excavations both of smaller sites (Hauptmann 1993; Meijer 1977; Voigt and Ellis 1981) and centers (e.g., Algaze et al. 1992; Matthiae 1978) in northwest Mesopotamia provide a broader perspective on economic organization than could be gained through a single excavation, making it possible to recognize general patterns of production and exchange. The archives from Ebla (e.g.,

Archi 1982; Pettinato 1991) provide detailed data on aspects of the political economy not generally available through excavation. This unusual combination of regional survey, excavations at centers as well as at towns, and texts documenting the political economy made it possible to obtain a broader and more detailed view of economic organization in an early state society than is possible in many regions of the world in which early state societies arose.

This study is based on excavation of houses at Kurban Höyük. However, results of surveys and excavations at nearby sites provided valuable insights into how the economy of one ancient regional system was organized. In this chapter I present the background to the site, area, and period. I then discuss the aims of the excavations conducted for this study and present a brief summary of the results.

MID-THIRD MILLENNIUM B.C. POLITICAL CENTRALIZATION IN NORTH MESOPOTAMIA AND THE KARABABA BASIN

Kurban Höyük is located at the northwest edge of the region where north Syro-Mesopotamian states formed, in the Karababa Basin of the Euphrates Valley, Urfa Province, Turkey (Fig. 1; Plate 2). The area forms a transitional zone between the north Mesopotamian steppe and the Taurus foothills (Fig. 2). Material collected on an extensive regional survey (Özdoğan 1977) revealed that the Karababa Basin marks the northern boundary for the north Syro-Mesopotamian third millennium states in terms of material culture as well as geography, with sites in the Karakaya Basin more similar to Anatolian highland sites, such as Arslantepe in the eastern Taurus.

The settlement patterns documented in the region surrounding Kurban Höyük paralleled trends on the north Mesopotamian steppe, although it was on a smaller scale in the Turkish Euphrates Valley, where agricultural land was more limited. The high density of third millennium B.C. settlement along the southern Turkish Euphrates River was not fully realized until salvage projects were carried out in the mid-1970s and 1980s because of dam construction (Özdoğan 1977; Whallon 1979; Wilkinson 1990). A survey undertaken along the middle Euphrates Valley of Turkey (including both the Karababa Basin and the Karakaya Basin 160 km upstream) established that more than 200 major sites would be flooded as a result of construction of two hydroelectric dams on the Euphrates River (Özdoğan 1977); most of these sites, including Kurban Höyük, have subsequently been inundated.

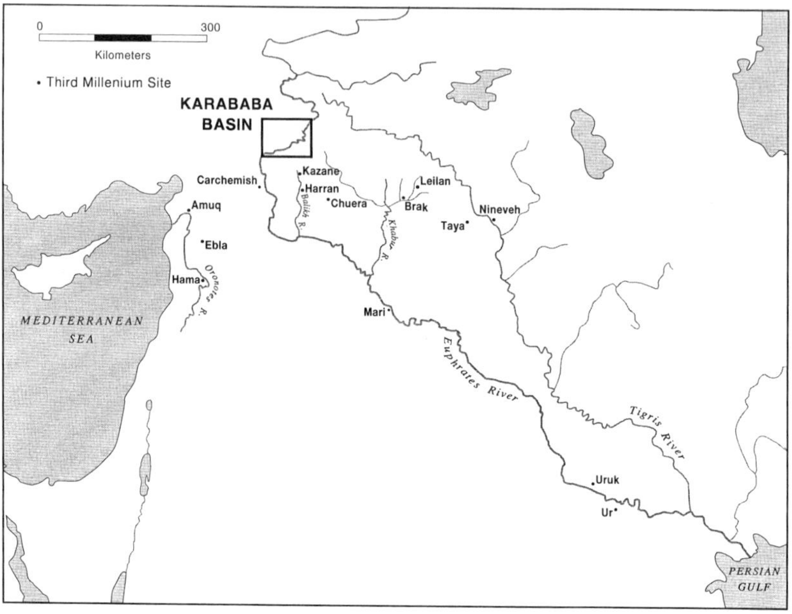

Figure 1. Map of the Near East, Showing the Location of the Karababa Basin and Selected Third Millennium B.C. Sites.

Prior to recent excavations connected with an international salvage effort, the third millennium B.C. in the Karababa Basin was only known through limited excavation in adjacent regions. To the south, work was conducted at Carchemish (Woolley 1952), and at Harran a deep sounding was excavated (Prag 1970). To the west, test excavations on the Amuq Plain yielded material similar to that from the Karababa Basin (Braidwood and Braidwood 1960). More recently, a number of excavations in southeast Turkey have expanded our knowledge of this part of the Near East (e.g., Algaze 1990a; Algaze et al. 1992; Hauptmann 1993; Wattenmaker and Mısır 1994).

Surveys by Özdoğan (1977) and Wilkinson (1990) provide an overview of broad changes through time in the settlement patterns of the Karababa Basin. The first evidence for state formation comes from the Late Chalcolithic Period (late fourth to early third millennium B.C.; Kurban Period VI). During this time, a three-level settlement hierarchy of a center (Samsat), towns (e.g., Kurban), and villages (e.g., Karatut Mevkii) emerged in the Karababa Basin. Extensive excavations of Late Chalcolithic/Uruk remains in the Karababa Basin were undertaken at only one small site, Hassek Höyük

Plate 2. Kurban Höyük is one of the many town-sized sites that arose in the mid-third millennium B.C. Photograph courtesy of the Oriental Institute.

(Behm-Blancke 1984, 1992). Test excavations and soundings uncovered remains from several other sites (Ingraham 1986; Özten 1984; Schwartz 1988a), but thus far few studies of sociopolitical complexity in the Karababa Basin during this period have been undertaken. Large regional centers (e.g., Tell Brak, Samsat) formed across the north Mesopotamian steppe during this time, paralleled by the emergence of a complex and partial centrally administered economy at Arslantepe in the highlands (Palmieri 1985, 204–5); it is likely that state societies emerged during this period in the Karababa Basin as well. If so, centralization in the mid-third millennium B.C. (the focus of this study) would represent an episode of state resurgence rather than initial state formation.

The late Chalcolithic period of expansion was followed by a period of decentralization and declining settlement density (Wilkinson 1986, fig. 7; 1990). The settlement pattern in the first part of the Early Bronze Age (early third millennium; Kurban Period V) was characterized by dispersed villages and hamlets of up to 1 ha. Thus far no early third millennium B.C. regional center has been located.

This period of population decline and decentralization was succeeded by a more than threefold increase in aggregate settlement area during Kurban

Figure 2. Map Showing the Location of Kurban and Nearby Excavated Mid-Late Third Millennium B.C. Sites.

Period IV—the mid-late third millennium B.C.[1] Although the total number of sites decreased, settlement differentiation increased considerably (see Wilkinson 1990; tab. 4.1). The mid-late third millennium B.C. settlement pattern included a regional center at Titriş Höyük (43 ha.; see Matney and Algaze 1995; Plate 3), large and small towns (e.g., Lidar Höyük, ca. 15 ha; Kurban, at least 6 ha.; Plate 4), and villages or hamlets (e.g., Saskan Böyüktepe, ca. 1.1 ha; Yaslica, 0.3 ha).

Excavations in the Karababa Basin support the inference from settlement pattern data that political centralization and major reorganization of the economy occurred during this time. A possible fortification wall at Kurban Höyük dates to this period, and a major fortification system at Titriş may also date to

Plate 3. Titriş Höyük. General view toward the southeast along Outer Town street, part of excavated Late-Early Bronze Age domestic area. High mound of Titriş in background. (Photograph courtesy of Guillermo Algaze)

this period (Algaze et al. 1995, 21). An extensive ceramic workshop of 19 kilns from four third millennium B.C. strata were uncovered at Lidar Höyük (Hauptmann 1984, 205–6), providing evidence for major craft specialization. Excavations from Titriş have documented the construction of large and carefully planned buildings at this time (Algaze et al. 1995, 37). Burials from the Lidar Höyük cemetery suggested social differentiation (Hauptmann 1983a, 255), and graves from Titriş include those with relatively simple offerings of pottery (Algaze et al. 1995, 20, 25) and those with offerings of bronze, silver, and shell jewelry (Algaze et al. 1995, 28; Plate 5). The chance surface find from Titriş of a 1-mana weight with the inscription of a high official under Shu-Durul, the last King of the Akkadian Dynasty,[2] suggests that the region may have had official relations with Akkadian Mesopotamia by the end of this period (Algaze 1990b, 344–5). Although excavated data point to a socially stratified and highly specialized society, the scale of sites are smaller than expected for a state society in mid-third-millennium greater Mesopotamia.

The relatively small size of sites in the Euphrates Valley led to the impression that mid-third-millennium societies were less politically centralized and eco-

Plate 4. The town site of Lidar Höyük (see Hauptmann 1983). Note Gritille Höyük (see Voigt and Ellis 1981), a village site in Adiyaman Province, across the Euphrates River. Photograph courtesy of Gil Stein.

nomically specialized than contemporaneous societies of north Syria and north Iraq (Stein 1987, 101). However, the fairly modest scale of urbanism in the Euphrates Valley may well be a result of the relatively limited agricultural land, rather than the nature of sociopolitical organization. Much of our understanding of the development of complex societies in southeast Turkey is based on the relatively extensive coverage of the Euphrates Valley, at the expense of broad agricultural plains. Just 40 km to the southeast of the Euphrates Valley, on the agriculturally rich and extensive Urfa Plain, there is a very different settlement pattern for the third millennium. During this period, the site of Kazane grew to 100 ha (Wattenmaker and Mısır 1994), revealing that urbanism in this region was on a scale equal to that elsewhere in north Mesopotamia. Third millennium texts from Ebla document that the site of Harran, only 38 km south of Kazane, was clearly an important political and economic center during this time as well (Archi 1988). Parallels in the ceramic assemblages from the Karababa Basin and the Urfa Plain (see Algaze 1990b; Hauptmann 1983b; Wattenmaker and Mısır 1994; Prag 1970) indicate that sites in the Euphrates Valley were closely connected to, or perhaps even part of, the highly centralized societies on the Urfa Plain.

Plate 5. View, after cleaning, of plundered Mid-Early Bronze Age tomb (Locus 006) in Extramural Cemetery area at Titriş Höyük (interior scale = 1 m). (Photograph courtesy of Guillermo Algaze)

KURBAN HÖYÜK: BACKGROUND TO THE SETTLEMENT AND RESEARCH

Kurban Höyük is a 6-ha double mound (Plates 5 and 6) that, subsequent to excavations, was inundated by the Ataturk Lake, which provides irrigation water for the region. The site is located in the Bozova district of Şanlıurfa Province. Before the Ataturk Lake was filled, Kurban was situated approximately 0.25 km from the left bank of the Euphrates River, on a low river terrace, and was visible 5 m to 10 m above the plain. The plain on which Kurban sits is bordered to the south by a higher terrace marking the boundary between the Euphrates Valley and upper steppe. Although the site is surrounded by the upper terrace to the south and east, the plain widens to the west. To the north of the region, the Taurus mountains limit traffic northward to a small number of narrow routes. However access to the south is much easier, with the Incesu Basin, just 4 km east of Kurban Höyük, leading toward Urfa and the Urfa Plain, Balikh Valley, and north Syria (Wilkinson 1990).

A spring between the two mounds of Kurban Höyük probably attracted the original inhabitants to the site, although it had dried up by the mid-third

Plate 6. Kurban Höyük (note high and low mound).

millennium B.C. The site may have served as a river-crossing point along with the site of Biricek, on the west bank (Wilkinson 1990, 101). As recently as A.D. 1560, the nearby village of Cümcüme served as a ferry-crossing point (Yananc and Elibüyük 1983, 431), although this part of the river was not an ideal crossing point during the time of excavation.

The Karababa Basin falls within the dry-farming zone of north Syro-Mesopotamia, receiving a mean rainfall of 400 mm to 470 mm per year, mostly between the months of October and May. In broad terms, the climate of the area is classified as semi-arid, although it varies within the region and is dry subhumid along the Euphrates (Wilkinson 1986, 39; 1990). A study of the plant remains from nearby Titriş and an analysis of sediment units from the surrounding area suggest that the region was either moister than in present times, had a heavier vegetation cover, or both in the mid-late third millennium B.C. (Algaze et al. 1995, 36–7).

Excavations at Kurban Höyük were conducted by the Oriental Institute from 1980 through 1984 under the direction of Leon Marfoe (see Fig. 3). The excavations carried out in 1984 specifically for this study were conducted to expand on what was learned from the 1980 to 1983 seasons about the third millennium settlement at Kurban Höyük. This chapter provides the background to the 1984 horizontal excavations of the mid-third-millennium

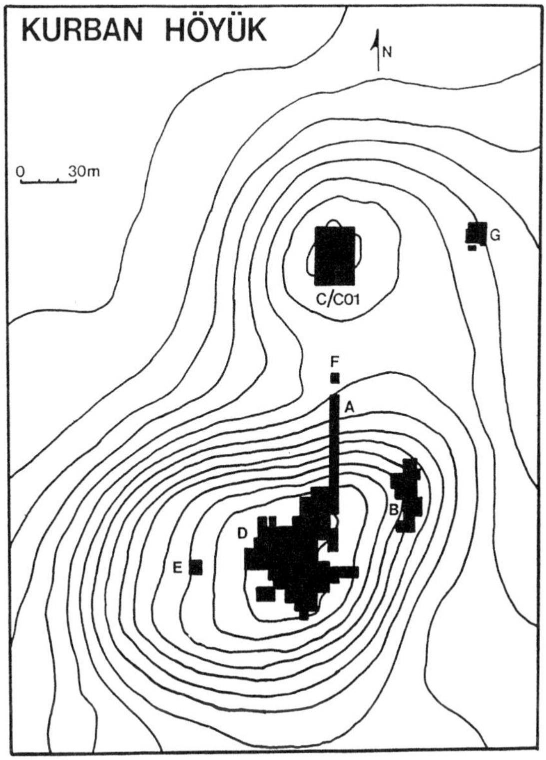

Figure 3. Map of Kurban Höyük, with Excavated Areas Shown.

settlement (in Areas B and G), which were conducted specifically for this study of non-elite production and consumption and have not been fully published. The results of the stratigraphic excavations at Kurban Höyük have been published in considerable detail (e.g., Algaze 1990a), and are not discussed in this section. Horizontal exposures of the mid-third-millennium community conducted from 1980 to 1983 aimed to fulfill objectives of the overall project, such as establishing an occupational sequence for the site and studying the spatial layout of the town (see Marfoe 1990a, 7–8). Fortunately, the data collected for these purposes were recorded and analyzed in a way that made them useful for this study of economic organization. As will be seen, excavations from all seasons form an integral part of this study.

Kurban Höyük was initially selected for excavation because it had mid-third-millennium B.C. deposits just below the surface, making it an ideal site

Plate 7. A mid-third-millennium b.c. neighborhood on the lower town (note high mound and step trench in background). Photograph courtesy of the Oriental Institute.

for a study of north Syro-Mesopotamian state development (Marfoe 1990a, 2). After the first two seasons, project efforts shifted from the third millennium settlement to a later (ca. 2000 B.C.) village that capped much of the larger mound, as well as deep soundings outlining the settlement history of the site (see Marfoe 1990b, 11). The probes revealed unsuspected occupational remains beginning in the fifth millennium located below the modern surface of the plain. The site was occupied fairly continuously through the third millennium B.C., with the locus of settlement alternating between the two mounds. Only during the late fourth millennium/Late Uruk and the mid-late third millennium B.C. were both mounds occupied. Kurban Höyük was abandoned by the early second millennium B.C. and was not reoccupied until a medieval khan was constructed on the large mound. Late medieval burials postdate the khan (see Algaze et al. 1986).

Findings from 1980 to 1983 indicate that in the mid-third millennium B.C. Kurban grew sixfold, with settlement expanding from the smaller mound to both mounds (Plate 7). This growth coincided with the construction of a fortification wall and monumental architecture on the large mound. Architecture and artifact distributions revealed variability in productive activities and status of occupants in different residential areas of the site. Ceramic slag, wasters, and lithic debris suggested that craft manufacturing was concentrated on the small mound (Marfoe 1982, 106). Faunal remains indicated the presence of a tributary economy and increasing specialization in food production (Wattenmaker and Stein, 1986; Wattenmaker 1987). These results, combined with the evidence from surveys and other sites mentioned previously, suggested to me that Kurban Höyük was an excellent site for a study of changes in domestic production accompanying regional centralization. However, additional excavations were needed to obtain the necessary data on the spatial distribution of economic artifacts.

EXCAVATION OF PERIOD IV DOMESTIC SECTORS: RESEARCH AIMS AND RESULTS

The excavations conducted specifically for this study of production and consumption focused on the period of political centralization, Kurban Period IV, and built on an extant body of data from previous field seasons. Earlier excavations were concentrated toward the center of the site, where relatively elite areas were more likely to be represented. To complement earlier findings, I expanded exposures toward the edge of the site, where non-elite residences were more likely to be found. Several factors indicated that the site was appropriate for a study of domestic economic reorganization. First, because Kurban is a fairly small site with relatively unspectacular architecture, success in locating non-elite residential architecture was likely. Earlier excavations had already identified two non-elite residential areas (B and G) that were promising in terms of accessibility and preservation. These excavations were expanded for this study. Second, three deep soundings undertaken by project members in previous seasons provided a continuous sequence from the approximately 400 years of mid-late third millennium B.C. occupation (spanning 8 m of deposit). An additional sounding, Area E, yielded Period IV materials, but artifact samples from this small exposure were not large enough to be of use. Findings from Areas A, C01, and F provided an opportunity to study change through time in production organization in relation to increasing sociopolitical complexity. Finally, 400 m^2 of Period IV occupational remains had already been cleared in one residential area, Area C, providing an already extant and substantial body of data from one part of the site for comparison with future excavations.

Decisions about where to excavate were guided by the fact that previous excavations of Period IV deposits had focused on three areas toward the center of the site (on a north–south longitudinal axis), Areas A, C/C01, and F. All of these areas had relatively substantial high-status buildings that appeared to be nonresidential (see Chapter 4), as well as more modest structures. Limited excavations toward the edge of the mound suggested that lower status site sectors and non-elite residential architecture, the focus of this research, were concentrated on the periphery of the site. Two areas that had been explored in previous seasons were targeted: Area B, on a spur to the east of the large mound, and Area G on a small spur on the east slope of the smaller mound. In addition to providing comparative data from each of the two mounds, the research would complement findings from the potentially higher status areas closer to the center of the site. Previous research identified three subperiods of Period IV, defined by architectural changes in the Area A step trench. From earliest to latest, these were IVC (the levels preceding the fortification wall), IVB (the subperiod in which the fortification wall was constructed and architecture was fairly massive), and subperiod IVA (characterized by relatively flimsy architecture believed to postdate the fortification wall; Algaze et al. 1986). On the basis of architectural similarities between deposits from the middle part of Period IV (IVB) in Area A and those in the more shallow occupational deposits of the small mound (8 m in Area A versus less than 2 m in Area C01), the project staff inferred that a major expansion of the site occurred during this central subperiod and that in the beginning and final subperiods settlement was confined to the large mound (see Ingraham 1986, fig. 11). The expectation that areas on the small mound or toward the edge of the large mound all dated to Period IVB, combined with the apparent similarities in ceramic assemblages from the three areas, led to the tentative conclusion that Areas C and G on the small mound, and Area B on the outskirts of the large mound, were contemporary, dating to the period of expansion. Therefore, I expected that expansion of excavations of Areas B and G would result in broad clearances of three roughly contemporaneous areas for a study of intracommunity economic organization. These areas could be compared with material from soundings for a study of change through time in economic organization.

Additional excavations were planned with the aim of recovering several categories of data crucial to this project. On the most general level, larger artifact samples were needed to determine the range of activities carried out in each area. Although ceramics were well represented in Area B, where 130 m^2 had been previously cleared, larger samples of less abundant materials, such as animal bones and sickle blades, were required. The 28 m^2 sounding from Area G was too small for an assessment of production and consumption patterns in this part of the site.

Most of the previously excavated deposits in Areas G and B were from room interiors. Because courtyards, pits, and other exterior loci often have higher concentrations and different types of artifacts than do interiors, additional excavations were aimed at locating the exterior areas associated with previously cleared rooms. Further excavation was also needed to obtain greater exposures of structures and associated work areas, so that the full range of artifacts in each sector would be recovered. The combined findings from all seasons did indeed allow a study of changing economic organization as the town grew. Detailed descriptions of Areas B and G are presented in Chapter 4. A brief summary of the excavation results and an overview of each area is presented next.

Excavation procedures generally followed those used for the site as a whole (see Verhaaren 1986, 67–8). For recording purposes, a 10-m^2 grid system was used. Actual horizontal excavation units within trenches were rectangular "strips" varying in size between 2 m^2 and 16 m^2; loci were used to mark the stratigraphic units. In keeping with the project policy, surfaces were excavated in 1-m^2 units, called *fine grids,* although such small units were not necessary for this particular study. Surface and feature deposits were screened in a 0.5 cm mesh. For less secure deposits, such as "fill," only a portion of the locus was screened (usually 1 : 5 or 1 : 10). The screening ratio was recorded, and material collected from screens was bagged separately from hand collected material so that differences resulting from recovery strategy could be controlled for. Samples were also sieved in a finer mesh in an effort to control for the loss of smaller pieces of lithic debitage, animal bone, and other small artifacts. In general, the density of artifacts was low, and we found that most material was recovered as it was excavated, rather than in the screen. Flotation samples were collected from surfaces and features, although seed preservation was poor in these areas because of their proximity to the surface.

In four weeks of excavation, 121 m^2 were cleared from Area G and approximately 230 m^2 from Area B (see Plate 18). Area B yielded four occupational subphases, three dating to Period IV. Expansion of the excavations confirmed previous assessment of the area as a densely occupied low-status domestic area. Rooms and structures were very small, and houses were built wall to wall, creating a maze-like appearance (see Fig. 29). The only space not contained within walls was a narrow cobbled street. Fortunately, the street was used as a trash disposal area, so that the artifacts from the street provided the information on economic activities that we had hoped to find from outdoor work areas. Because rooms in three of the excavated trenches (B62, B71, and B72) were reused in the following Period III, resulting in the mixing of artifacts, only the north part of the excavated area is included in this study.

Although Area G was selected for excavation because previous testing suggested that it was well-preserved and easy to excavate, our findings in the area adjacent to the test probe were the reverse. Three subphases were represented, all dating to Period IV. The uppermost level of Period IV had been largely destroyed by plowing, so that only isolated features remained. Postoccupational wall robbing made it difficult to define the limits of rooms or to determine where one structure ended and another began. Fortunately, wall robbing did not cause significant disturbance of the occupational surfaces; plaster and packed dirt surfaces were well preserved with pots found in situ. Portions of three rooms and a courtyard were excavated. Although excavations did not yield well-preserved architecture, they did retrieve critical data for this study of domestic economic activities. The modest remains from Area G provided an important contrast to other parts of the site.

Excavations from all seasons resulted in three areas of horizontal clearance (Areas B, C, and G) and three deep soundings (Areas A, C01, and G; see Table 1). Because of time constraints, it was not possible to excavate entire structures in any of the areas. Moreover, structures were often not completely preserved (because of erosion, plow destruction, wall robbing, etc.). Therefore this study is based on results from a small number of rooms per structure; many of these rooms were only partially excavated. Because houses were only partially sampled, it is not possible to draw conclusions about the composition of households (e.g., nuclear families, extended families). Nor can it be assumed that the full range of economic activities carried out within structures or households were represented. Fortunately, this study focuses on production and consumption of products that were widely and regularly used, such as pottery and chipped stone, and these categories of artifacts were recovered in most or all of the excavated rooms. Moreover, many of the patterns regarding production and consumption were duplicated from room to room within a site sector, suggesting that even partial exposure of structures was sufficient to identify key temporal trends in the reorganization of production and consumption. This repetition in artifact distributions from room to room may indicate that many of the materials recovered, particularly broken pottery and animal bones, came from secondary depos-

Table 1
Alternative Relative Chronologies Proposed for Kurban Höyük

	Results based on seriation			Results based on architecture[a]			
	Areas, phases			Areas, phases			
Period	South mound	Saddle	North mound	South mound	Saddle	North mound	Period
IV.1	A18–20, A15, B	F13–14	C01 16	A16–20, B			IVA
IV.2	A16–17	F8–12	C01 15 C11, G				
IV.3	A13–14		C01 11–14	A13–14	F8–14	C01, 11–14 CII, G	IVB
IV.4	A11–12	F2–7		A11–12	F2–7		IVC

[a] Based on Marfoe and Algaze 1990, table 50.

its—trash thrown into rooms after they were abandoned, as is often the case in densely occupied multiperiod sites. It is likely that the goods had been used in the immediate vicinity of the houses in which they were deposited, so that the artifacts recovered reveal a great deal about economic activities in particular neighborhoods, although they may be less useful for documenting activities conducted in specific rooms and structures.

In assessing the strengths and shortcomings of this sample, it is important to emphasize that Kurban Höyük is currently the only mid-third-millennium B.C. site in the northern part of Greater Mesopotamia that has relatively broad exposures of domestic areas, thorough publication of both excavations and well-provenienced ceramics, and partially published or unpublished but thoroughly documented studies of several other artifact categories. At present, Kurban Höyük remains our best opportunity for understanding changes in production and consumption among the non-elites during this key period when polities became more centralized and urban systems formed. It is hoped that future excavation of complete structures from other sites in the region will make it possible to further evaluate many of the hypotheses on domestic production and consumption resulting from this study. Broader exposures of houses obtained at Titriş will allow a detailed study of household economic organization at an urban center during a slightly later phase of the mid-late third millennium B.C. than those examined here (see Algaze et al. 1995).

As mentioned previously, prior to the 1984 season we believed that Areas B, C, and G were roughly contemporary, dating to the middle of Period IV (IVB). However, the discovery that Area B buildings were reused in Period III indicated that the Area B Period IV deposits were later than we had thought. This called into question the assumption that all Period IV occupational remains on the small mound and settlement periphery dated to IVB. Dating the Period IV excavation areas relative to one another became a major subproject of this research.

A RELATIVE CHRONOLOGY FOR THE MID-LATE THIRD MILLENNIUM B.C. (PERIOD IV) LEVELS AT KURBAN HÖYÜK

3

Working in a relatively unexplored region has the advantage of many unexpected findings but the disadvantage of poorly defined ceramic sequences. Although earlier excavations in north Syria and Turkey identified the mid-late third millennium B.C. ceramic assemblage (e.g., Braidwood and Braidwood 1960; Fugmann 1958; Prag 1970; Woolley 1952), changes in ceramics within this approximately 400-year period had not been identified. The eight meters of deposit and ten occupational phases in Area A at Kurban suggested that the Period IV deposits represented a significant time span. Moreover, the settlement history of the site suggested that major changes occurred in sociopolitical organization in the region during this time, making it necessary to control for chronology before artifacts from different levels and areas could be used to study economic organization. Because the various excavation areas were not stratigraphically linked, a ceramic seriation was conducted to date the Period IV deposits relative to one another.

THE PERIOD IV CERAMICS

The Period IV ceramic assemblage belongs to a well-documented tradition that spans from the Amuq Plain in the west (Amuq I, Braidwood and Braidwood 1960, 406–19) to the Balikh Valley to the east (Kühne 1976; Prag

Plate 8. Cooking pot. Photograph courtesy of the Oriental Institute.

1970; Wattenmaker and Mısır 1994), northward approximately 50 km along the Euphrates from Kurban Höyük, toward the Karakaya Dam (see Özdoğan 1977), and southward as far as Hama (Hama J2–6; Fugmann 1958, 49–85) and Tell Mardikh (IIa; Matthaie 1979, 30; see Yakar 1985, 341–2, 345–6). The most common wares are handmade, generally grit-tempered burnished ware, Cooking Pot ware (Plate 8; Figs. 4–5; Kühne 1976, plate 38, Prag 1970, 83), and a wheel-made grit-tempered buff or reddish Plain Simple ware (Braidwood and Braidwood 1960, 406–13; Plates 9–11). Additional wares include Horizontal Reserve Slip ware (Figs. 8 and 10; Braidwood and Braidwood 1960, 413), Metallic or Stone ware (Plate 10; Figs. 9, 11–12; Prag 1970, 81; Kühne 1976, 33, and plates 2–8), Combed Wash ware (Plate 11; Fig. 13; Prag 1970, 83–5), Painted Band ware (also Fig. 13; Kühne 1976, plate 35), and Karababa Painted ware (Fig. 14; Thissen 1985, 92–5; see Algaze 1990b, 311 for a detailed description of the Kurban Period IV ceramics).

Although no radiocarbon dates are available from Kurban Höyük, five radiocarbon dates from Titriş provide an approximate date for the final phases of Period IV. These dates come from deposits at Titriş that have been correlated with a building phase at Kurban that immediately follows Subperiod IV.1 (Phase 21 in Area A) (G. Algaze, August 25, 1997, personal communication). Although one date is clearly too early for its context, three dates indicate that buildings from this phase were occupied in the last 300 years of the third millennium. A single date from the earlier building phase that correlates with Period IV at Kurban is centered in the middle of the third millennium (Matney and Algaze 1995, 39–40). Some scholars have proposed that the Akkadian expansion played a strong role in the formation of north Mesopotamian

Plate 9. Plain Simple Ware beaded-rim bowls (sherds) (Area B).

urbanism, but the single early date from Titriş suggests that the center grew to urban dimensions prior to the historically documented Akkadian expansion (Matney and Algaze 1995, 50). The major growth and reorganization at Kurban apparently predated the Akkadian expansion as well.

In terms of the best represented forms and wares, the Kurban Period IV ceramics (and mid-third-millennium B.C. ceramics from the lower Turkish Euphrates Valley in general) closely resemble those from the Balikh Valley to the southeast (Kühne 1976; Prag 1970; Wattenmaker and Mısır 1994; Table 2). There are also strong parallels with sites along the Euphrates to the south, in the Tabqa Dam area (Dornemann 1988; Meijer 1977, 122–3; Orthmann 1981, plates 53, 64–6) and the Amuq Plain (Braidwood and Braidwood 1960). The ceramics are less similar to those from sites to the east of the Khabur River, such as Tell Leilan (Schwartz 1988b). Some of the most common Plain Simple ware (Figs. 6–9) and Stone ware vessel forms (Figs. 9–12) at Kurban are well represented at Tell Brak (Fielden 1977, 250), although the composition of the Plain Simple wares are somewhat different at Tell Leilan (see Schwartz 1988b, 40–1). With respect to other wares in Kurban Period IV deposits, there appears to be little overlap between the assemblages from the Turkish Euphrates Valley and those from the Khabur region.

Horizontal Reserve Slip ware (see Plate 12), generally found west of the

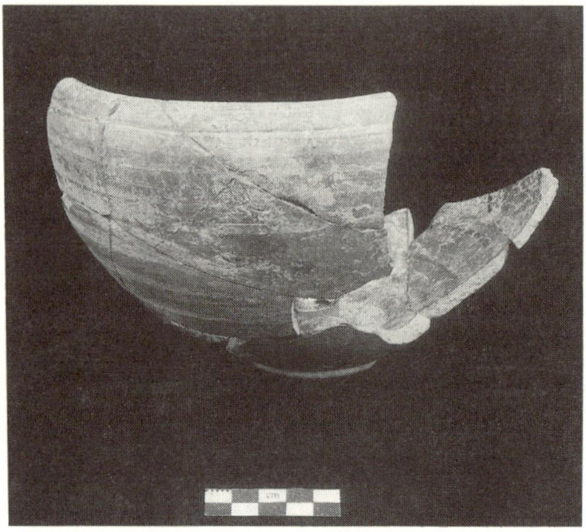

Plate 10. Stone ware bowl (Area B).

Euphrates River in inland and coastal Syria (Braidwood and Braidwood 1960, 413; Mazzoni 1985, 2), is well represented in Kurban Period IV deposits (Figs. 8 and 10). The Kurban assemblage overlaps with that from Tell Mardikh IIB1–2, although the sequence of use of various forms and wares may differ. Wares such as Plain Simple ware and Combed Wash ware (Fig. 13; Plate 13) link the Kurban Period IV assemblage with sites to the south of the Karababa Basin. However, the Karababa Painted ware (Fig. 14) may be related to the Early Bronze Age painted wares used in the Keban region of the Anatolian highlands to the north (Thissen 1985, 94–5; e.g., see Hauptmann 1979, fig. 31; Whallon 1979, figs. 17–19).

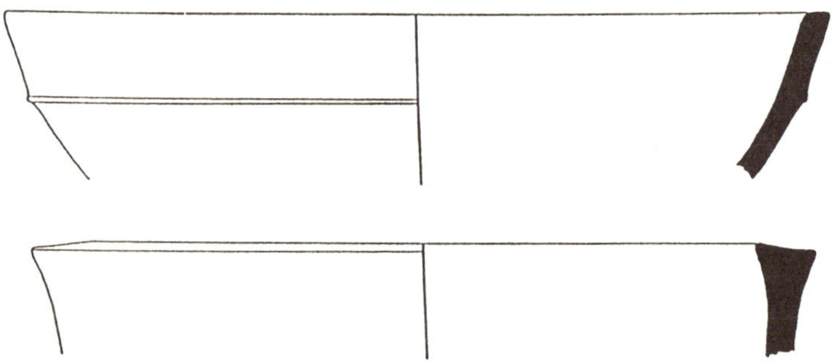

Figure 4. Handmade Grit-Tempered Burnished Ware Open Vessels (from Algaze 1990b; scale 2 : 5).
(A) 106-07-021. Orange paste, large sized grey grits, both surfaces grey, lower surface largely burnished, upper body rough.
(B) A07-05-035. Orange paste, large white grits and quartz flakes visible. Exterior surface mottled brown-black, well burnished.

Plate 11. Combed Wash Ware cup (Area C). Photograph courtesy of the Oriental Institute

Plate 12. Examples of Horizontal Reserve Slip ware (Area B).

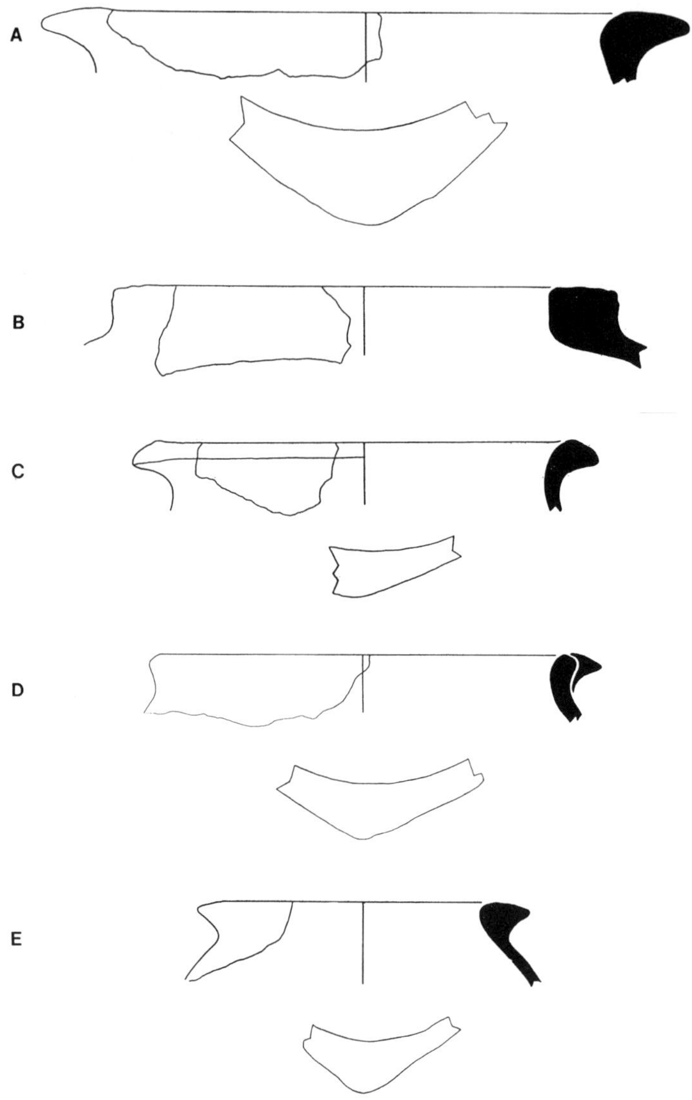
A
B
C
D
E

Figure 5 *(on facing page).* Handmade Grit-Tempered Burnished Ware Lugged Vessels (scale 2 : 5).

(A) G64-04-001. Evenly fired reddish-brown with coarse sand/quartz temper. Surface burnished. Mottled in firing. Mostly light brown with patches of dark grey.

(B) B01-04-018. Evenly fired reddish-brown paste with coarse sand/quartz temper. Exterior surface burnished up to inner edge of rim. Interior surface light grey, smoothed. Exterior surface mottled in firing-color ranges from greyish-brown to light brownish-grey.

(C) C66-01-003. Unevenly fired reddish-brown core tending to dark grey toward exterior surface. Interior surface smoothed light yellow-brown. Exterior surface burnished, mottled in firing, light yellow-brown to dark grey.

(D) G65-0203-009. Evenly fired very dark grey paste with coarse grain sand/quartz temper. Interior and exterior surfaces burnished. Mottled in firing exterior surface ranges from greyish-brown through light brown to dark grey. Interior surface light brown.

(E) B81-02-013. Unevenly fired greyish-brown core tending to brown toward exterior surface. Interior surface smoothed greyish-brown. Exterior surface horizontally burnished (extending over top of lip), grayish-brown. Medium to coarse sand/quartz temper.

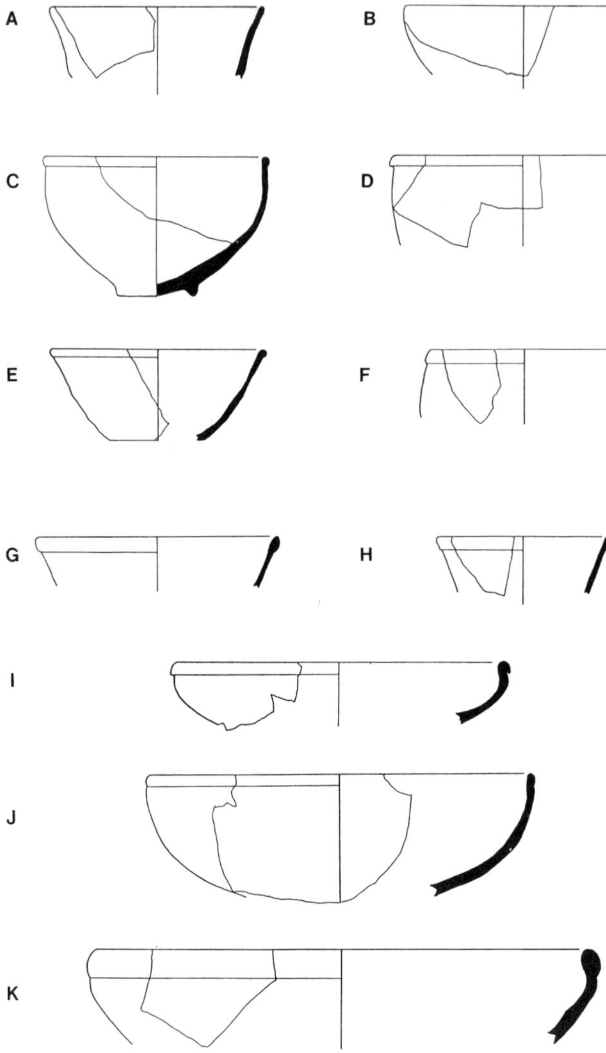
A
B
C
D
E
F
G
H
I
J
K

Figure 6 *(on facing page)*. Wheel-Made Grit-Tempered Plain Simple Ware Open Vessels (scale 2 : 5).

(A) B02-03-018. Brown paste with fine to medium sand and limestone temper. Evenly fired. Exterior slightly smoothed, pale brown.

(B) B02-03-018. Pale brown paste with fine to medium grit temper with fine limestone inclusions. Evenly fired. Interior plain matte. Exterior slightly smoothed, very pale brown.

(C) B03-02-018. Evenly fired pale brown paste with fine to medium sand temper and occasional fine grain limestone inclusions. Closely spaced wheel marks on interior and exterior surfaces. Top four centimeters of outer surface smoothed, bottom plain matte.

(D) B81-02-013. Evenly fired very pale brown paste with fine to medium grain sand temper. Exterior surface smoothed matte, undecorated.

(E) G64-05-010. Unevenly fired light brownish-grey core tending to reddish-brown toward exterior surface. Fine to medium grain sand temper. Closely spaced wheel marks on exterior surface. Plain matte undecorated light reddish-brown exterior.

(F) B02-03-018. Very pale brown paste, evenly fired with medium sand temper. Plain matte undecorated surface.

(G) G65-02-009. Evenly fired light brown paste with fine to medium sand temper. Surface plain matte undecorated, very pale brown.

(H) B02-03-018. Pale brown paste, evenly fired. Fine grit temper with fine limestone grit inclusions. Exterior surface slightly smoothed very pale brown.

(I) B02-04-018. Evenly fired light grey paste with medium grain sand temper. Interior and exterior surfaces plain matte undecorated very pale brown.

(J) G65-0203-009. Evenly fired light grey paste with medium sand grit temper. Wheel marks on interior surface. Exterior surface smoothed, matte undecorated, very pale brown.

(K) B01-04-018. Evenly fired light grey paste with medium grain sand temper. Interior and exterior surfaces plain matte, undecorated very pale brown.

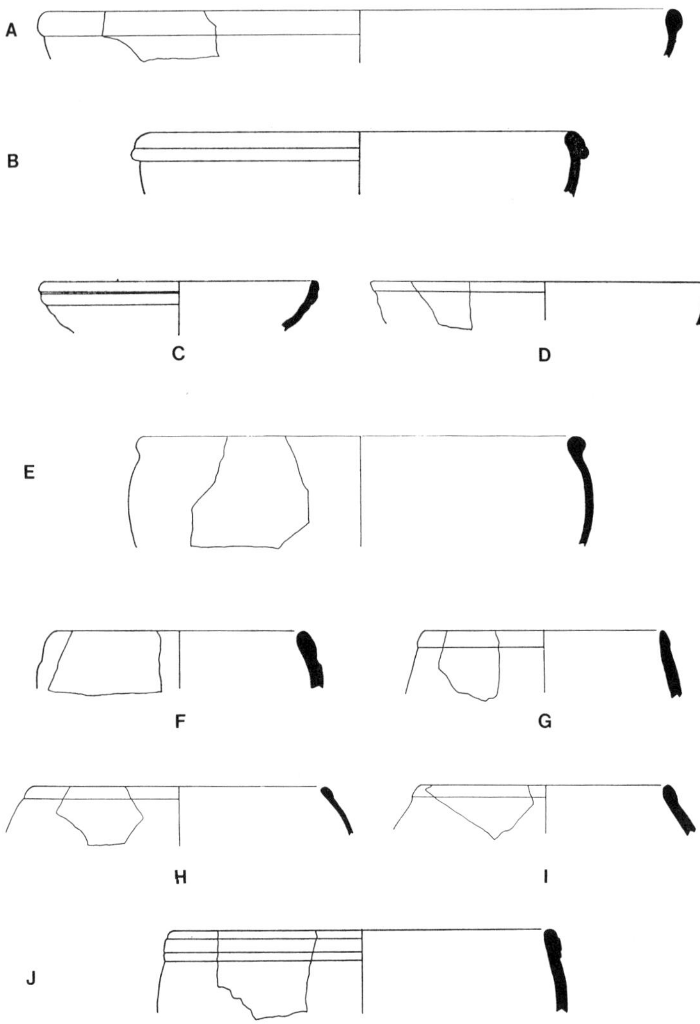
A
B
C
D
E
F
G
H
I
J

Figure 7 *(on facing page)*. Wheel-Made Grit-Tempered Plain Simple Ware Vessels (figures B and C from Algaze 1990b; scale 2 : 5).
(A) G64-0456-012. Evenly fired pale brown paste with medium grain sand and limestone temper. Closely spaced wheel marks on interior surface. Exterior surface smoothed matte, undecorated.
(B) A07-15-065. Fairly dense buff clay, small sized white grits.
(C) A05-05-017. Green buff paste, small sized grits.
(D) G65-02-002. Evenly fired dark grey paste with fine sand and limestone temper. Surface matte grey.
(E) C66-0336-012. Unevenly fired light yellowish-brown core tending to very dark greyish-brown toward interior surface and to light red toward exterior surface. Medium grain sand temper. Closely spaced wheel marks on interior and exterior. Exterior surface smoothed light red matte.
(F) G64-04-026. Evenly fired light grey paste with medium sand temper and occasional coarse inclusions. Surface plain matte, undecorated, light grey.
(G) B01-04-018. Evenly fired light grey paste with medium grain sand temper and medium grain limestone inclusions. Exterior surface smoothed, matte undecorated, very pale brown.
(H) G64-0218/19-013. Unevenly fired reddish-brown core tending to dark grey toward interior surface and to red toward exterior surface. Exterior surface plain matte, undecorated, red.
(I) B02-03-018. Light brownish-grey core tending to light reddish-brown toward interior and exterior surfaces. Very fine grit temper with occasional mica inclusions. Smoothed exterior surface.
(J) G64-03-011. Unevenly fired light grey core tending to light brown toward interior and exterior surfaces. Exterior surface smoothed, matte undecorated very pale brown. Medium sand temper.

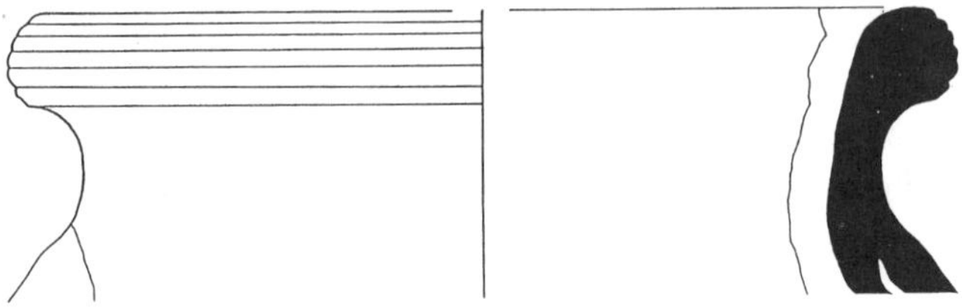

A

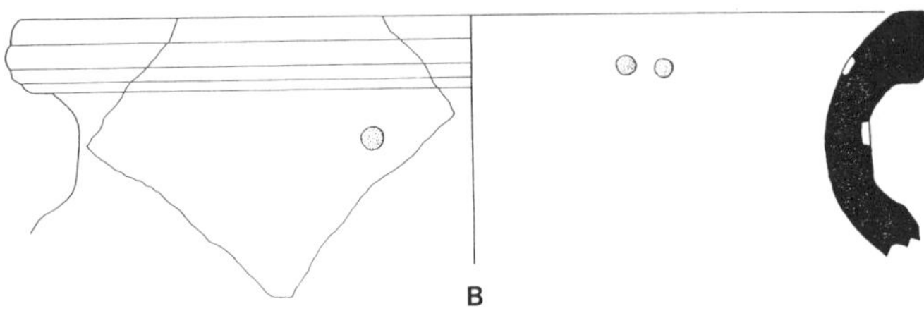

B

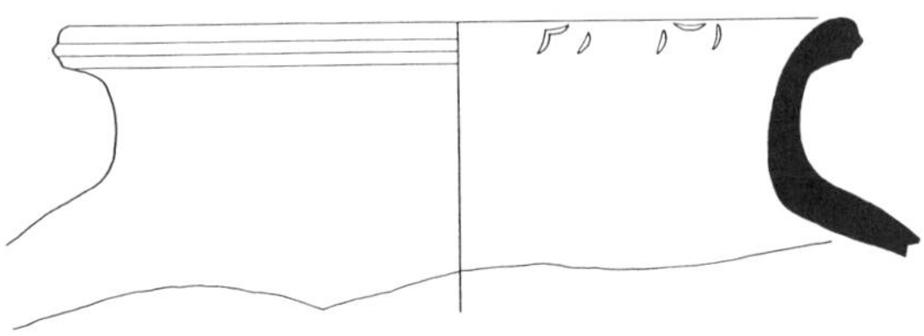

C

Figure 8 *(on facing page)*. Grit-Tempered Plain Simple Ware and Horizontal Reserve Slip Ware Jars with Wheel-Made Rims and Handmade Bodies (scale 2 : 5).
(A) B02-04-018. Rim diameter 41 cm (not to scale). Unevenly fired light grey core tending to very pale brown toward interior and exterior surfaces. Medium grain sand temper. Surface plain matte undecorated, very pale brown. Rim and body manufactured separately and joined before firing; thumb impression visible on vessel interior at point of joint. Wheel marks visible on rim and neck, shoulder of vessel scraped on exterior.
(B) G64-04-026. Unevenly fired light grey core tending to very pale brown toward exterior surface. Medium grain sand temper. Two impressed holes (possibly potter's marks) 2 mm deep on neck interior and one impressed hole on neck exterior. Wheel marks on exterior. Exterior plain matte undecorated, very pale brown.
(C) B81-0117/27-006. Evenly fired pale brown paste with medium grain sand temper. Rim interior has potter's marks (six fingernail impressions). Exterior surface of shoulder and neck decorated in horizontal reserved slip forming alternate light and dark bands 1 mm to 3 mm wide. Surface is very pale brown.

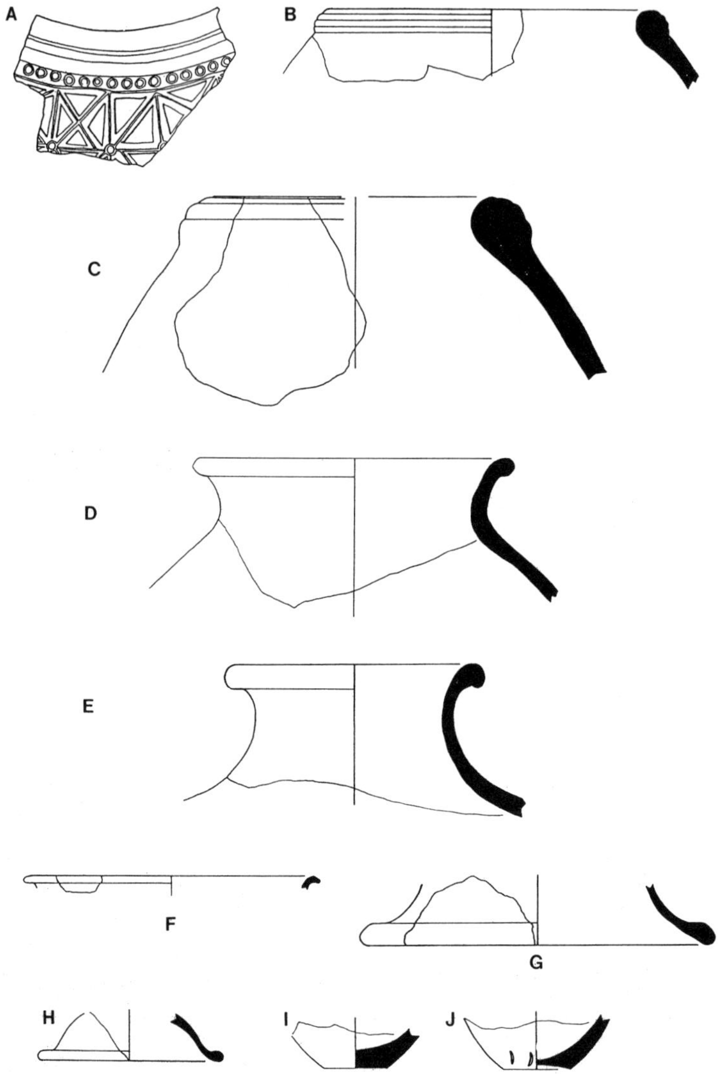
A
B
C
D
E
F
G
H
I
J

Figure 9 *(on facing page)*. Plain Simple Ware and Stone Ware Jars, Pedestals, and Bases (scale 2 : 5).
(A) B01-05-018. Evenly fired light reddish-brown paste with medium grain sand temper. Surface decoration of punctated circles, incised lines, and excised triangles. Surface is light reddish-brown.
(B) B01-03-018. Unevenly fired pale brown core tending to light yellowish-brown toward exterior surface. Fine to medium sand temper. Finger impression on vessel interior. Exterior surface plain matte undecorated, very pale brown.
(C) B81-0115/16-012. Diameter uncertain. Unevenly fired pale brown core tending to light grey toward surfaces. Interior scraped. Exterior smoothed, light grey.
(D) G64-0998-034. Evenly fired light yellowish-brown paste with medium grain sand temper and medium limestone grit inclusions. Surface very pale brown.
(E) B81-0335-017. Evenly fired light grey paste with medium sand temper. Rim profile varies from everted to slightly overhanging. Exterior surface plain light grey.
(F) G64-0338-012. Stone ware. Evenly fired grey paste with fine to medium sand temper and occasional medium grain limestone inclusions. Top of lip burnished. Interior and exterior surfaces are otherwise smoothed, undecorated grey. Closely spaced wheel marks on interior.
(G) B01-05-018. Evenly fired light grey paste with medium grain sand temper. Closely spaced wheel marks on interior surface. Exterior smoothed, very pale brown.
(H) B81-04-018. Evenly fired light grey paste with medium sand temper. Wheel marks visible. Exterior smoothed, very pale brown.
(I) B01-04-018. Evenly fired light grey paste with medium grain sand temper. Slightly smoothed exterior surface. Very pale brown matte undecorated.
(J) B01-04-018. Unevenly fired light grey core tending to light reddish-brown toward exterior. Medium grain temper. Closely spaced wheel marks on exterior. Exterior smoothed, very pale brown. Two fingernail impressions on surface as potter's marks.

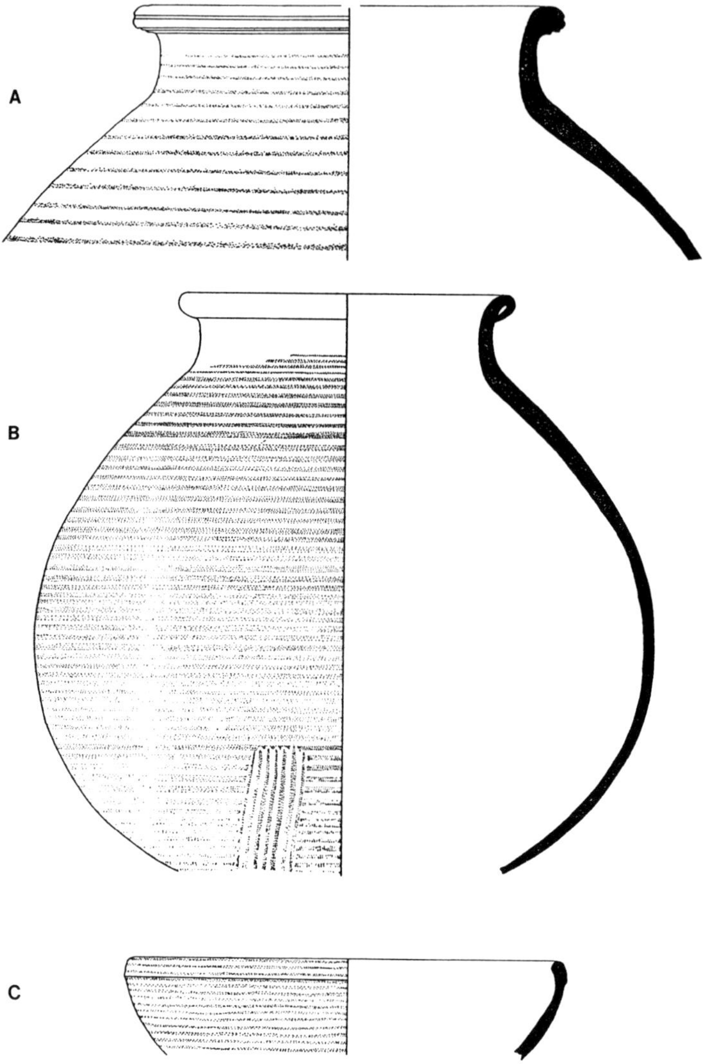

Figure 10. Wheel-Made Grit-Tempered Horizontal Reserve Slip Ware Vessels (from Algaze 1990b; scale 2 : 5).

(A) C55-09-023. Buff paste, small sized grits. Buff slip on exterior surface, horizontally reserved.

(B) C35-02-014. Buff paste, small sized grits. Buff slip on exterior surface, horizontally reserved.

(C) A01-06/01-036. Reddish-buff clay, small sized white grits. Exterior surface covered with greenish-buff slip, horizontally reserved.

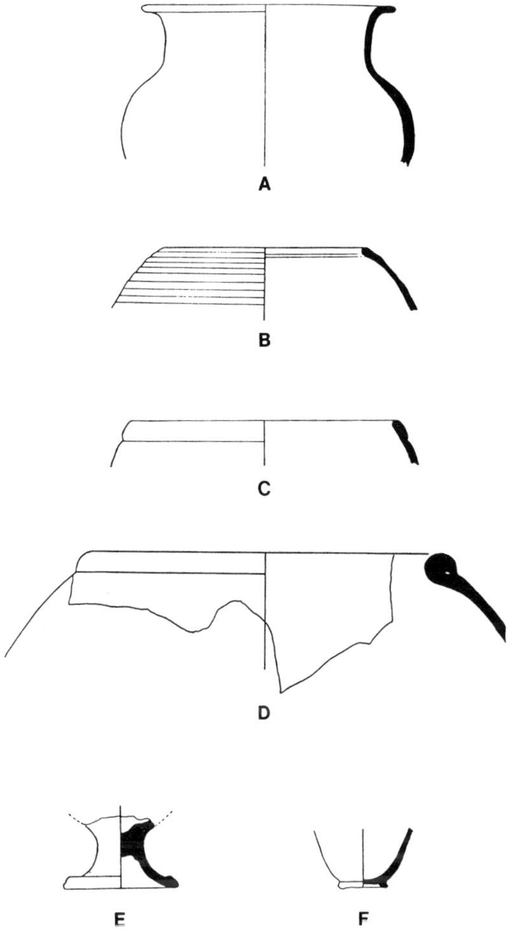

Figure 11. Wheel-Made Grit-Tempered Stone Ware Vessels (from Algaze 1990b; scale 2 : 5).

(A) A07-05-014. Dense orange on interior surface, reddish on exterior. Neck and rim are grey. Lightly burnished with horizontal strokes.

(B) B02-03-015. Dense reddish clay. Exterior surface is burnished.

(C) B01-05-014. Dense. Toward interior clay is greyish. Reddish toward exterior. No visible temper.

(D) G64-03-011. Unevenly fired, medium sand temper. Red, tending to grey toward interior surface.

(E) B03-05-002. Dense grey clay. No visible tempering other than occasional white grits.

(F) B02-03-004. Reddish clay. Small sized white grits. Exterior surface is black.

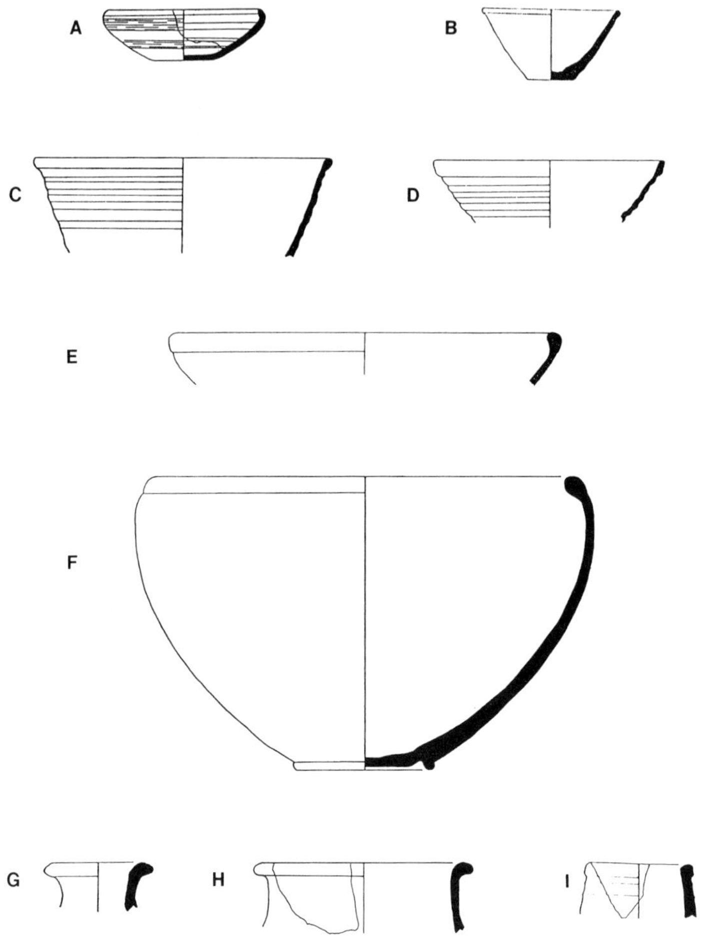
A
B
C
D
E
F
G
H
I

Figure 12 *(on facing page)*. Wheel-Made Grit-Tempered Stone Ware Vessels (from Algaze 1990b; scale 2 : 5).
(A) B01-03-018. Black paste, evenly fired with fine grit temper. Burnishing (incomplete) on rim interior and exterior, vessel interior. Scrape marks on exterior.
(B) C35-02-014. Dense light brownish-buff clay with grey core. A few small sized scattered white grits visible.
(C) B02-03-004. Dense reddish clay with occasional scattered small sized grits. Blackish on exterior top of vessel, reddish on lower part.
(D) B03-05-002. Dense brownish-buff clay, occasional scattered small sized grits.
(E) F01-04-009. Dense reddish clay.
(F) B02-0508-021. Unevenly fired with pale brown core tending to reddish-brown toward exterior and to very dark grey toward interior. Interior surface ranges from very dark grey at bottom to reddish-brown at rim. Exterior surface reddish-brown and burnished horizontally over upper half of vessel, fine grit sand temper.
(G) G64-0326-012. Evenly fired dark brown paste with medium sand temper. Exterior smoothed, light reddish-brown.
(H) G64-0327-012. Evenly fired dark brown paste with fine sand temper. Exterior surface smoothed matte undecorated light reddish-brown.
(I) B02-02-018. Evenly fired light brown paste with fine sand temper. Wheel marks visible on interior and exterior surfaces. Exterior surface slightly corrugated, pink.

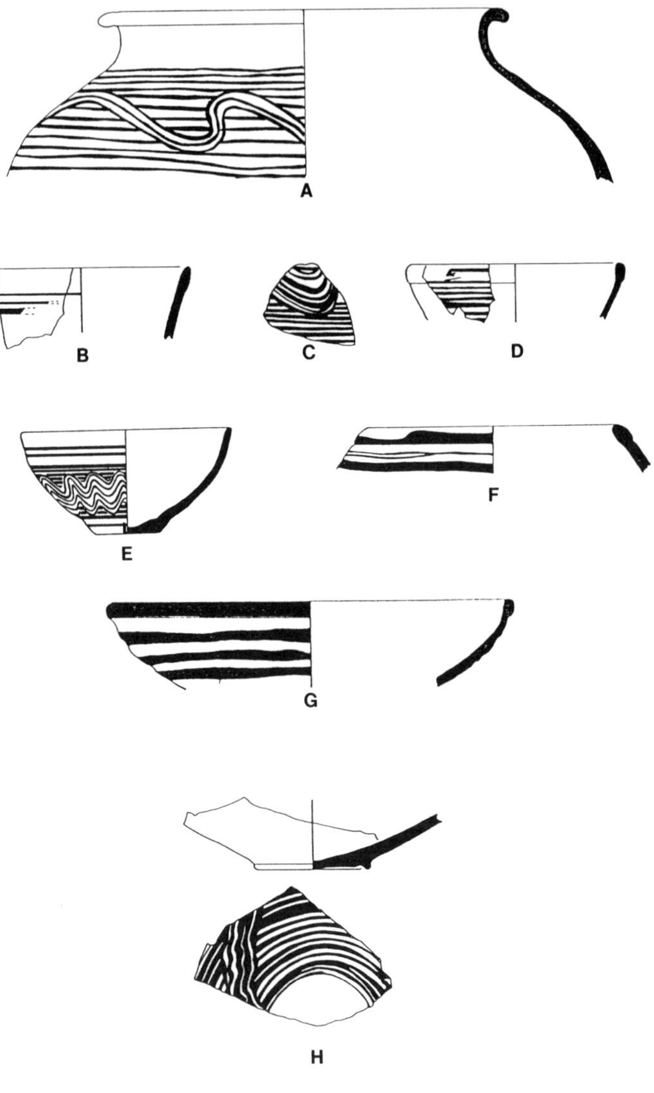
A
B
C
D
E
F
G
H

Figure 13 *(on facing page)*. Wheel-Made Grit Tempered Painted Band and Combed Wash Wares (after Algaze 1990b; scale 2 : 5).

(A) B02-03-015. Dense greenish-buff clay. Small sized grits. Olive-brown paint.

(B) G64-0218/19-013. Evenly fired pale brown paste with fine to medium sand temper. Closely spaced wheel marks on interior surface. Exterior surface smoothed very pale brown with painted bands of grayish-brown.

(C) B81-00116/17-006. Unevenly fired with interior well fired (almost Stone ware) and exterior Plain Simple ware. Fine grit temper. Exterior smoothed, pale brown. Paint varies with thickness from red-brown to brown.

(D) B02-03-018. Evenly fired pale brown with fine to medium sand temper and occasional fine limestone inclusions. Wheel marks visible on interior. Exterior surfaces very pale brown. Painted with brown bands.

(E) B02-03-015. Dense orange-reddish clay. Very small white grits, red paint.

(F) B01-0213-015. Greenish-buff clay, small sized grits. Brown paint.

(G) B02-03-010. Greenish-buff clay, small sized grits, black paint.

(H) C66-02-007. Evenly fired light grey paste with medium-grain sand temper. Surface painted with horizontal bands, cut through by diagonally combed or smeared lines.

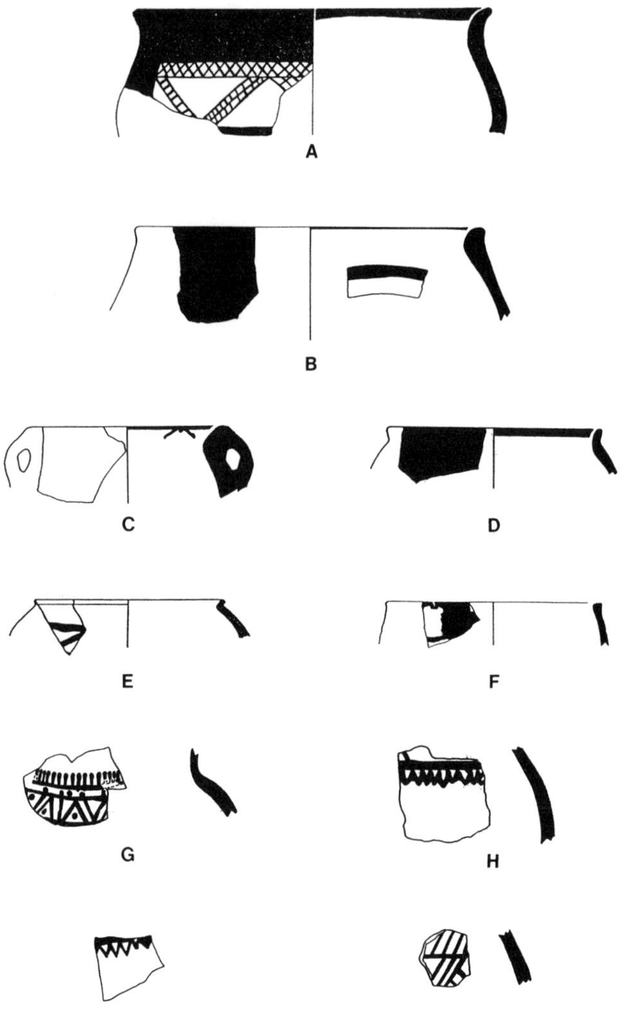
A
B
C
D
E
F
G
H
I
J

Figure 14 *(on facing page)*. Grit-Tempered Karababa Painted Ware (A, E, F, and G from Algaze 1990b; scale 2 : 5).

(A) B72-05-017. Brownish-buff clay. Medium sized white grits. Thick cream slip with black paint.

(B) B01-04-018. Reddish-brown paste with medium lime grit temper, evenly fired. Exterior paint weak. Marks on rim interior possibly from slow wheel.

(C) B02-04-018. Unevenly fired pale brown core tending to light brown exterior surface. Medium grain sand and limestone temper. Rim interior has reddish-brown painted design. Exterior surface painted very dark grey and possibly burnished as well.

(D) C66-01-003. Light brown paste with medium sand temper and occasional limestone grit inclusions. Evenly fired. Paint varies with thickness of application from reddish-brown to dark grey. Paint extends over lip interior.

(E) B02-04-004. Dense brownish-buff clay. No visible tempering. Lighter buff slip. Paint is brownish.

(F) B01-05-018. Evenly fired light gray with medium grain sand temper. Exterior painted dark grey.

(G) B02-03-018. Evenly fired light grey with medium sand temper. Exterior surface painted dark grey.

(H) B01-04-018. Light grey to very pale brown paste with medium lime grit temper. Evenly fired, exterior painted brown. Exterior unpainted surface is smoothed, possibly with light burnish. Shallow finger impressions on interior.

(I) B01-04-018. Unevenly fired with pale brown core tending to very pale brown at interior and exterior surfaces. Exterior surface smoothed very pale brown with brown painted triangles hanging from horizontal bands. Color varies with thickness of application. Medium sand and limestone temper.

(J) B01-04-018. Very pale brown paste with medium sand and limestone grit temper. Evenly fired. Exterior painted brown in two registers of cross-hatching.

Plate 13. Karababa Painted ware bowl from Area B. Photograph courtesy of the Oriental Institute.

INTRODUCTION TO THE PROBLEM OF AN INTERNAL CHRONOLOGY: MONITORING CHANGE WITHIN PERIOD IV

Because the chronological relationships used in this analysis differ in part from those presented in the final excavation report on Kurban Höyük (Marfoe and Algaze 1990), I will briefly outline the latter approach and the reasons for my reinterpretation. In the report on Kurban excavations, various Period IV excavation units and building levels were linked chronologically on the basis of similarities in architecture and, in some cases, depth below the mound surface. This was necessitated by the lack of stratigraphic connections between different site sectors (see site plan, Fig. 3), as well as temporal homogeneity in the ceramic assemblages (Algaze 1986, 58; 1990b, 335). As discussed in Chapter 2 (Algaze 1990a; Ingraham 1986), Period IV was divided into three subperiods on the basis of changes in Area A architecture (see Table 2). The Phase 13 fortification wall and Phase 14 public building defined Period IVB as one characterized by a large-scale building program (Ingraham 1986, 51, see tab. 4; Marfoe and Algaze 1990; Marfoe and Ingraham 1990, 61–2). Period IVC predated the fortification wall, and IVA post-dated its use (ibid.). Under

Table 2

Tentative Relative Chronology: Kurban Period IV

Timeline	Kurban	Amuq	Hama	Ebla	Chuera	Brak	Leilan
	III	J		IIB2			
2100 B.C.							
	IV.1						
	IV.2	I	J	IIB1 (palace)	Kleiner Antentempel	Agade	
	IV.3				Steinbau		II
					Houses	ED III	
	IV.4						
2500 B.C.							
	V	H		IIA			III

Note: Compiled from Braidwood and Braidwood (1960), Matthiae (1981, 66), Mazzoni (1985, 10), and Schwartz (1988b, 67).

the assumption that the IVB architecture in Area A represented an episode of settlement expansion and construction of a major wall system throughout the settlement, Area C/C01 [which had relatively massive architecture (in C35/45 and especially C01 Phases 11–14)], was dated to IVB (Ingraham 1986, 52; Marfoe and Evins 1990, 141). The two major building phases of Area C01 were correlated with two major building phases of Area A IVB (Phases 13 and 14). The dating of the Area C/C01 deposits on the small mound to Period IVB led to the conclusion that the small mound was only occupied in that subperiod. A wall segment 1.2 m wide in Area F served to correlate Phases 8–12 with Area A IVB (Ingraham 1986, 51; Marfoe 1990a, 176). As with Area A, levels predating this wide wall in Area F were assigned to Period IVC, and levels postdating the wall were dated to Period IVA.

Although the architecture in Area G was not massive, it was assigned to Period IVB, because it was located on the small mound, believed to have been occupied only in IVB. Moreover, the Area G deposits were just below the mound surface, as were those in Area C (Ingraham 1986, 51; Marfoe 1990b, 188). Initially Area B was placed in Period IVB because of its location away from the center of the large mound (which was believed to be the locus of settlement during this time), as well as parallels with Area C in building construction. It was reassigned to IVA when it became clear that the buildings had been reused in the following Period III (Ingraham 1986, 51; Marfoe 1990b, 181).

It was not possible to cross-check the Kurban relative chronology based on architecture and depth below surface with available results from Algaze's analysis of the Kurban ceramics from the deep soundings and Area C. An initial study of ware frequencies and broad vessel categories in each subperiod did not indicate changes through time in the ceramics examined (Algaze 1986, 58; 1990b, 335). Algaze isolated good chronological indicators for Period IVC on the one hand, and Periods IVB and IVA on the other, but he concluded that it was not possible to separate IVB and IVA levels on the basis of ceramics (Algaze 1990b, 339). Some differences between ceramics of Periods IVB and IVA were observed in assemblages from the deep soundings, but these criteria were discarded when ceramics from horizontal excavations, dated by project members on the basis of architecture, contradicted those findings (Algaze 1990b, 338). One reason for the apparent homogeneity in ceramics throughout most of the sequence may be that ceramic assemblages from horizontal excavations were dated on the basis of architecture. These assemblages were then compared with those from the deep soundings to verify the results of the ceramic chronology based on stratigraphic excavations, rather than vice versa. The apparent ceramic homogeneity was then used to justify the use of a relative chronology based on architecture.

Although the resulting chronology based on architecture served to provide a general framework for analysis of broad trends in the settlement history, the present study of change through time in production and consumption patterns required a relatively secure correlation of deposits across the site. For a number of reasons, I preferred a relative chronology based on ceramics to one based on architecture. First, if the locations of public buildings or elite neighborhoods shifted through time, buildings might have been interpreted as contemporary on the basis of similarities in scale, when in fact they may have represented elite buildings from different subperiods. Second, architecture might have varied as a result of location within the settlement, rather than chronology. For example, space may have become unavailable toward the center of the large mound, resulting in small, closely spaced structures on the large mound and larger but contemporary ones on the small mound. Third, wall robbing in Areas C and G on the small mound may have altered considerably the appearance of buildings in those areas, making it risky to date them on the basis of architecture. Fourth, factors such as the leveling of areas prior to construction of new buildings, more intensive occupation in one part of the site, and dispersed settlement during other periods would invalidate the use of depth below surface in establishing chronological relationships, as was done for Areas G, C, and the north part of Area B. Finally, similarities in scale of architecture served to place some

Plate 14. The Area A deep sounding.

deposits within subperiods, but it was not possible to link them with phases within subperiods. This made it difficult to place levels just before or after those with fairly massive architecture within subperiods.

In an effort to establish an internal relative chronology that was not based on the assumption of architectural homogeneity within subperiods, I undertook a ceramic seriation based on the relative frequencies of nine ceramic forms as well as four ware categories (see Appendix). I isolated these forms and ware categories by examining change through time in ceramic distributions from stratified deposits in the Area A sounding (Plate 14). I then checked the reliability of these ceramic attributes by using them to seriate deposits within each of the two other soundings. The results of the seriation are in close agreement with the stratigraphic evidence available in all but one case (Area

C subphases), providing solid support for the relative dating of deposits for which no stratigraphic linkages were obtained. On the basis of results of both excavations and the seriation, I divided the Period IV deposits into four subphases for the analysis (see Table 2). From earliest to latest they are as follows: Subperiod IV.4, the earliest levels of Period IV, predating the fortification wall ("village phases," see Fig. 39, v1, v13, later in the book), Subperiod IV.3, when settlement seems to have expanded and monumental architecture was constructed ("town formation phases," Fig. 39, v2, v6, v3, v7); Subperiod IV.2, when the site may have reached its maximum extent in size and maximum variability in the status of residents ("town development phases"; Fig. 39, v8, v17, v14, v4, v10, v11); and Subperiod IV.1, when population density may have increased and space on the large mound appears to have been limited ("town nucleation phases"; Fig. 39, v12, v9; v16; v5; v15).

With the exception of layers from the deep soundings, the excavated deposits date to the last two subperiods, as we might expect, given that excavations focused on deposits just below the surface. Most reasonably well-preserved deposits close to the surface of the small mound were assigned to Subperiod IV.2, whereas those close to the surface of the large mound represented Subperiod IV.1. The absence of coherent late Period IV occupational remains on the small mound may indicate a contraction of settlement with the population concentrated on the large mound during this time (Marfoe and Algaze 1990, 429). However, the presence of a poorly preserved Period IV occupational phase above the IV.2 levels of the small mound, combined with the late relative dating obtained for ceramics from C01 Phase 16, suggests that the small mound was occupied in IV.1 but that the architecture was largely destroyed. On the large mound, later occupational remains and wash layers served to protect IV.1 levels from weathering and from destruction by plowing. In contrast, there was no post-Period IV occupation on the small mound,[1] and the uppermost levels were vulnerable to destruction from plowing, weathering, and wall robbing.

This evidence for continued occupation on the small mound during Period IV, combined with evidence for increasing population density of the large mound, presented in the following chapter, illustrates that shifting settlement patterns at the site in the later part of this sequence were more complex than that of a simple population decline. Having placed the various Period IV deposits within a relative chronological framework, it is now possible to examine more closely the nature of the evidence from each subperiod, as well as changes in the architecture and community organization during Period IV.

THE MID-LATE THIRD MILLENNIUM TOWN AT KURBAN HÖYÜK 4

During the Early Bronze Age, Kurban Höyük went through numerous phases of growth, contraction, and reorganization, as revealed in the chronological analysis in the preceding chapter. In this chapter, I examine the nature of the settlement during each of these subphases. Archaeologists generally assume that small town and village-sized sites were composed largely of farming and herding families of relatively modest resources. In fact, excavations in the Near East and elsewhere have revealed that even smaller sites were diverse in terms of the function of buildings recovered, status of residents, and activities they carried (cf. Schwartz and Falconer 1994). To recognize any variability that may have existed in function of buildings and status of occupants at Kurban Höyük, I examine the excavation results from each area. I use findings to provide an overview of the function of various site sectors, changes through time in the nature of the settlement, and the archaeological contexts of the artifacts used to study economic trends, which are presented in Chapters 5 and 6.

EXCAVATION AND INTERPRETATION OF MID-THIRD MILLENNIUM B.C. DEPOSITS AT KURBAN HÖYÜK

The following interpretations of the Period IV remains are based on data presented in unpublished field records and published reports on the deep soundings at Kurban Höyük (Algaze 1990a).[1]

PUBLIC BUILDINGS AND PRIVATE DWELLINGS

Mid-third millennium building remains from Kurban Höyük varied according to size, architectural plan, and presumably purpose of construction. Features and artifacts found in association with archaeological deposits were diverse. Before examining the extent of specialization among the non-elites and comparing production and consumption patterns between elites and non-elites, it is necessary to establish whether excavated areas were indeed residential and to consider the social ranks of residents.

Residential structures and special-purpose buildings can be differentiated on the basis of architecture and associated artifacts. When entire buildings are exposed, it is usually not difficult to distinguish domestic structures from other kinds of architecture. However, at Kurban Höyük, the depth of the deposits and incomplete preservation resulted in only partial recovery of building plans, which meant identification of building function was more difficult. Both ethnoarchaeological data and data on complete buildings excavated in east Anatolia and north Syria have provided guidelines for identifying domestic structures.

Domestic structures and associated trash deposits are likely to have a high proportion of artifacts used in food preparation, serving, and consumption. In addition, domestic structures might have a wider range of materials than structures that served a specific function, such as workshops. For example, in households we might find artifacts used in hunting, fishing, agricultural production, food storage, processing and preparation, carpentry, sewing, games, personal ornamentation, and ritual activities. In contrast, artifacts associated with a workshop might be confined to tools and raw materials used to manufacture a specific category of goods.

Watson (1979, 161–73) listed standard items found in nearly every household at the western Iranian village of Hasanabad. Most of these, such as adobe storage chests and storage pits, mortars and pestles, and pots played a role in food procurement, storage, preparation, and serving. We would expect a similar range of features and artifacts in archaeological contexts. Weaving and sewing were household activities at Hasanabad, and spindles and needles were found in houses (ibid., 173). The distribution of spindles in an archaeological situation would depend on whether spinning was a household activity, as well as whether spindle whorls were made of perishable wood or more durable materials. Clothing and personal ornaments were among the materials represented in the Hasanabad houses. Although textiles would generally not be preserved, other materials used in personal ornamentation, such as beads, might be. Each house had at least one hearth in the living room and many households had a second hearth. In the modern city of Şanlıurfa, near Kurban Höyük, traditional shops in the bazaar are not heated, because winter days are relatively mild. Hearths might be located primarily in houses, where they would be needed for food preparation and heat during winter nights.

Specialized workshop areas are often obvious because of concentrations of manufacturing implements, by-products, or quantities of finished products. For example, the ceramic workshop at Lidar Höyük included kilns, large quantities of wasters, and ash deposits (Hauptmann 1982, 18). This workshop was spatially separate from the residential area, but workshops associated with domestic structures may also be recognizable. For example, a house found in a different part of the settlement, probably a potter's residence, included an unusual quantity of sherds used as house construction material. Adjacent to the house was an ashy deposit similar to that found in the kiln area but not found elsewhere at the site (Hauptmann 1984, 227; 1985, 205).

Documented plans of north Syro-Mesopotamian public buildings and temples have been summarized by Crawford (1977, 45–61; 1991); it is sufficient to note that many public buildings can be recognized by their scale, quality of construction, specific architectural features, and associated artifacts. Public building such as palaces or temples can often be distinguished from houses because of their relatively large size, massive walls, careful construction, and regular plan. They are often located in or near the center of a settlement. Examples include the Norsuntepe palaces (Hauptmann 1979, 57, 59) and the Tell Mardikh palace and temples (Matthiae 1981, 43). Smaller administrative buildings and modest temples may be more difficult to recognize and may be confused with residential structures (Crawford 1977, 47–8, 53–4). However, even in smaller structures, features such as benches and altars are often found in shrines (e.g., Tell Chuera; see Kühne 1976, plan 1), and administrative artifacts such as discarded clay sealings from containers or doors might be associated with either temples or administrative buildings (see later discussion).

Building size was *not* a useful indicator of function at Kurban Höyük, because structures were only partially excavated, and the areal extent of buildings could not be determined. Instead, wall thickness, construction techniques, building plan, features, and room contents provided insight into building function as well as the socioeconomic status of occupants. The walls of public buildings are generally more massive than those of domestic structures. For example, walls from the palace at Tell Mardikh measured approximately 2.5 m in width (Pinnock 1984, plate V). Most walls of the large third millennium B.C. public building of Level VI at Norsuntepe in east-central Turkey measured between 1 m and 2.5 m, although a few small interior walls were less than 1 m. House walls from the same period measured between .5 m and .8 m (Hauptmann 1979, 37, 39). Broad excavations of mid-final third millennium B.C. residential structures at Selenkiheye in the Euphrates Valley of north Syria revealed what appeared to be a primarily residential district. House walls ranged in width from approximately .6 m to 1.1 m (van Loon 1979, fig. 8). At Kurban Höyük, mud-brick walls were preserved only in the deep excavations, but stone foundations were generally intact, so that wall thickness could be measured.

Because ancient Near Eastern public buildings were often carefully planned and followed a standardized layout, they may have been more regular in plan than domestic structures; houses were often constructed incrementally as more space was needed. Prior to construction of public buildings, areas were often cleared and leveled. In domestic areas, builders made do with available space, so that walls were often not constructed at right angles. For public buildings, the construction was generally more elaborate, with features such as wall buttresses, pillars, mud-brick rather than packed dirt courtyards, and painted walls.

Temples may have had offering platforms and benches lining the walls, such as in the inner cella of the early second millennium structure, Sanctuary B2, at Tell Mardikh (Matthiae 1979, 19, fig. 5). The walls were sometimes massive and the plan more symmetrical than was the case with domestic architecture. Some early second millennium shrines from Tell Mardikh were relatively small in areal extent but had walls 3-m and 4-m thick (Matthiae 1978, 21; Matthiae 1979, 18, fig. 4). The simple building plans and massive walls contrasted with the closely spaced domestic structures with much thinner walls built at irregular angles.

The artifacts in public buildings and temples differ from those in domestic structures. Clay sealings were often used to monitor or restrict access to rooms or the contents of containers (see Wright and Johnson 1975, 271–2). Although seals or sealings may be found in private houses, they are more likely to be concentrated in public buildings, which served as collection, storage, and reshipment nodes for large volumes of tribute and trade goods. For example, at Arslantepe, large quantities of sealings had accumulated on the floors of late fourth millennium B.C. public buildings (Frangipane and Palmieri 1988/1989). Sealings did not prevent access, but broken seals served to alert officials or owners to the unauthorized opening of rooms or containers. Therefore, seals are most effective in situations in which the identities of potential intruders are known, such as when workers have access to rooms or messengers are delivering goods. When goods were sent between households, it is more likely that transactions occurred directly between the parties involved, obviating the need to seal goods. In contrast, gifts, trade goods, or tribute sent to public buildings would more likely be delivered via messengers, rather than directly by the sender. For example, if tribute goods were sent by officials of a dependent polity, it is likely that they would have been delivered by messengers, rather than the officials ultimately responsible for the collection and delivery of goods. In such cases, containers might be sealed to prevent removal or substitution of contents by messengers. The sealings would then be discarded in or near the public building after delivery, as the contents were checked. Another reason sealings were more common in public buildings was that larger numbers of unauthorized individuals have the opportunity to gain access to goods stored in a public building than in houses, necessitating the use of container and door sealings.

Evidence for many of the same activities might be found in both houses and public buildings. However, these activities might have been more spatially discrete in public buildings, where they were more likely to have been conducted on a larger scale by specialists (e.g., see Zeder 1988, 243–5). Public buildings are more likely to have concentrations of goods made of scarce materials or even of unworked raw materials. Finally, elite and public buildings are often disappointing in terms of artifact yields, with most debris having been swept up and discarded (e.g., see Wright 1981, 178). However, through a combined consideration of architectural scale, features, and artifacts, it is often possible to distinguish public from domestic structures, even when buildings are only partially cleared.

ARCHAEOLOGICAL INFERENCES ON HOUSEHOLD RANK: DOMESTIC ARCHITECTURE AND ARTIFACTS

A key source of variability I tried to control for in this analysis was differences between households in ranking, as expressed in the material remains. Ethnographically, there seems to be a positive correlation between house size and family wealth in the Near East, even in villages where architecture is relatively homogeneous (e.g., Kramer 1982, 127; Watson 1979, 292). Hasanabad families ranked by Watson as "wealthiest," "middlin," and "poorest" on the basis of animals owned, the condition of houses (but not size), and other possessions (1979, 229–30) had house compounds that averaged approximately 330 m^2, 245 m^2 and 220 m^2, respectively.[2]

Archaeological support for a positive relationship between house size and wealth comes from the central Mesopotamian town site of Khafajah. Late-early Dynastic houses judged relatively wealthy on the basis of associated artifacts were larger than average (Henrickson 1981, 70). Tombs tended to occur in houses greater than 200 m^2, and simple pit graves were more common in houses of less than 200 m^2 (ibid., 73).

Although there is a positive correlation between house size and family wealth, the areal extent of houses could not be used as an indicator of family wealth in this study, because only portions of structures were cleared. Individual room dimensions do not appear to be reliable indicators of family wealth, because dimensions will vary with function and total number of rooms per house. Ethnographically, a poor family may have only one room both for their own use and for receiving guests, whereas a wealthier family may have separate rooms, each of which is smaller than the single room of the poorer family (Watson 1979, 126, 230, and figs. 5.6–5.29). Using the data from Hasanabad, I calculated the mean living room areas of "wealthiest" and "next wealthiest" families as 19.3 m^2, of "middlin" families as 15.3 m^2 and of "poorest" families as 18.9 m^2; the lack of a consistent positive correlation may be related to the small sample size.

In the absence of data on total structure size at Kurban Höyük, I used wall thickness as an indicator of wealth. Thicker walls require greater amounts of building material as well as labor but provide greater protection from heat and cold. Moreover, wealthier families might be more likely to have second stories (Watson 1979, 292), which require thicker walls. At one Iranian village, walls for single-story houses were .50 m to .60 m, whereas walls with second stories were, ideally, at least 1 m thick (Kramer 1982, 132). If an upper story was added after construction of the original house, the ground floor walls were thickened by the addition of abutting walls.

Unfortunately, there may not always be a strong relationship between family rank and house wall thickness. External walls of Hasanabad houses had a mean thickness of .62 m for "wealthiest" and "next wealthy" households, .63 m for "middlin" houses, and .58 m for "poorest" houses (Watson 1979, 230, figs. 5.6–5.29). Internal walls were almost all about .50 m regardless of family ranking; contrary to expectations, walls less than .50 m were found in three households categorized as "wealthiest." The landowner's building, occupied by the village headman, provides a striking exception to this pattern of homogeneous or seemingly random wall thickness, regardless of wealth. This large structure (960 m^2) housed the village leader and sharecroppers, as well as the landlord when he visited, and served as a storage area for the landlord's share of the harvest. In addition to being more than twice as large as the next largest compound, this structure has external walls of almost 1 m in thickness compared with an average of .61 m for the other village houses. The internal walls measured .70 m, whereas the average for other houses was .47 m. These results suggest that although wall thickness may not be useful for recognizing relatively minor variations in wealth, it does serve to isolate structures serving a combined residential and administrative function for elite families.

At the modern village of Aliabad, in the Iranian Zagros, second-story living rooms are considered desirable in hot weather, presumably because they receive more of a breeze (Kramer 1982, 135). However, the association between family wealth and the presence of an upper-story room was only moderately strong. Kramer attributed this weaker than expected association to the fact that families having second-story rooms tended to fall into two categories: relatively wealthy families who did not need the extra space but desired a second-story living room and relatively poor households with small compounds and no space for horizontal expansion. Poorer families with fairly spacious compounds tended not to have second stories (Kramer 1982, 134–5). Living rooms of the poorer landless families were larger than those of the landed, and Kramer suggested this may reflect long-term plans on the part of the landed to add rooms (Kramer 1982, 129). Perhaps plans for expansion would be evident in the thickness of walls as well. Relatively wealthy families, expecting to add second stories, might have initially built fairly massive walls. In contrast, poorer families having to add second stories when their compounds became too crowded might have had to thicken their ground floor walls by adding abutting walls. By differentiating between walls that were initially constructed fairly massively and double walls, it might be possible to identify houses that were occupied by relatively wealthy families.

Artifacts provided an additional line of evidence for cross-checking inferences on household rank based on architecture. Poorer households tend to expend a greater proportion of resources on subsistence goods (see Douglas and Isherwood 1979, 155). I expected low-status houses to have a greater proportion of artifacts dealing directly with subsistence, and higher ranking houses to have more materials not directly related to subsistence, such as ornaments and artifacts used in information-processing activities. High-ranking households would be more likely to have goods made of scarce material, such as metal. At Kurban Höyük, such artifacts were rare in general, and it was not always possible to determine if the locations of such objects were a result of chance (e.g., accidental loss of an object), rather than status of occupants. Moreover, many objects of scarce materials were found in streets, where they could not be linked to specific structures. Nonetheless, the density of "sumptuary goods" and information-processing artifacts (such as seals) was somewhat greater in the vicinity of the more substantial buildings.

The data from Hasanabad discussed previously suggest that without largely complete house plans it would be difficult to recognize relatively minor variations in household rank, but that *major* distinctions might be evident even with small sections of a structure. In the following consideration of architectural evidence, I interpreted especially thick walls as one line of evidence that a building was not a low-status domestic structure and then examined the associated artifacts and features to cross-check findings from architecture, as well as to determine if the building was residential and/or public.

THE KURBAN PERIOD IV ARCHITECTURE

The extensive exposures of Period IV deposits in Areas B and C provided detailed information on the nature of architecture and spatial layout of neighborhoods during this period. Most of the houses in these areas and elsewhere in the Period IV settlement had stone foundations rising above the floor. The wall superstructures rarely survived intact, but findings from the deep soundings, where architecture was better preserved, revealed that the stone foundations had been capped with mud-brick. In areas with good preservation, floors and walls were plastered white. A few walls were made entirely of mud-brick and some floors consisted of packed mud. In both Areas B and C, houses flanked a cobble and pebble street.

In Area C, the most extensively excavated part of the Period IV settlement, at least two houses had foyers that led to courtyards. However, in the fairly extensive clearance of Area B, no courtyards were recovered. Houses from this area had less carefully constructed wall foundations made of smaller stones. Structures were built against one another. The street appeared to be the only exterior area in the immediate vicinity of the houses, unless courtyards were located outside of the excavation area.

Viewing the Period IV evidence as a whole, there was relatively little differentiation within this community in the scale and elaboration of construction. With the exception of the building from Area A Phase 14, and possibly that of Area A Phase 13, most building remains seem to have been houses occupied by the non-elites. Although the community appears to have been relatively homogeneous on a most general level, detailed examination of architecture reveals significant variability within periods, as well as change through time, in the plans of non-elite houses and neighborhoods.

SUBPERIOD IV.4: VILLAGE PHASES

Exposures from the earliest Period IV phases inform about the antecedents of the Early Bronze Age town that developed in the following subperiod. Excavations were limited to Area A on the large mound and Area F in the saddle. Although a sounding on the small mound, Area C01, was completed, no Subperiod IV.4 occupational layers were recovered from this area, perhaps indicating that the site was only partially occupied during this subperiod (Marfoe and Algaze 1990, 427) or that the density of occupation was fairly low. Based on the limited available evidence indicating that Kurban Höyük was a village-sized site at this time, the settlement of this subperiod is referred to as a "village." However, as will be discussed later, differences were observed in the amount of labor invested in architecture, and possibly in the status of the residents as well. Moreover, the settlement may have been larger than the available evidence suggests; a single sounding is insufficient for establishing a lack of settlement on the north mound. Thus, I leave open the possibility that a town-sized settlement had already formed by this period.

Area A yielded an exterior passageway between two structures and a surface without associated architecture in a 22-m^2 exposure (ca. 1 m of Subperiod IV.4 deposits). Remains from a 3.74-m^2 exposure (just over 1 m deep) in Area F include a series of stratified surfaces (both interior and exterior deposits) and one floor deposit within a structure. Because of the limited exposures, very little is known about Subperiod IV.4, the least documented subperiod of Period IV.

AREA A: PHASE 11

The earliest Period IV occupational phase was represented by an exterior passageway bordered on either side by walls from adjacent structures (Fig. 15). Neither of the structures were excavated, and only one room corner was exposed (Unit 11.1). The small exposure of Unit 11.1 (25 m^2) yielded a series

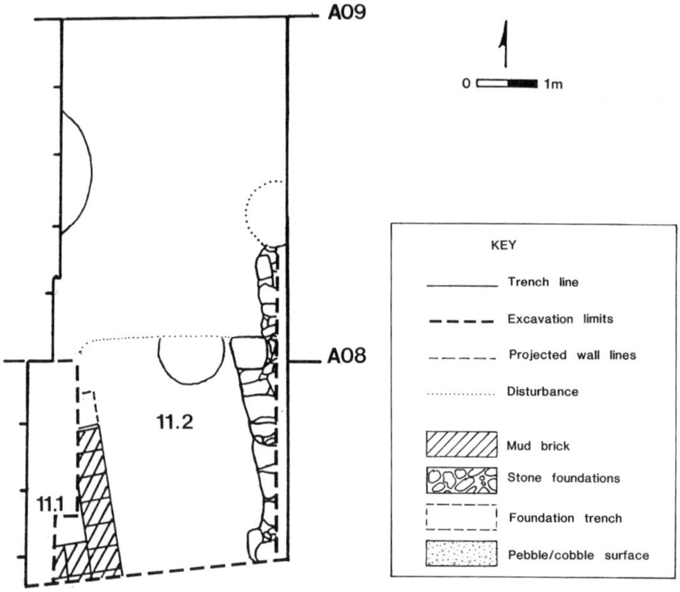

Figure 15. Plan of Area A Phase 11. After Marfoe and Ingraham 1990. (Plans of Figures 15 to 24 and 26 to 29 represent simplified plans after Algaze 1990a. The key applies to Figures 15–22, 24–28, and 30–32)

of white plaster floors, seen only in section. The walls were made of alternating beige and red-brown mud-bricks, a relatively elaborate style not found elsewhere at the site. In contrast to walls from the later subperiods—when most walls had stone foundations rising above the floor level—the wall of Unit 11.1 was made entirely of mud-brick without stone foundations (see Marfoe and Ingraham 1990, 35–36). The artifacts, primarily chipped stone, ceramics, and bone, suggest a domestic function. The only artifacts indicating a possible specialized function are two pierced limestone artifacts recorded as "weights," perhaps loom weights (see Wright 1981, 149).

Unit 11.2 was an open area of compacted earth, possibly a passageway. The unexcavated unit to the east of Unit 11.2 was represented by a wall foundation of limestone blocks overlaid with mud-brick. This construction style—a stone foundation rising well above the floor and capped by mud-brick—is typical of Period IV (Marfoe and Ingraham 1990, 35–6).

Although the exposed wall of Unit 11.1 appears fairly elaborate, without more extensive exposures from this subperiod it is not possible to determine if it is common or unusual for this subperiod. However, differences between

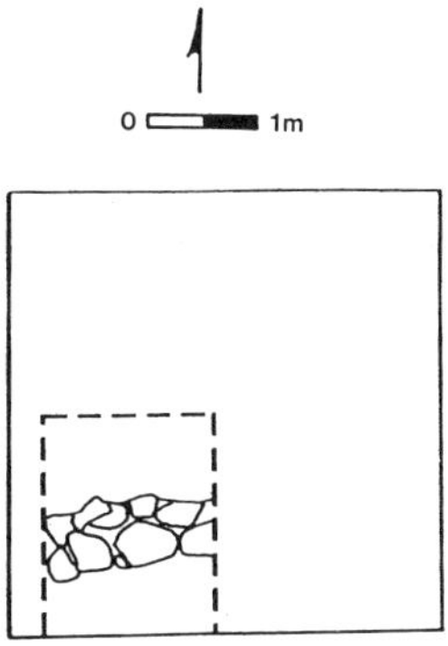

Figure 16. Plan of Area F Phase 6.

the walls of Unit 11.1 and the wall along the eastern edge of Unit 11.2 would suggest that the building may not have been typical.

AREA A: PHASE 12

Phase 12 (no plan available) was separated from the earlier one by approximately .85 m of collapse. It was poorly preserved, a result both of erosion and disturbance from major construction in the subsequent phase, and represented only by a compacted earth surface with two hearths. The only wall, an unassociated fragment of a mud-brick wall, apparently without stone foundations, was .35 m thick (see Marfoe and Ingraham 1990, 37). The packed earth surface, narrow wall, and hearths, combined with the recovery of pottery, chipped stone and bone from the surface, suggest that this was a domestic area. It appears to have been more modest than Unit 11.1, although this may be a result of poor preservation.

AREA F: PHASES 2 TO 7

Because of the limited areal exposure (3.75 m^2), the first five phases are known from occupation surfaces with no associated architecture. Phase 2, the earliest Period IV.4 level, was defined by a pebble layer, perhaps a street or exterior work area (Fig. 16). It was overlain with an ashy silt deposit. Two stratified plaster floors, separated by a thin layer of occupational debris, represented Phases 3 and 4. It is likely that these were interior surfaces; other examples of white plaster floors from well-preserved Period IV contexts came from interior contexts. Phase 5 consisted of an approximately .25-m series of surfaces, including two ash lenses and a pebble surface.

Phase 6 provided a stone wall foundation and an associated plaster floor. The final phase of this subperiod, Phase 7, included a surface of pebbles and limestone, perhaps associated with the same wall as the Phase 6 surface (Marfoe 1990b, 170–1).

The limited exposure from this part of the site makes it difficult to determine the functional nature of the deposits or status of the occupants. All artifacts suggest a domestic function; the excavated wall is within the size range expected for a non-elite domestic structure. The only evidence for specialized manufacturing is a single piece of vitrified kiln material associated with the pebble surface of Phase 5, perhaps indicating proximity to a ceramic or metallurgical workshop. A drilled shell pendant made from *Arcularia*, a Mediterranean shell species (Reese 1990, 410–1), came from a mixed context from the earliest phase, and may derive from the underlying Late Chalcolithic deposits.

An absence of settlement on the small mound during Subperiod IV.4 was suggested by the relatively shallow Period IV deposits in Area C01 and the absence of an early Period IV ceramic assemblage (Marfoe and Evins 1990, 130). The results of the Area C01 ceramic seriation supported this interpretation. Although the areal clearance from this period was very limited, available evidence suggests that the settlement during these early phases was a small village-sized settlement. The exposure is too small to determine if elite domestic architecture or public buildings were present at the settlement during this time. However, the relatively elaborate construction of Unit 11.1, compared with that of Units 11.2 (eastern wall), 12.1, and those in Area F, indicates variability in domestic architecture and socioeconomic diversity even during the earliest phases.

Major differences appear to have existed in the scale of excavated architecture in this earlier subperiod and the subsequent one (Marfoe and Ingraham 1990, 37–8), although this may be a result of the limited excavations of the earliest phases. The total exposure for Subperiod IV.3 in Area A alone was approximately 80 m^3, compared with only approximately 26 m^3 from Subperiod IV.4 deposits in both Areas F and A. Within Area A, the apparent differences in scale of architecture between Subperiod IV.4 and the subsequent Subperiod IV.3 (Phases 13 and 14) may be at least partially related to differences in preservation conditions in excavated areas of each period. The Phase 11 occupational layers in Area A had been truncated because of erosion of mound deposits. The Phase 12 deposits were even more badly disturbed, both because of erosion and disturbance from Phase 13 construction. In short, little is known of the antecedents of the Subperiod IV.3 town. Thus, although Subperiod IV.3 (or IVB in Algaze 1990a) is viewed as a period of political reorganization and social change, the limited exposure of the earliest Period IV settlement makes this interpretation highly tentative, especially given the elaborate nature of the Area A Phase 11 architecture. Future excavation at other sites may well push back the date of political centralization and urbanism to the earliest phases of this period.

SUBPERIOD IV.3: TOWN FORMATION PHASES

This subperiod was represented in two of the three deep soundings, Areas A and C01. The architecture in these areas defined the subperiod (IVB in Algaze 1990a) as one of major construction and expansion. Data from Areas A and C01 that serve as the basis for interpretations are derived from excavation reports (Marfoe and Evins 1990; Marfoe and Ingraham 1990). Exposures from this subperiod include (1) part of a building (or portions of three smaller structures) in association with a massive wall from a 68-m^2 clearance from Area A Phase 13; (2) part of a carefully constructed and relatively elaborate building from the subsequent building phase (Area A Phase 14); and (3) five phases of interior and exterior surfaces from a house and associated enclosed courtyard, recovered in an approximately 18-m^2 sounding in Area C01.

AREA A: PHASES 13 AND 14

The total exposure of Area A Phases 13 and 14 remains reached a maximum of 50 m^2 at the base and was 3.5 m deep (Marfoe and Ingraham 1990, 37). A sounding .5 m to .6 m below a substantial Phase 13, interpreted as a fortification wall, produced ashy fill, leading to the suggestion that there was no public architecture in this part of the mound prior to Phase 13 (ibid., 38).

Two interpretations are offered for the Phase 13 architecture. In one view, the architectural plan was essentially that shown in Figure 17, with some disturbance caused by a Phase 14 foundation trench to the north of Unit 13.6. The plan has been interpreted as a series of modest structures, with a newly founded major fortification wall serving as the north wall for two of these building (see Marfoe and Ingraham 1990, 38–41). However, I propose

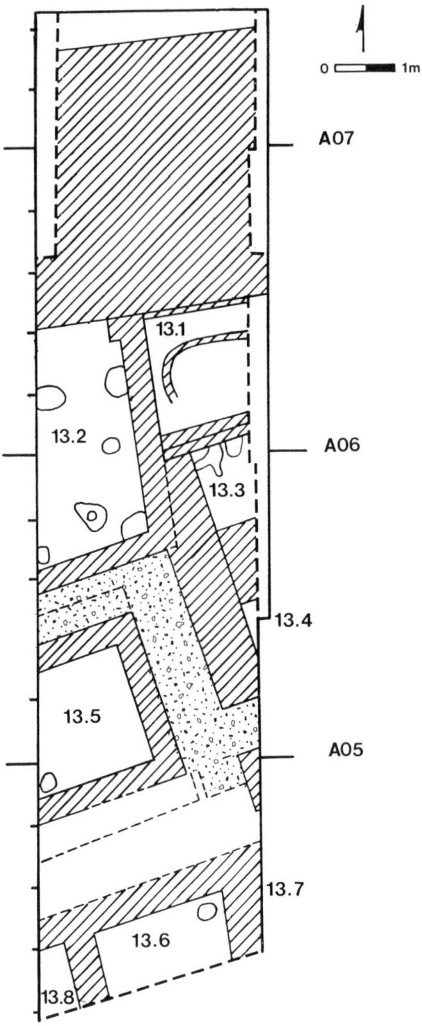

Figure 17. Plan of Area A Phase 13.

that the Phase 13 architecture may have originally been a more substantial building, similar to that of Phase 14 (Fig. 18). The seemingly less substantial walls of Phase 13, and gaps between units, may be attributed to disturbance from foundation trenches for the Phase 14 walls. A more substantial structure in Phase 13 than the plan suggests would help account for juxtaposition of the building and a massive wall. In both interpretations the area was residential, although if the second view is correct, the area was probably inhabited by high-status residents in Phase 13 as well as Phase 14.

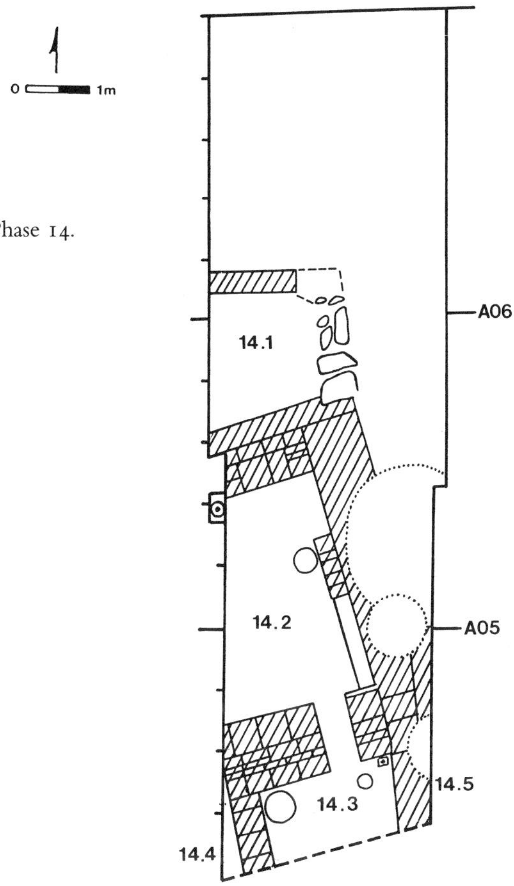

Figure 18. Plan of Area A Phase 14.

AREA A: PHASE 13

The data from this phase have been interpreted as evidence of a major building program that surpassed the scale of construction in the previous period (Marfoe and Ingraham 1990, 37–8). A 4.5-m-thick east-west mud-brick wall led to the characterization of Phase 13 as one of a substantive building program. Only a small section of the wall was excavated, but the scale alone suggested that it may have been part of a fortification wall surrounding the south mound. The interior face of the massive wall was plastered, and the wall served as the north wall for two partially cleared rooms, Units 13.1 and 13.2 (ibid., 38–9). Given the absence of evidence for occupational remains on the small mound during the early part of this subphase, it is possible that the settlement was confined to the area within the wall. Alternatively, only part of the settlement was fortified during this time. By Phase 14, if not before, houses were located outside of the wall on the lower town, and the wall may have served primarily to mark off an elite area from other parts of the site. Finally, the wall may simply represent the outer wall of an elite precinct or building. Although it is substantially larger than one might expect from a wall serving such a purpose, a roughly contemporaneous 5-m-wide exterior wall of an elite building was recovered from the center of Kazane. Although it seems unlikely that such monumental architecture would be located at a small site such as Kurban Höyük, we know remarkably little about elite sectors of town sites in this part of the Near East.

Unit 13.2 was separated from Unit 13.1 by a mud-brick partition wall; there was no doorway connecting them. Like several other Phase 13 walls, the south wall of Unit 13.2 had stone foundations with a mud-brick superstructure (Marfoe and Ingraham 1990, 39). All three walls had plaster faces. Mud-bricks were used as flooring, indicating more investment in floor construction than has been found in other Period IV rooms and supporting the interpretation that this area was occupied by higher ranking residents than the fragmentary remains suggest. Overlying the mud-brick flooring was a series of four plaster floors. Hearths were associated with the first three floors (the third one had two), and the earliest floor had a small plaster-lined pit and hearth. The unit appeared to have been burned during or shortly after the final floor level was in use. The walls were burned red and the fill over the floor was ashy (Marfoe and Ingraham 1990, 39). Although the walls of Unit 13.2 suggest that it was constructed somewhat haphazardly, making use of the fortification wall in an ad hoc fashion, this may be a result of incomplete wall preservation.

Although in the plan Unit 13.5 appears as a freestanding unit, it may originally have been part of the same structure as Unit 13.2. In section, the foundation stones of the north wall of Unit 13.5 can be seen to have originally extended further north (Marfoe and Ingraham 1990, 40). The excavators interpret this as evidence for a reduction of the room size, but it is also possible that the outer section of the wall was destroyed, perhaps when it was rebuilt in Phase 14. Although it has been suggested that the stone paving to the north and east of Unit 13.5 was either a street or *packing* (fill packed behind the fortification wall) (ibid., 41), it is also possible that it represents foundations for sections of Phases 13 walls that had been destroyed. Disturbance to the south of Unit 13.5 was caused by a foundation trench for a Phase 14 wall. Given that considerable continuity between architecture of the two phases was noted by the excavators (ibid., 43; see figs. 20 and 21), it may be relevant that these gaps between the Phase 13 walls occur below Phase 14 walls. The fact that in Phase 14 the two walls were rebuilt as one large one supports the interpretation that the Phase 13 walls had originally been more substantial. If the two walls originally did join in Phase 13, they would have totalled 2.30 m in thickness, perhaps including a bench (see Phase 14 plan in Figure 18). The walls of Unit 13.5 consisted of stone foundations and mud-brick, with plaster on the interior faces. The floor was plastered and contained a hearth (Marfoe and Ingraham 1990, 40). Because of the obvious disturbance to the south end of Unit 13.5, and the suggested disturbance to the east and north, it was not possible to establish the relationship between Unit 13.5 and other Phase 13 rooms.

The white plaster floor of Unit 13.1 ran up to the fortification wall, providing a clear stratigraphic link between the room and wall. An oval-shaped plaster basin had been set in the floor (Marfoe and Ingraham 1990, 39). Because the walls separating Units 13.1 and 13.3 are narrow partition walls, it is probable that the two rooms formed part of the same building.

In Unit 13.3, two features, a hearth or oven and a bin-like mud-brick feature containing ash, were placed along the north wall. The floor was of compacted earth (Marfoe and Ingraham 1990, 39–40). This seemed incongruent with the fairly substantial walls. This unit shared its southern wall with Unit 13.4. Although the rooms were separated by a relatively massive 1.3-m-thick wall (providing support for the view that the structure was originally more substantial than the building remains indicate), the similarity in orientation and shared western wall suggest they were part of the same structure.

Only a small corner of Unit 13.4 was cleared, and the floor seemed to be plastered (Marfoe and Ingraham 1990, 40). A break in the western wall, interpreted as a possible doorway to the proposed street (alternatively interpreted here as foundations), may in fact have been caused by disturbance from a pit cut into the wall during a later phase of occupation (see Phase 14 plan in Figure 18).

Because of the placement of a Phase 14 foundation trench just north of Units 13.6, 13.7, and 13.8, it is not possible to establish the relationship between these rooms and other Phase 13 architecture. Judging from the Phase 14 rebuilding of the area, which incorporated the walls of Units 13.6, 13.7, and 13.8, the rooms would have been part of the same structure as Unit 13.5. Because of erosion of deposits in the eastern-most part of Phase 14 (Areas A05, A06) there is no relevant Phase 14 architecture to use for understanding the relationship between Units 13.6, 13.7, and 13.8 on one hand, and 13.3 and 13.4 on the other. The Phase 14 foundation trench appears to have truncated the northern wall of these three units.

Units 13.6, 13.7, and 13.8 share a wall, suggesting they belonged to the same structure. Moreover, the east and west walls of the central room are shared with rooms on either side. All walls had stone foundations capped with mud-brick. None of the wall interiors seem to have been plastered. Two floors were excavated in Unit 13.6. The lower floor of compacted earth was covered with ash, pebbles, and occupational debris. A hearth was associated with this floor level. Debris separated an upper floor and lower floor (Marfoe and Ingraham 1990, 40–1).

The artifacts and features from this area suggest a clearly domestic function. Artifacts from each cluster of units include pottery, chipped stone, and bone. The presence in Unit 13.2 of hearths in Floors 1 to 3 (Floor 1 is the earliest), a mortar and a sickle blade on Floor 3, and possible pestles and a sickle blade above Floor 4 suggest that the unit was occupied by farmers and that food processing and preparation took place in the room. The complex represented by Units 13.1, 13.3, and 13.4 yielded two hearths or ovens (in Unit 13.3) as well as a bone awl and probably agricultural tool (both from Unit 13.1), findings consistent with the interpretation that this building was used as a house. Finally, for Units 13.6, 13.7, and 13.8, a hearth in the first unit, combined with the recovery of bones, chipped stone, and pottery, suggests a domestic function for this group of rooms.

Overall, the available information on status of the residents in this part of the site is conflicting. If the settlement extended beyond the wall during this phase, the houses of higher ranking residents may have been located within the wall. However, there is currently no solid evidence for occupation outside the wall during this part of Subperiod IV.3 (see Table 1). Some features, such as the mud-brick floor base of Unit 13.2 and the relatively massive walls of Units 13.3 and 13.4 suggest a fairly high investment in construction and perhaps the presence of upper stories; the high volume of collapse separating the Phase 13 and Phase 14 structures may represent debris from a second story. On the other hand, much of the preserved architecture, such as the walls associated with Unit 13.5, appears modest. This conflicting evidence probably results from considerable disturbance of Phase 13 building remains; the Phase 13 rooms may in fact have housed high-ranking occupants. The rooms may have originally been part of a single substantial building complex, similar in plan to the Phase 14 rebuilding. As discussed in Chapter 6, the faunal remains are consistent with the interpretation that residents of this area were of relatively high status. However, it is also possible to interpret the architectural remains as representing four separate buildings (13.2, 13.5, 13.1–13.4, and 13.6–13.8)—three of which were fairly modest (13.2, 13.5, and 13.6–13.8)—if we assume that the use of the fortification wall as the north wall of Unit 13.2 was opportunistic.

Unless we interpret Phase 13 architectural remains as the remnant of what was once a more substantial complex, evidence from this period for construction of monumental architecture is confined to the fortification wall. The architecture of Phase 13 as shown in the plan appears to have grown incrementally, rather than having been the result of a large-scale centrally coordinated construction program. With the exception of the fortification wall, the wall thicknesses were not greater than in earlier phases, averaging approximately .55 m (excluding the fortification wall) compared with .60 m in the preceding phases.

In conclusion, unless one accepts the interpretation of Phase 13 architecture as having been more substantial than it appears on the plan, evidence suggests that modest houses of agricultural families were located in this part of the site. However, Units 13.3 and 13.4 may well have been occupied by fairly high-ranking residents.

The presence of hearths in so many of the excavated rooms may indicate that they were occupied by separate social units (Marfoe and Ingraham 1990, 41). Because at least some of the rooms had multiple floor levels, it is not possible to determine which of the hearths from various units were in use at the same time. Nonetheless, the recovery of so many hearths when rooms were only partially cleared may indicate that the area was occupied by several families. Regardless of how one interprets the remains from this phase, the artifacts and features do suggest that a major shift occurred in the use of this area between Phases 13 and 14. During Phase 13 it appears to have been a fairly elaborate residential area, with no signs of administrative activities. In Phase 14 the area seems to have had combined public and residential functions.

The uppermost levels of two rooms contained burned materials and all rooms were filled with collapse. Although the collapse may indicate that the structures were abandoned for a short period before they were rebuilt, the excavators noted that the original building plan was largely maintained in the second phase (ibid., 43); this may not have been the case if the building had been abandoned for some time. In summary, the architectural remains from Phases 11 through 13 have provided some evidence for social differentiation, even though the exposures were fairly limited. By Phase 14, this division in status of residents appears to have intensified, leading to the spatial segregation of an administrative elite. Thus, the Phase 13 and 14 remains may document the elevated status of a specific family as the settlement grew and became more differentiated.

AREA A: PHASE 14

Five rooms excavated within a 35-m^2 exposure were assigned to Phase 14. An additional 17.5 m^2 to the north of the rooms represented an erosional deposit. Because of the erosion, this phase was not as extensively preserved as was Phase 13, although the portion that was preserved was less disturbed than the Phase 13 deposits.

Because Phase 14 deposits in Trench A06—in which we would expect to find the fortification wall—had been eroded, the excavators could not be certain that the wall continued in use during this phase. However, the sharp slope of the collapse layers at this elevation suggest that the wall did remain in use during Phase 14 (Marfoe and Ingraham 1990, 43). It may well have served as the northernmost wall of the complex, as it did in Phase 13.

Some of the Phase 14 rooms were located directly above Phase 13 rooms, with the earlier foundations used. Room 14.1 was built over the collapse of Room 13.2. The south wall of 13.2 was reused, but the east and north walls were entirely rebuilt. The north wall was constructed entirely of mud-brick, in contrast to the other walls that had stone foundations. The floor was plastered white, and plaster traces were found on the interiors of the north and south walls (ibid.). It is not clear if Unit 14.1 was separate from the more formally constructed major Phase 14 building (referred to here as Structure 1). Although the wall between Units 14.1 and 14.2 is a double one, the space between Unit 14.2 and the presumed location of the fortification wall may be too small for a second structure (3.2 m, north-south).

Unit 14.2 was the most extensively cleared room of Structure 1. Although it appears longer than Unit 13.5, it was built directly above the earlier room, and the walls were similarly oriented (ibid.). The eastern wall of Unit 13.5 (which I have suggested may have been a bench) formed the foundation for a bench and crenelated feature along the eastern wall of Unit 14.2. The southern wall was built against the reused northern wall of Unit 13.6/14.3. The east and south walls both had three courses of foundation stones covered with mud-brick. The walls were quite substantial (.95 m to 1.2 m) and could have supported an upper story. The walls and floor had been replastered numerous times.

A crenelated trough-like mud-brick feature, perhaps a hearth, rested at the north end of the Unit 14.2. A large cooking pot was found nearby. A door socket against the north wall may have been associated with an unexcavated passageway between Units 14.1 and 14.2. (Marfoe and Ingraham 1990, 44).

The three excavated walls of Unit 13.6 were rebuilt to form Unit 14.3, and a plaster floor was set where the old and new wall segments met. A large storage jar was embedded on the floor; two clay door-lock sealing fragments were found nearby. A door socket rested near the doorway to Unit 14.2 (ibid.).

The near absence of domestic installations such as hearths and mortars, combined with the substantial nature of the architecture, the recovery of a storage jar and sealings, suggested to Marfoe and Ingraham (1990) that the building served an administrative function, or at least belonged to a high-status group (ibid.). This contrasts with findings from the underlying Unit 13.6, which included a hearth and artifacts expected from a domestic context, and illustrates the changing nature of the area through time. The use of door locks on an internal door in Unit 14.3 suggests potentially greater access to the room than might be the case in an exclusively residential structure.

Although the thick walls and careful construction of the building, sealings, and faunal remains (see Chapter 6) do suggest that the building may have been a public one, the presence of a hearth and cooking pot in Unit 14.2 suggest the building had a combined residential and administrative function. Artifacts from Unit 14.3 include those that might be found in domestic contexts, such as two bone awls, three ground stone objects of unknown function, a figurine, and ornaments. Bones, pottery, and chipped stone were found in all rooms. The shift from an exclusively domestic function for this area in Phase 13 to a combined administrative and residential function in Phase 14 coincides with the hypothesized period of settlement expansion onto the lower town and evidence for increased socioeconomic diversity at the site. The significance of the burning of the Phase 13 building is not clear, but it opens up the possibility that this community reorganization was not entirely a peaceful one. The fairly elaborate structure is contemporary with the earliest known Period IV construction on the small mound, found in Area C01.

AREA C01: PHASES 11 TO 14

A 3 m x 9 m vertical sounding on the low mound (see Marfoe and Evins 1990, 118) provided a sequence of surfaces from a domestic complex that was occupied and periodically remodeled throughout this subperiod and into the following one (Figs. 19 and 20). Although the exposure is small, a broad

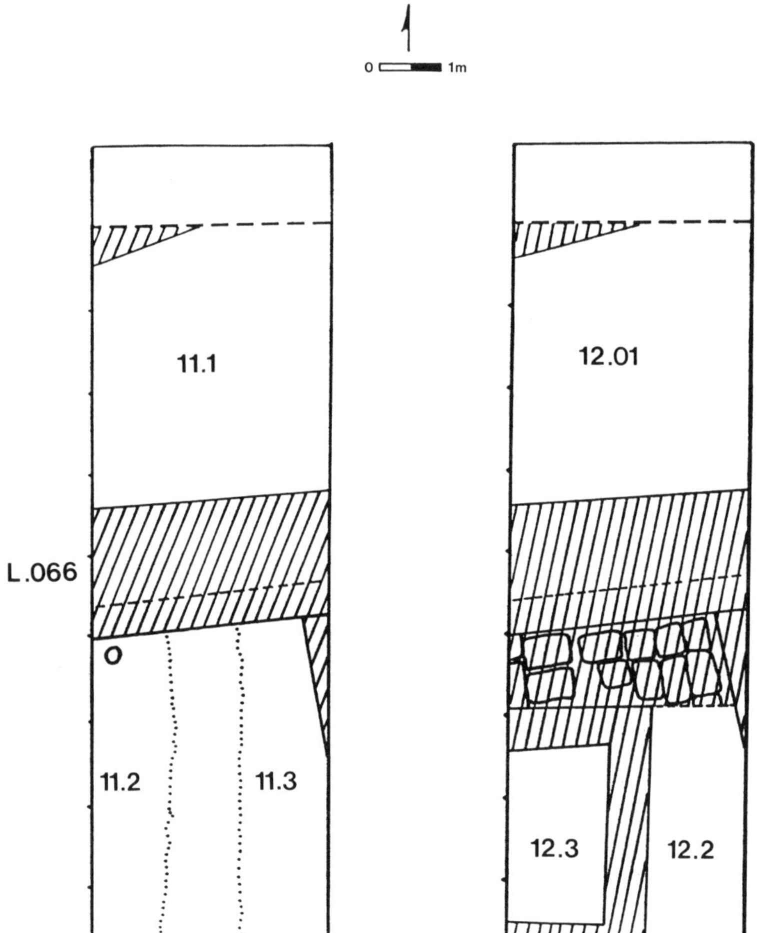

Figure 19. Plans of Area C01 Phase 11 and C01 Phase 12 (after Marfoe and Evins 1990).

exposure in Area C, which incorporates Phase 15 of the C01 deep sounding, provides a plan of the same structure at a later date. Although the building had undergone many changes, the plan provides a useful guide for interpreting the nature of architecture and surfaces in earlier phases from Area C01. The walls were less substantial than those of Area A, Phase 14, the construction was less elaborate, and the building was not kept as clean. It probably represents a domestic structure rather than a public building.

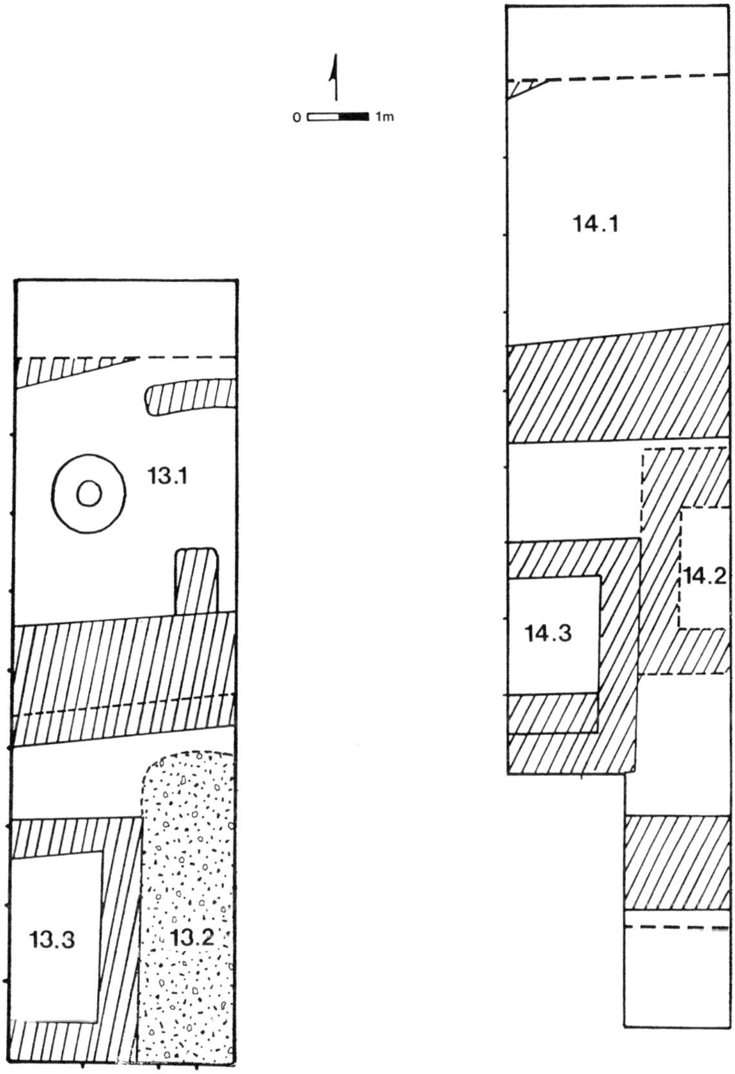

Figure 20. Plans of Area C01 Phase 13 and C01 Phase 14 (after Marfoe and Evins 1990).

Architectural continuity from Phases 11 through 14 is indicated by the use of Wall C01: 066 throughout the sequence. This substantial wall, 1.2 m to 1.4 m wide, divided the trench into north and south segments. It formed the southern wall of a fairly large and continuously rebuilt room that remained in use throughout both major construction phases, C01 Phases 11–14, and C01 Phase 15 (Unit 11.1/15.1). The Area C excavations, which encompassed the upper phases of the C01 sounding, provided additional contextual information on the deposits from Area C01. The Phase 15 remains are part of a large building complex that included a series of rooms and a courtyard. The evidence for architectural continuity within the C01 sequence suggests that the Area C building plan may be useful in interpreting the limited exposures of earlier phases of the building excavated in C01 Phases 11 to 14. If so, then the excavated rooms and exterior area would represent part of a large structure, and the exterior surfaces part of an associated courtyard.

Wall C01: 066, which formed the southern border throughout the sequence, was composed of a foundation of large limestone rocks and a pise or mud-brick superstructure. Unit 11.1 had a burned floor overlain with ash (Marfoe and Evins 1990, 131). Unit 11.2 shared Wall C01: 066 with Unit 11.1; later Area C plans indicate that the two rooms belonged to the same structure. A second wall-like feature, possibly a bench, ran along the south side of the wall. The area was partially disturbed by a Phase 12 foundation trench; the proposed interpretation of the relationship between Units 11.2 and 11.3 is partially based on the Phase 12 plan. Unit 11.2 contained a high density of chipped stone debitage and other artifacts. In later phases this area was an unroofed passageway or section of a courtyard. The high density of debris in Unit 11.2 is consistent with the interpretation that this was an enclosed but unroofed area during this phase as well. A white plaster floor, presumably the interior of a room, was located to the west of a disturbed area. An ash-filled pit had been set in the floor (Marfoe and Evins 1990, 132). The fairly massive walls of Unit 11.1 could have supported a second story. The scale of the architecture suggests it may have been inhabited by a high-ranking family.

With the exception of three pieces of vitrified kiln material, the artifacts (querns, a possible grinding stone, animal bones, etc.) are consistent with expectations for a domestic area. In the preceding Area C01 Phase 9 (Period V) occupation, proximity to a kiln area was indicated by high concentrations of ash, vitrified kiln material, ceramic wasters, and finished vessels (Marfoe and Evins 1990, 127). The Phase 11 kiln wasters may indicate that the excavated area was adjacent to a workshop, although no additional evidence for ceramic production or metal working was found in association with this structure. The Phase 11 ceramic assemblage included only a few intrusive Period V ceramics, but it is possible that the vitrified clay samples had been redeposited from Phase 9 deposits. Alternatively, the samples may have been collected from a nearby workshop for use in paving, construction, and so on, in much the same way that pebbles were used in Period IV occupational areas.

A high concentration of chipped stone debitage was noted by the excavator. However, the chipped stone assemblage from this structure was not studied, so it is not possible to determine if specialized chipped stone production took place here. Flint debitage was prevalent in other Period IV exterior contexts that were not specialized workshops, and families apparently manufactured most of their own flint tools (see Chapter 5). Therefore, the high concentration of chipped stone may have resulted from production for household use in the courtyard area, rather than surplus production for exchange. Available data suggest that this structure served as a residence, possibly for a high-ranking family that may have been involved in some specialized craft activities (such as ceramic production, metal working, or perhaps even stone tool manufacturing).

The Phase 12 remains follow the same plan as those from Phase 11, with the addition of a brick path built along the central wall (see Fig. 19). The floor of Unit 12.1 consisted of a series of burned plaster surfaces. A possible hearth uncovered in the Phase 13 excavation may originally have been built in this phase (Marfoe and Evins 1990, 134). A mud-brick surface ran along the north side of the central wall, joining with Unit 12.2 to form an L-shaped passageway or courtyard area. Three walls of Unit 12.3 were at least partially cleared. The room floor was not plastered. On the basis of results from the more extensive Area C excavations, the excavators propose that Unit 12.3 was an anteroom.

Artifacts suggest this area continued to serve as a residential structure. A range of domestic activities are indicated by the recovery of a bone awl, a possible spindle whorl, and a quern, as well as ceramics, chipped stone, and bones.

Phase 13 was again similar to earlier levels but better preserved (see Fig. 20). The floor of Unit 13.1 was the uppermost of the sequence of burned plaster floors from Unit 12.1. A heavily plastered mud-brick feature extended across the southeast corner of the trench. A small platform or bench abutted the northern wall of the room. A small circular plastered hearth was placed in the floor (Marfoe and Evins 1990, 133–4).

To the south of the central wall, the small room and corridor continued in use (Units 13.2 and 13.3). However, the mud-brick paving was replaced, largely with plaster. The surface of Unit 13.2 consisted of a layer of pebbles and artifacts. During this phase Unit 13.2 may have been an enclosed corridor or courtyard (Marfoe and Evins 1990, 134).

The hearth and artifacts, such as grinding stone fragments and a shell pendant, suggest that this area continued to be residential. However, it may have served as a workshop as well. Four samples of ceramic slag may be from a nearby kiln. Three pierced ground-stone objects may represent loom weights used by weavers.

Phase 14 was generally similar to previous phases, although there were numerous modifications to create more interior space (see Fig. 20). A room (Unit 14.2) was added where the exterior area had been. The northern wall of Units 11.1 to 13.1 had been rebuilt, increasing the room width by .2 m. The floor was plastered (ibid., 135–6).

The surface space increased on the south side of the central wall as well. The bench or mud-brick feature along the south side of the central wall (C01: 066) had been removed, presumably to make space for the new room. A mud-brick bench was added against the south wall of Unit 14.3. In other respects, the structure was identical to the one in earlier phases. The floor was plastered. The north and south walls of Unit 14.2 were entirely of mud-brick. The floor of the room was not found (ibid.).

In the area surrounding Unit 14.3, the plaster and pebble surfaces of Phase 13 had been covered over. The surfaces were poorly defined, but the surface south of Unit 14.2 consisted of white concretions covered with small stones and broken ceramics (ibid.).

Ceramics from C01 Phase 14 were anomalous (see Appendix, Fig. 39, v8), but were most similar to those from Area A Phase 14. For that reason, the Area C01 Phase 14 deposits were included in this section on Subperiod IV.3. Although the Phase 15 architecture closely resembled that from previous phases, the excavator noted that most of the walls had been rebuilt. In this analysis, I placed Area C01 Phase 15 deposits in a separate subperiod on the basis of the ceramic assemblage. Whereas Phases 11 to 13 were closely correlated with ceramics from Subperiod IV.3 in Area A (Phases 13 and 14), the ceramic assemblage from Phase 14 was almost intermediate between Area A Phase 14 and Area A Phases 16 to 17. Assemblages from two other areas (Area G, F 9–12) fell into this category, and all three areas are included in the section on Subperiod IV.2. Area C01 Phase 15 (also assigned to Subperiod IV.2) is grouped with Area C, to which it is stratigraphically linked.

It is possible that by the end of the subperiod (IV.3) the site had already reached its maximum size; the apparent absence of remains dating to Subperiod IV.3 in Area F may be a result of the limited size of the excavation area or an error in dating the Area F deposits, perhaps because of the small sample size of artifacts. Differences between Areas C and A in architecture and artifacts suggest an increased diversity in status of occupants during Subperiod IV.2, but this may be a result of the greater exposure of deposits from this subperiod. In short, the deep exposures were too limited in scale to allow a precise dating of the period of expansion, but by Subperiod IV.2, if not before, Kurban Höyük was a socioeconomically diverse, town-sized settlement.

SUBPERIOD IV.2: TOWN DEVELOPMENT PHASES

Subperiod IV.2 is the best sampled of all the subperiods, with more than 600 m^2 cleared from Areas A, C, C01, F, and G. All parts of the site tested through deep soundings yielded deposits dating to this subperiod, indicating either an increased density in occupation during this time or an expansion of the settlement. Exposures include samples from three separate structures in Area A, three houses bordering a cobble street in Area C (including Area C01 Phase 15), interior and exterior surfaces in Area F, and two rooms, an outdoor cobble surface, and a possible courtyard in Area G.

AREA A: PHASE 16

Phases 16 and 17 yielded deposits 2 m thick, although the remains were very fragmentary as a result of erosion. Phase 16 had two subphases, preserved only in the southern part of the trench (Fig. 21). The lower phase was represented by a room (Unit 16.1) with a white plaster floor and bench. The only preserved wall of this room was built of mud-brick. When the room was rebuilt in the upper phase, the wall was widened and a new plaster floor and bench were constructed (Marfoe and Ingraham 1990, 50).

A second structure, Unit 16.2, predated Unit 16.1. It was represented by the fragmentary remains of two walls. A pebble surface, possibly a path, separated the two rooms. Both walls of Unit 16.2 had stone foundations covered with mud-brick. A series of plaster floors were associated with the walls.

Unit 16.3 shared the north wall of Unit 16.2. The north wall of Unit

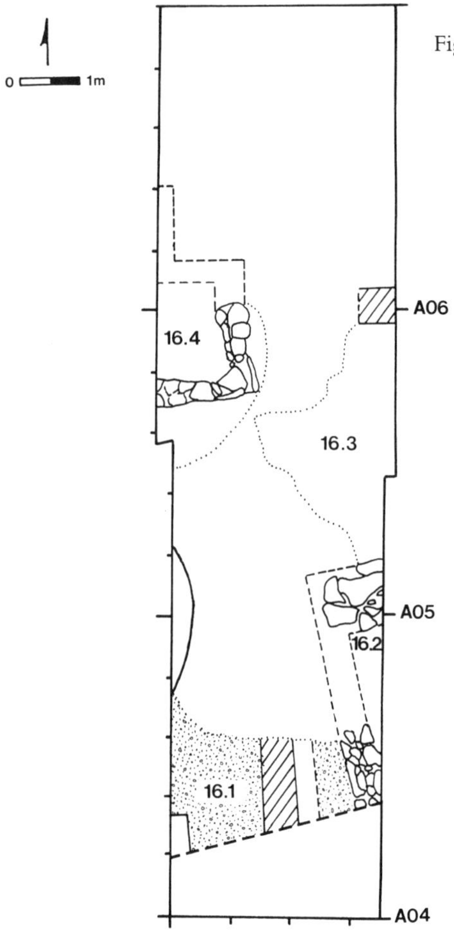

Figure 21. Plan of Area A Phase 16.

16.3 was built entirely of mud-brick. Two plaster floors were associated with the room. The lower one was associated with the two walls. The upper floor ran over the north wall, indicating that the room had expanded in size (ibid.).

Two walls formed the southern and eastern borders of Unit 16.4, found only in the upper subphase. These walls were each represented by a single course of stone foundations. The room had a plaster and pebble surface (ibid., 51).

In earlier Area A phases, the architecture tended to be oriented on a north-northwest-south-southeast axis. During this subperiod, some walls were oriented on a north-south axis. This shift appears to have occurred elsewhere at the site as well, as old structures were replaced. New walls in

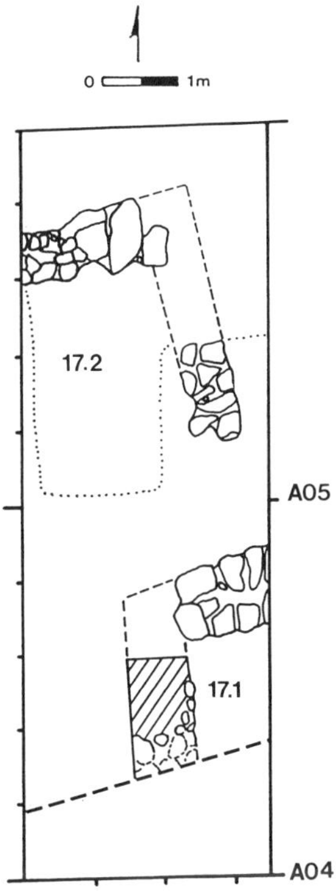

Figure 22. Plan of Area A Phase 17.

Areas C and C01 (Phase 15) were oriented north-south. In Area F the orientation of architecture did not shift.

Given the considerable disturbance, it is difficult to determine either the nature of this area or the status of occupants on the basis of artifacts. Although the architecture appears to be fairly modest, this may be because of incomplete preservation. Artifacts recovered from this area are consistent with the interpretation that this was probably a residential area.

AREA A: PHASE 17

Portions of two rooms were preserved in Phase 17. Unit 17.1 was bordered on the west and north by walls constructed of stone foundations and mud-brick superstructures (Fig. 22). Although the floor of the room was not preserved, the limestone used in leveling the surface indicated where the floor had been. Sections of the foundation stones for the north and east walls of a possible second room, Unit 17.2, were recovered. A compact surface with localized ash deposits (Unit 17.3) provided evidence for an

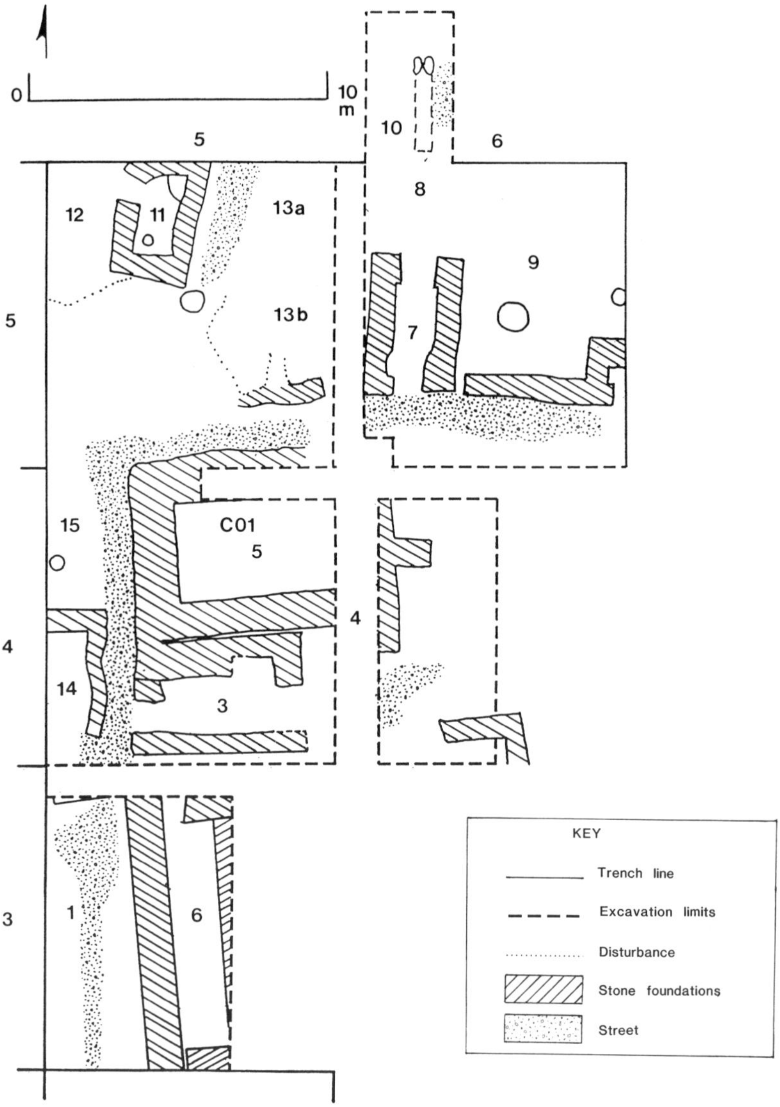

Figure 23. Plan of Area C/C01 Phase 15 (after Verhaaren 1986).

Plate 15. Area C. Photograph courtesy of the Oriental Institute.

exterior surface between Units 17.1 and 17.2 (ibid., 51). As with Phase 16, the area appears to be a non-elite residential sector, but this may be a result of incomplete preservation.

AREA C

Area C (Fig. 23; Plate 15) provided the most extensive exposure of Period IV remains at Kurban Höyük (see Marfoe 1990b, 186). Approximately 420 m^2 were excavated to a depth of .3 m to 1 m, and two main phases were represented. The final phase, Phase 1, was just below the modern ground surface and consisted of isolated features that had been badly disturbed. The major phase, Phase 2, had two subphases, defined primarily by two stratified street surfaces. Ceramic analyses indicated that the Phase 1 occupation had been more substantial than the spatially restricted intact deposits suggested (see Chapter 3). The clearance of Phase 2 deposits yielded the partial remains of four structures lining an L-shaped cobbled street. The architecture and streets followed a north-south orientation, in contrast to architecture in Area C01 Phases 11 to 13.

The excavators cleared 20 m of a cobbled street running east-west and 20 m of the cobbled street that ran north-south. The best preserved building (partially excavated as Area C01) included at least three rooms (Structure 1). One of the rooms, a foyer, led to a courtyard and was flanked on either side by larger rooms. The entrance room seems to have been slightly more substantial than the others in the area. It is hard to determine if this house was representative of contemporary houses in other parts of the site, because the narrow soundings in Areas A and F did not yield complete house plans, and in Area G much of the architecture had been destroyed. However, the plan seems typical for this part of the site. Judging from the evidence in Area C01, the earlier architecture (Subperiod IV.3 remains) from this area followed the basic plan of an entrance room and courtyard found in Area C Phase 2.

Phase 15 of Area C01 was located within Structure 1 of Area C (see Fig. 23), and included part of the northernmost room (Unit 15.1; Area C Unit 5), the foyer (Unit 15.3, Area C Unit 3), and part of the courtyard (Unit 15.2, Area C Unit 4). The foundations of the south wall of Unit 15.1 were built of large limestone blocks and were 1.2 m to 1.4 m wide (Marfoe and Evins 1990, 137). Judging from the wall thickness, Unit 15.1 may have included a second story. The floor was of well-preserved plaster. The north wall of 15.1 bordered the northern street excavated in Area C (Unit 2). The southern wall bordered the courtyard area, Unit 15.2. The west walls of Room 15.1 and 15.3 also ran alongside a street (Unit 1).

The walls of Unit 15.3 (Area C, Unit 3), the entrance room, had stone foundations. The floor was plastered white. All three walls were poorly built compared to those of the earlier Area C01 phases (ibid., 138). The decreased formality in construction parallels architectural trends elsewhere at the site.

Unit 15.2 (Area C Unit 4) was probably a courtyard. The surface was packed earth and contained an artifact scatter, in contrast to the well-cleaned room floors of this structure (Marfoe and Evins 1990). A copper/copper alloy tool, possibly a reamer, was recovered from the surface (Yener 1990, 407). The third and southernmost room of the structure (Area C, Unit 4) was excavated as part of Area C. The floor was plastered.

The excavated part of the structure was 20 m long and 9 m wide (180 m^2). Unless the entire structure was substantially larger than the portion excavated, its dimensions fall within the range of modern Near Eastern village houses (see Watson 1979; for a different interpretation, see Marfoe 1990b, 188). The size does approach that of some high-status houses in the Diyala region of ancient Mesopotamia (see Henrickson 1981, 70–73). The thick walls and possible second story suggest the building was occupied by a fairly prosperous family. Artifacts include those expected in domestic contexts, such as an agricultural tool, bone awl, and quern, as well as four samples of vitrified kiln material. Although the density of artifacts within the structure was low, objects recovered from the street just outside support the interpretation that this structure was inhabited by a relatively high-status family, possibly craft specialists. The artifacts are diverse and include several objects unrelated to food or craft production, such as a cattle figurine, a clay house model, and a shell ornament. Although metal objects were very rare at the site, with only six pieces recovered from Period IV deposits, four were found in the vicinity of this structure. In addition to the tool from Unit 15.2, three copper/copper alloy objects, a toggle pin, a pin or needle, and the shank fragment of a pin were found in the street (see Yener 1990, 406–7). Four additional pieces of vitrified kiln material had been deposited in the street (Area C35 Unit 1).

Directly across the street, to the west of the first structure, excavators found another structure, represented by Unit 14. Only one wall of Unit 14 and traces of two cross walls were recovered. Judging from these wall fragments, the structure seems less substantial than Structure 1. The outer wall of Unit 14 appears to have been .60 m, compared with approximately 1.30 m for Structure 1.

With the exception of the clearly defined street (Unit 1), the area north of Structures 1 and 2 was difficult to interpret, because of the proximity of the excavated levels to the surface. The remains of a third unit (Structure 3, Unit 11), on the north side of the east-west street, were interpreted as a "monocellular structure" (Marfoe 1990b, 187; Verhaaren 1986, 70). The plaster surface east of it (Unit 13, north) was identified as an associated courtyard.

For several reasons, I interpret Unit 11 as part of a larger architectural complex, the remainder of which was no longer preserved, rather than as an isolated single room structure. The small internal dimensions of the room (4.16 m^2) argue against it being a self-contained unit; it may have been a storage room belonging to part of a larger building. A bin was located in the northeast corner of the room and a pot rested on the floor. Among artifacts found inside the room were a dolomite axe or hammer and a possible mace head.

Unit 11 may have been associated with unexcavated rooms to the north or rooms to the south that were not preserved. There was evidence that wall foundations had been removed elsewhere in Area C, either through plowing or stone robbing; it is possible that some wall foundations originally associated with Unit 11 were similarly destroyed. In 1984, a small sounding was excavated in Trench C66 to clarify the relationship between the apparent exterior plastered surfaces and associated monocellular structures. It provided support for the view that the buildings of Area C had been disturbed. The probe uncovered a cobble and stone threshold resting against the plastered surface (Unit 10). However, the threshold was no longer associated with any walls. Had it not been for the entrance way, we would have interpreted the plaster surface as an open outdoor area, but the threshold indicated that it had originally been enclosed. Wall robbing was a potential source of disturbance in the vicinity of Unit 11. In addition, any walls in the badly disturbed area to the south of the room would have been destroyed. The area directly north of the room was not excavated, and it is possible that the structure continued northward. Evidence for stone robbing was also found in Area G (see later discussion), indicating that the wall destruction in Area C was not an isolated example.

Only one door of Unit 11 was located, arguing against the likelihood that this room, like Unit 3, was the foyer of a larger structure. However, a pebble surface alongside the east wall of Unit 11 may in fact have been a threshold of an undetected doorway. A round pebble feature, possibly a hearth base, was built just outside the southeast corner of Unit 11.

In thickness, the walls of Unit 11 were comparable to those of Unit 3, but the room is substantially smaller. Given the limited remains of this structure and uncertainties about the purpose it served, it is not possible to make inferences about the relative status of the people who used this area. With the exception of a single sample of vitrified kiln material, artifacts suggest the area was residential.

Unit 11 was separated from a white plaster surface (Unit 13a) by the pebble strip mentioned previously. It is not clear with which structure this plaster surface was associated.

Structure 4 (Unit 7) was represented by a single room, also interpreted in the excavation report as a monocellular structure (ibid.). However, the small size of the room, the entrance from the street, and the second doorway leading to a courtyard all suggest that the room had served as the entrance room to a larger structure. The room plan parallels that of Unit 3, both in terms of room dimensions and the locations of doors. A wall to the east of Unit 7 may have formed the southern boundary of a second room of the proposed compound. A plaster surface to the northwest of Unit 7 (Unit 13a) may have been associated with a room of the complex. A courtyard surface to the east of Unit 7 (Unit 9) had an associated hearth and drain to the street.

Given the fragmentary nature of the remains, it is difficult to establish whether this structure, like Structure 1, was a more elaborate building. Although the walls of the anteroom were .80 m to .90 m thick (slightly wider than those of Unit 3), the room was somewhat smaller. The outer wall that borders the street was less substantial than that of Structure 1, and probably did not support a second story. Apparently this structure was more modest than Structure 1. With the exception of a single vitrified kiln sample and a stone stamp seal, artifacts included those expected in a residential area, such as pottery, bones, chipped stone, a grinding stone, quern, animal figurine, and two Mediterranean shell ornaments. There were a few stone and clay objects of unknown function. The stone stamp, found in the courtyard just north of Unit 7, is one of the few recovered from Period IV contexts. It may indicate linkages between the residents of this building and other economic units and involvement in activities other than simple production for household use, such as the transshipment of surplus goods from this area. Because seals were probably valued, and may have been discarded only for ritual purposes (such as burials) or when broken, they may have been used more often by households than suggested by their near absence in the Kurban contexts. However, the low occurrence of both seals and sealings recovered from the now extensive exposures in the region do suggest that they were used only by a subset of the population in restricted contexts. For example, the clearance of more than 2,000 m from a somewhat later phase at the center of Titriş Höyük yielded only two cylinder seals and one cylinder seal impression (G. Algaze, November 1996, personal communication; see also Algaze et al. 1995, 19). Excavation of mid-late third millennium deposits at Kurban Höyük yielded only two stamp seals; sealings were limited to the door locks from Area A discussed previously (see Yener 1990). Overall, the evidence from Structure 4 suggests that this was a residential complex whose occupants, like those in Structure 1, may have engaged in some activities in which the poorest families were not involved.

Available evidence indicates that Area C was a residential sector whose inhabitants appear to have been better off than those further from the center of the site (see Area G discussion later). Differences may also have existed in the status of families within Area C, with the residents of Structure 1 better off than those from Structure 4. The vitrified kiln material suggests proximity to a workshop, and some residents of this area may have been specialized craft producers. However, no workshop features were located.

AREA F: PHASES 8 TO 12

Architectural evidence for Phases 8 to 11 was limited to one wall and associated surfaces (Fig. 24). The wall was relatively massive and had a

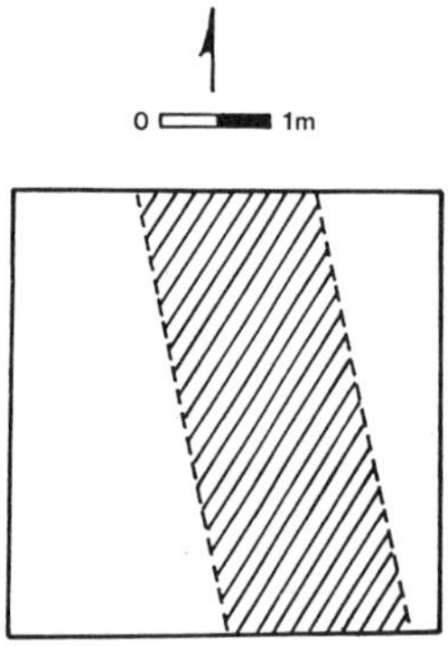

Figure 24. Plan of Area F Phase 12.

foundation consisting of two outer layers of limestone blocks encasing a core of small stones. Phases 8 to 11 are represented by a series of four white plaster floors to the west of the wall and two to three exterior surfaces to the east of the wall. The lowest floor may not be associated with the wall (Marfoe 1990a, 172). The width of the wall and careful construction suggest it was part of a relatively substantial building, perhaps with an upper story. Artifacts indicate it was a residential structure. Finds from Phases 8, 9, and 11 include primarily ceramics, chipped stone, and bones. In addition, a copper/bronze pin and green stone pendant fragment were recovered from Phase 10. The scale of architecture, combined with the presence of ornaments made of relatively rare materials, suggests the residents of this building were of relatively high status.

In Phase 12 a new wall was constructed to the west of the earlier one. It followed the same orientation and was similarly constructed, but it was .10 m to .20 m wider. The surface to the west of the wall was unplastered and recognized as a floor largely on the basis of flat-lying pottery. The lack of plaster suggests it was an unroofed area. An unpaved corridor ran between the structure on the west side of the trench and a second one represented by a wall to the east (ibid., 173–4). Artifacts indicated the residents of this area continued to be relatively high status, compared to, for example, those in Area G. Among the utilitarian goods expected in domestic contexts were ceramics, chipped stone, bones, a quern fragment, and a spindle-whorl fragment. Less frequently found artifacts suggesting this may have been an elite area included an elaborate pot stand or model tower, a diorite stamp seal, and the fragment of an unidentified copper artifact. The stamp seal is similar to those documented from the Ubaid and Halaf sites, raising the possibility that it may have been intrusive (Yener 1990).

Plate 16. Area G.

AREA G

Area G (Fig. 25; Plate 16) yielded the most extensive clearance of non-elite architecture from Subperiod IV.2. Unfortunately, most of the architecture was not well preserved because of the proximity of the deposits to the mound surface, the disturbance of the best preserved phase (Phase 3) by later features, the deliberate removal of foundation stones for reuse, and the extremely compact sediment, which was not conducive to preservation. Walls were incomplete and surfaces were sometimes fragmentary. A pit cut into the south wall of Unit 1, just at the point where a segment of the stone wall had been removed, was probably a result of stone robbing. The stone foundations were probably removed and used in construction during a later phase.

The lower of the two main phases, 3a and b, was assigned to this subperiod. This phase was represented by a room (Unit 1) with a plaster floor, bordered by a cobbled exterior area (Unit 4) to the east and an ashy exterior trash deposit to the south. An additional room (Unit 2) and possible courtyard (Unit 3) bordered the northern side of the room (see Fig. 25).

The evidence presented previously for stone robbing suggests that the fragmentary nature of the architecture can in part be attributed to mining for foundation stones, perhaps during the final third to early second millennium B.C. or medieval occupations, when settlement was restricted to the

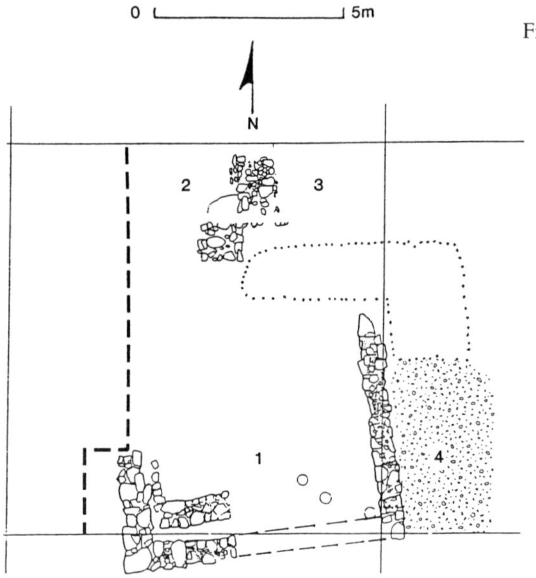

Figure 25. Plan of Area G.

large mound. The northern wall stones had also been removed. Although the associated white plaster floor had a straight edge where the north wall had been, only the brick collapse from the wall could be traced. Three pots were set into the floor.

Units 2 and 3 were separated by at least one wall and a second wall or bench. Unit 2 had a plastered floor with few artifacts. The southeast corner of the room rose to form a platform. The floor of Unit 3 was of compacted mud and contained an unusually high concentration of pottery. The absence of plaster on the floor and high density of debris suggests the area may have been part of a courtyard.

To the east of Unit 1 was an exterior area or courtyard (Unit 4). The Unit 4 surface was partially cobbled; the unpaved portion consisted of a packed mud surface with a relatively high density of debris. Two pebble features and a pot were found on the surface. One of the pebble features was covered with plaster and had been burned. It may have been a hearth or oven base. The function of the second feature, a low platform composed of small pebbles and limestone slabs, is unknown.

In addition to the major exposure of Phase 3b deposits, a few isolated deposits were uncovered from the earlier Phase 4. They include the northwest corner of a room below Unit 1 and an unassociated plaster floor underlying a Phase 3b exterior surface.

The area appears to have been a non-elite residential one. Although few walls were recovered, those that were preserved averaged only .64 m, indicating that the architecture was fairly modest in scale. Although the exposure was relatively large, the artifacts were almost exclusively those related to food production, processing, or consumption. Exceptions were one stone ornament, stone tools (and debitage from their manufacture), groundstone objects of an unknown function, and one piece of sealing clay that did not have an impression.

Excavation results reveal the diversity in architecture, and presumably the status of residents, during Subperiod IV.2. The large complex of Area C and the substantial, though minimally excavated, architecture from Area F reveal that relatively large-scale architecture existed beyond the large mound. The generally rare objects concentrated in these areas, such as metal ornaments and a stamp seal, point to both an uneven distribution of craft goods and variability in activities carried out by the residents of these buildings. In contrast, the structures in Areas A and G were relatively modest, and most of the artifact types recovered from them were well represented throughout the site. Thus, the decreased care taken in planning and constructing buildings in some parts of the site during this subperiod does not correspond to decreased complexity in the socioeconomic organization of the community. Rather, it may indicate increased differentiation in the houses of families of varying rank, as suggested by the careful construction in Area F.

SUBPERIOD IV.1: THE NUCLEATION PHASES

During the final phases of Period IV, the settlement plan shifted from a more open one in which houses had larger rooms and included courtyards to one in which buildings were closely spaced, exterior areas were almost exclusively confined to streets, and rooms within structures were subdivided to increase the number of rooms without increasing the size of the building. The most coherent building remains come from a broad clearance in Area B; small exposures of structures and exterior surfaces in Areas A and F provide additional information on this period. Only traces of features and surfaces in Areas C and G attest to use of the lower mound during this subperiod. Most excavated structures served a domestic function, but one building in Area A may have been a shrine. Conclusions about the nature of the settlement are tentative, because they are based on limited exposures and incomplete plans of houses. However the overall impression from the architecture is that the settlement plan is a highly nucleated one that might be found in a densely occupied town in which a wide range of economic activities were conducted, rather than a primarily agrarian community. Although the settlement may have contracted in size, we cannot conclude that the population of the settlement declined, given the apparently higher density of buildings.

AREA A: PHASE 18

Deposits from Phases 18 to 20 were 2 m in depth, but only the upper meter containing Phase 20 remains was well preserved. Phases 18 to 20 were linked by five superimposed floors in Trench A04 (Fig. 26).

Phase 18 remains were encountered in portions of Trenches A04 and A05. The exposure spanned just over 6 m in length, 3.5 m in width. The remains were only approximately 0.8 m below the ground surface and spanned less than a meter in depth (Marfoe and Ingraham 1990, 53). Proximity of remains to the surface resulted in relatively poor preservation.

Excavations uncovered part of a sizable room (Unit 18.1) with a plastered floor. A stone wall foundation marked the northern boundary of the room. The excavators suggested that Unit 18.1 may have continued to be used through Phase 20. The wall ran parallel to the walls of Unit 20.1 and was similarly constructed. They noted that the level of the Phase 19 surface is .5 meter below the nearest Phase 20 floor and suggested that this may have been a result of terracing of buildings (ibid., 57). In Area B, where there was a broad clearance of architecture contemporary with Phase 20, houses were terraced and adjacent rooms were at substantially different absolute levels. The Area B construction pattern lends support to the interpretation of Area A Phases 18 to 20 as a series of adjacent rooms that overlapped in time of use.

AREA A: PHASE 19

Phase 19 (Fig. 27) remains were confined to patches of three superimposed plaster floors above Unit 18.1. No associated walls were recovered. The uppermost floor was only 0.5 m from the mound surface (ibid., 54). I estimate the volume excavated from Phase 19 as .70 m^3.

AREA A: PHASE 20

Trenches A01, A02, and A04, all at the top of the step trench, yielded remains from Phase 20, the final occupational phase of Period IV. The comparatively

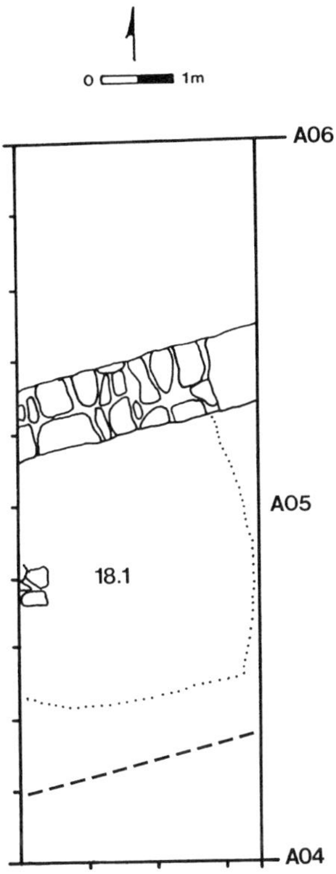

Figure 26. Plan of Area A Phase 18.

good preservation of this phase was attributed to the absence of later construction above this area (ibid., 55). The total volume of deposits was approximately 12.6 m^3.

Unit 20.1 was relatively large. The north wall foundation was made of sizable limestone slabs .80 m to .90 m wide. The west wall was 1 m wide. Judging from the plan, the south wall was between 1 m and 1.4 m thick. A mud-brick bench ran along all three exposed walls of the room, and a mud-brick platform extended from the central part of the western wall of the room. A limestone slab was located on the floor of the room to the south of the platform. The floor was coated with at least three layers of plaster that extended over the bench and up the walls. The mud-brick platform revealed a thin deposit of ash, bones, and pebbles (ibid., 56).

Unit 20.1 may have served a ritual, rather than domestic, function. Benches and platforms for offerings are often characteristic of temples and shrines. Although we do not know the scale and boundaries of the structure, it was not monumental. Unit 20.2 belonged to a separate structure, as indicated by the double wall separating the rooms and the differing con-

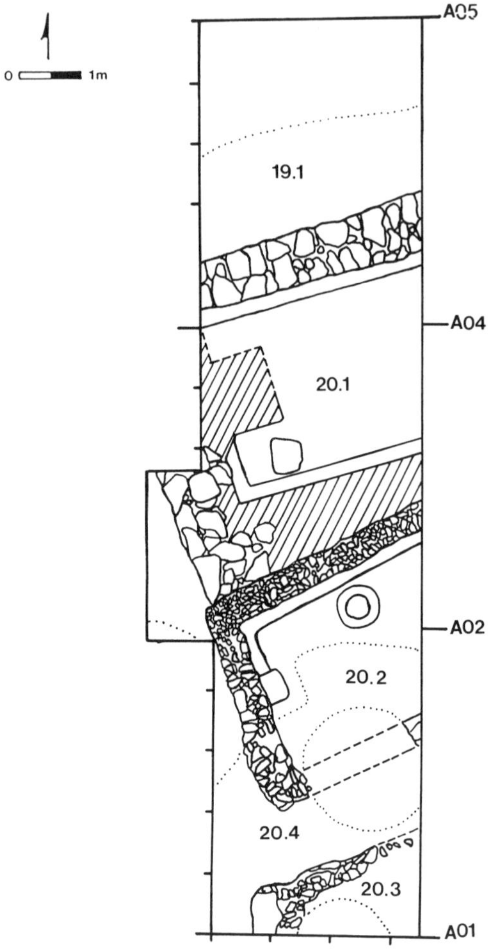

Figure 27. Plan of Area A Phases 19 and 20.

struction materials. The northern border of the structure that Unit 20.1 belonged to is unknown. The excavators suggest that Unit 19.1 may have continued in use in Phase 20; if so, it may have belonged to the same structure as Unit 20.1. The overall layout of Phases 18 to 20 architecture suggests that the area had a primarily domestic function. The buildings are closely spaced and the walls are not massive. Therefore, Unit 20.1 may have been a simple shrine in a residential area. The list of artifact categories represented in Unit 20.1 did not provide additional support for the interpretation of this room as nonresidential, although many of the finds may have been discarded after the structure was abandoned. Bones, pottery, and chipped stone were all recovered, as was a limestone object with two depressions and an animal figurine.

The north wall of Unit 20.2 ran along the south wall of Unit 20.1. Some of the features in Unit 20.1 were similar to those in Unit 20.2. A mud-brick bench ran along the north wall and at least the northern part of the western wall. A platform substantially smaller than the platform in Room 20.1 was found in a similar location toward the center of the western wall. In spite of the differences in building construction, the excavators interpret the two rooms as having a similar function (ibid., 56). However, a circular plastered basin or hearth was located toward the northern wall. This hearth-like feature combined with the small size of the platform makes the function of this room less clear than in the case of Unit 20.1. Again, artifacts did not clarify the function of this room.

The area to the south of Unit 20.2, Unit 20.4, was cut by a later pit, making it difficult to ascertain the nature of the deposits from this area. No surface was reached, but excavators suggest that Unit 20.4 may have been an exterior passageway (ibid., 56).

The corner of a third structure, Unit 20.3, was recovered immediately to the south of Unit 20.4. The north wall of the room ran parallel to the walls of Units 20.1 and 20.2. The construction technique employed for the wall foundations, the "rubble masonry technique," was the same as that used for Unit 20.2 (ibid., 56). These two structures dating to the final Period IV phase were more similar to buildings from the following Period III than to most Period IV structures (ibid.). The western faces of the three units appear to be aligned, as if they are bordering a street (see Area B plan).

Artifact categories are largely those expected in residential areas, and architecture is fairly modest. With the exception of Unit 20.1, the units from Phases 18 to 20 may represent non-elite domestic structures. The close spacing of the structures suggests a more nucleated settlement pattern than that of earlier subperiods.

AREA A: PHASE 15

Occupational remains from this phase were located near the exterior base of the fortification wall. Because the layers were not stratigraphically linked to the other Period IV deposits inside the wall, excavators dated Phase 15 (Fig. 28; Plate 17) remains only to the later part of the sequence (IVB/IVA = IV.3, IV.2, IV.1; Marfoe and Ingraham 1990, 45–6). Here, they are here assigned to Subperiod IV.1 on the basis of ceramics alone.

Plate 17. Area A Phase 15. Interior of Room 15.2 and doorway into Room 15.1. Photograph courtesy of the Oriental Institute.

The remains of this phase extended for approximately 7 m in Trenches A06 and A07. Some Phase 15 deposits rested on a layer of collapse from the fortification wall, indicating that Phase 15 postdated Phase 13, when the wall was built.

The external face of the fortification wall marked the southern boundary of the architecture from this phase; in the north part of the excavated area layers had been destroyed by erosion. The findings include two associated units. Units 15.2, a room, and 15.1, an associated courtyard or exterior surface, formed part of a house, as indicated by the wide range of domestic features and artifacts. Unit 15.1, the southernmost unit, had south and north boundary walls within the excavation area, but the east and west boundaries were beyond the trench lines. This unit cut into the fortification wall, indicating that the Phase 13 wall was no longer in use.

A step had been cut into the wall face and a second wall, interpreted as a retaining wall, was built against it. The wall did not entirely close off the south side of Unit 15.1; a passageway to the east of Wall A06: 022 provided access to a garbage pit that had been cut into the fortification wall and a pebbled hearth built on top of the fortification wall. Unit 15.1 had two superimposed surfaces. The lower one was made of flagstones and large pebbles, and the upper one was of flagstones, pebbles, and sherds. Several

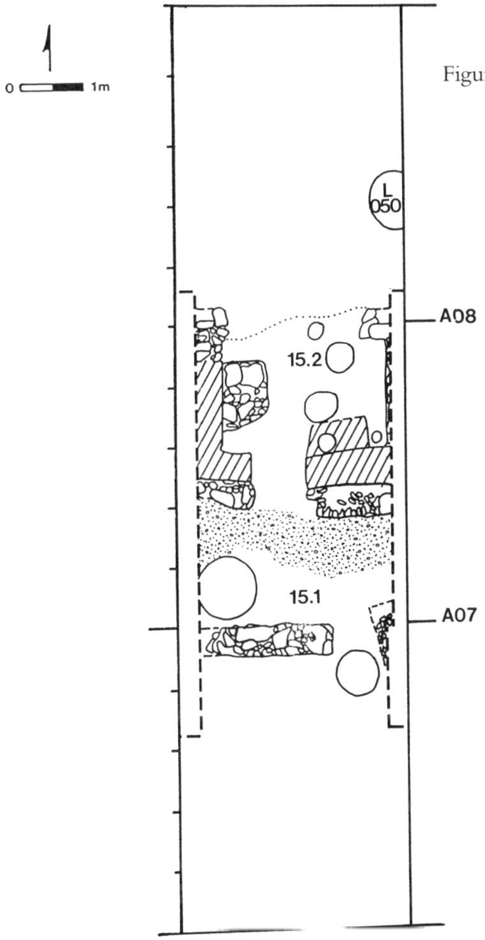

Figure 28. Plan of Area A Phase 15.

basalt querns rested on the upper paving. Excavators located a second garbage pit, 1.7 m deep, cut into the southwest portion of the exterior surface. Two low stone benches flanked the .90 m. wide doorway leading to Room 15.2 (ibid.). There were concentrations of lithic debris in the area and a complete cooking pot (ibid.).

The boundaries of Unit 15.2 were defined by the south wall and the interior faces of the east and west walls; the northern part of the room had eroded and the east and west walls ran into the balk. The foundation of the south wall was built of crude stone. The room floor and interior faces of all three walls were plastered (ibid.).

The room had several features. A small plaster-lined mud-brick platform, .28 m high, abutted the south wall east of the doorway. A large cooking pot was embedded in the platform. A second .18-m-high platform or bench, built of stone but also plastered, protruded from the west wall. Excavators noted the resemblance between this feature and some found in Period III, as well as between the crude wall construction in Unit 15.1 and the walls of Period III architecture. These similarities provide additional support for the dating of these deposits.

Other features include four pits. A small pit .45 m wide and .48 m deep was lined with the same layer of white plaster that coated the floor. Similar plaster-lined pits are described in the section on the contemporary Area B architecture. A shallow plastered depression in the floor directly east of the mud-brick platform contained two jars. Excavators interpreted a second shallow pit, located to the north of the first one, as a depression used to brace a large vessel, although the pot was not located. A third depression to the northeast of the stone platform was probably used for the same purpose. This pit was not in use during the final occupation of the room, because the plaster floor covered it. In addition to the features and associated pots, several complete or almost complete vessels and a pot stand were recovered from the floor. The artifact scatter was dense.

Excavators recovered a well 1 m to the north of the preserved Unit 15.2 floor, although erosion of the area in between the surface and well made it impossible to link them stratigraphically. The well measured approximately 1 m in diameter, as shown on the plan, and 6.5 m in depth. Because the floor of Unit 15.2 and the well were at roughly the same elevations, excavators posited that the well dated to Phase 15 (ibid.). The feature contained an abundance of well-preserved faunal and botanical remains. Unfortunately, the ceramics from the well had not been recorded and were not available for study, so it was not possible to use ceramics to date the other materials in the well. However, the ceramic specialist noted the presence of a number of examples of pottery (grooved-rim jars and Combed Wash ware) that date the contents to either Subperiod IVB or Subperiod IVA, the late subperiods of the sequence (ibid.). Because Combed Wash wares did not occur until IVA (IV.2, IV.1)[3] in the soundings, and grooved-rim jars were especially common in the final subperiod (IV.1), I assigned the well contents to IV.1, the same subperiod as the other Phase 15 remains.

The authors of the final report on the site noted that the architecture of Phase 15 differs from the earlier IVB (IV.3, Phases 13 and 14) architecture behind the wall. It is more similar to the later architecture in Areas B and G in terms of orientation and height of stone foundations in relation to the floor (ibid.). The area contrasted with contemporary levels in Areas A (Phase

20) and B in having a courtyard; in the upper trenches of Area A and in Area B, space seems to have been at a premium, and streets or passageways were the only exterior areas observed. The presence of the outdoor work area may indicate that space was at less of a premium further from the center of the mound, or that the occupants of this structure engaged in economic activities that required outdoor space. The spatial distribution of farming tools supports the second interpretation; as will be discussed in Chapter 6, sickle blades were absent from Area B but one was recovered from a pit in Unit 15.1. The modest architecture and predominance of artifacts used in food procurement, processing, preparation, and consumption suggest this was a non-elite domestic area. The recovery of a sickle blade from the exterior surface suggests that the occupants were involved in the harvest of crops.

Two activities possibly carried out in the outdoor area include grape pressing for juice, wine, or vinegar, and nut grinding for oil or meal. Several grinding stones were recovered from this area, and botanical finds from the well (A08: 050)—in particular, pressed grape samples, grape stems, nut shells with attached almonds—may have been the remains of grape pressing and nut grinding (Miller 1986, 89).

The excavators observed that the Phase 15 exposure yielded roughly the same number of pot sherds as did the much greater clearances of Area A Phases 13 and 14 combined (ibid.). This may be partially a result of the fact that exterior areas often have a higher density of materials than interiors; Unit 15.1 was an outdoor work area with garbage pits, whereas Phases 13 and 14 had only interior surfaces. Moreover, elaborate buildings often have well-swept surfaces, whereas trash is more likely to accumulate in non-elite domestic areas (for example, see Wright 1981, 178).

AREA B

Area B (Figs. 29 and 30 and Plates 18 and 19) provided the only broad exposure of well-preserved remains from the final subperiod. Findings included a series of partially excavated structures on either side of a cobbled street (Plate 18). Structures were built against one another on both a north-south and east-west axis, creating the impression that space in this part of the settlement was very limited.

Although much of the architecture in the south half of Area B dated to Period IV, the rooms had been reused in Period III (Period III rooms are shown in Fig. 29 but not Fig. 30; Plate 19). Most of the finds in this area dated to Period III and are not included in this study. Excavations in Area

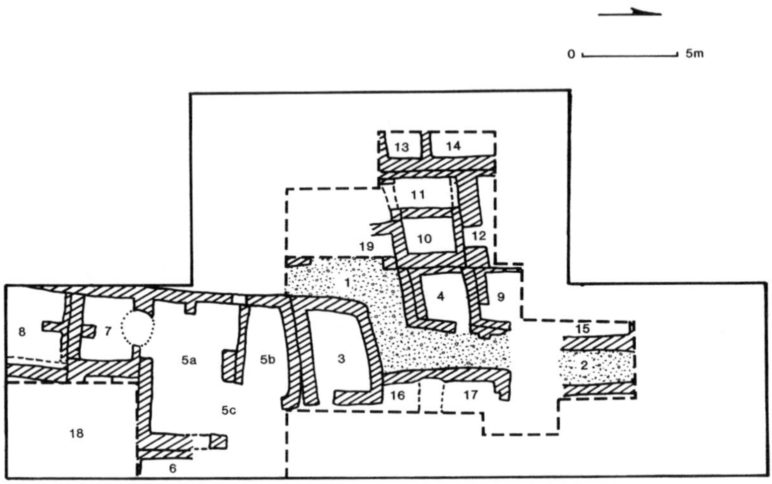

Figure 29. Plan of Area B Periods III and IV (after Verhaaren 1986). See key for Fig. 23.

B62/72 uncovered four Period IV rooms, three of which had been reused in Period III.[4]

Beginning in the south, only the wall foundations of the first room, Unit 8, were preserved (see Fig. 29). A stone feature resembling a wall foundation extended from the north wall of the room. It may represent the only preserved part of a curtain wall, or a feature of an unknown function. Similar features in the more extensively cleared part of the Period III settlement, Area D, were associated with hearths or ovens. The north wall had a mud-brick core, unlike most foundations in Area B, which were built entirely of stone. The wall of another unit (Unit 18) was constructed directly to the east, but this area was not excavated. Unit 7, built directly against the south wall of Unit 8, was approximately of the same orientation and length as Unit 8 and had a similar stone feature in the same relative location, but on the opposite side of the room. There were no doorways so we cannot say that the rooms belonged to the same structure. All the walls had stone foundations; the north, east, and west foundations were of medium-sized stones similar to most walls of Period IV, whereas at least part of the south foundation was composed of smaller stones characteristic of Period III. A large pit cut into the north wall foundation and south wall of Unit 5 may have destroyed traces of a doorway. A white plaster surface associated with the walls was dated to Phase 3 (Period IV) on the basis of associated ceramics. The surface in Unit 5 was dated to Period III on the basis of pottery. However, a test trench in

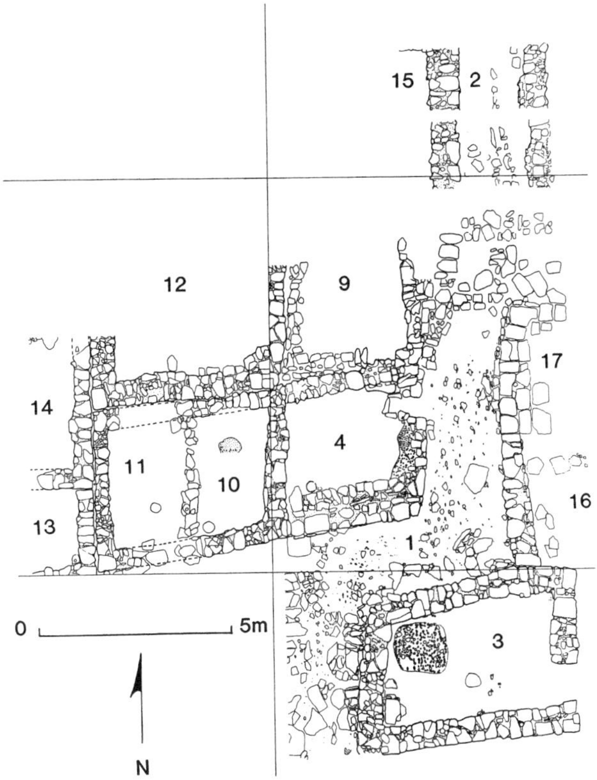

Figure 30. Plan of Area B Period IV.

the northwest corner of the room reached an earlier Period IV surface. No Period IV surfaces were excavated in Units 5c and 6.

The ceramics provided a Period III date for the surface of Unit 5b. A partially paved Phase III surface appears to run over the foundation stones of the north wall; the Phase IV foundation stones may have been incorporated into the Period III flagstone and rubble surface. Units 5a, 5b, and 5c may have been part of a Phase III courtyard or exterior surface. In Area D, where the architecture and surfaces were in a better state of preservation, courtyards contained platform hearths similar to one located in the southwest corner of Unit 5. One test trench in Unit 5b uncovered a Period IV wall. An adjacent test trench yielded Period IV artifacts and an early pebble surface.

In the north half of the excavated area, most of the architecture, surfaces, and artifacts dated to Period IV (see Fig. 30). Only isolated traces of Period III remained. Most of the Period IV architecture dated to two main sub-

Plate 18. Area B, general view. Photograph courtesy of the Oriental Institute.

phases: (1) 2b, the earliest phase, was characterized by relatively large structures; and (2) 2a, when the 2b structures had been subdivided into small rooms and doorways were blocked. The Area B street was in use during both subphases. Earlier architecture, dated to Phase 3, was characterized by wider wall foundations with similar orientations but different locations. At least some of the Phase 3 architecture continued in use during Phase 2.

Five of the rooms in the north part of Area B lined the Phase 2 street (Plate 19). The street surface was 0.5 m to 0.10 m thick and composed of small cobbles, sherds, and flint, with a small amount of densely packed sediment and occasional large flat stones. Along the edges of the street, flagstones, cobbles, pebbles, and large sherds formed a curb. The high density of debris suggests the street served as a trash disposal area for occupants of the adjacent structures. Three main segments of the street were excavated. Beginning in the southernmost section, the street ran upslope in a north-south direction for 5.10 m, and then turned east (and probably west as well, as indicated by the alignment of the southern walls of Units 4, 10, 11, and 13) for 5.20 m between the outer walls of Units 3 and 4. Finally, the street turned northward again. It may turn eastward just north of Units 16 and 17.

The wall foundations of Unit 3 were about .70 m thick. No definite doorways were identified. A gap in the east wall probably resulted from stone

Plate 19. Area B Period IV structures.

robbing, plowing, or erosion. A possible doorway may have existed between Units 3 and 16 and 17 at the east end of the northern wall, where the stones are smaller than elsewhere in the wall. Although the room was small, it contained several features from both subphases. A drain in the base of the west wall foundation opened onto the street. A limestone slab supported at either end by rock columns was placed above the drain. Small pebbles in the southwest part of the room indicated a lower surface. They probably served as leveling for a floor that was not preserved. Two white plaster-lined pits also dated to this lower subphase. The first, toward the center of the room, was a small double-chambered one. The second, in the northwest corner of the room, was a small circular pit with a plaster lining. The edges of the pit were burned and the pit fill was ashy, indicating that it may have been a fireplace. An oven base from an upper subphase covered the circular pit. The feature rested on a packed mud surface that was only preserved in the west part of the trench.

If a doorway did in fact exist in the northeast corner, then Unit 3 formed part of a larger structure that included Unit 16 directly to the north. The fact that they share a wall segment supports this interpretation. I believe on the basis of the double wall and absence of a doorway that Units 5 and 3 belonged to separate structures. Plowing and erosion destroyed the floors and sections of walls in the east part of the trench; it is possible that an additional room of the structure had been located east of Unit 3 but was not preserved.

The surfaces of Units 16 and 17 were .60 m below the level of the street with which they were associated, indicating terracing on the east side of the street. The only Unit 16 walls retrieved were the west wall, a portion of the north wall, and the segment of the south wall that was shared with Unit 3. A fairly massive wall (ca. 1.20 m) may have served as the north wall of Unit 16.

The relatively uniform size and shape of the Unit 17 foundation stones, and the relatively large scale of both the individual stones and foundation walls themselves, indicate that it may have been constructed at an earlier date than most of the other excavated Area B architecture, or that it was occupied by a family with access to skilled labor (the west wall was .80 m wide and the south wall 1.20 m). A possible north wall measured about .85 m. The eastern segment of the north wall was not located in a trench to the east, and the wall may have been removed by erosion. A white plaster floor was partially preserved.

Just north of Unit 17 the street may have turned eastward. Excavations indicated that the street continued northward as well. Walls on either side of the northernmost excavated stretch of street suggested that structures lined this segment of the street as well, although these were not excavated.

On the west side of the street seven rooms belonging to four structures provided evidence for terracing of architecture on the east slope of the mound. A large stone wall foundation was evident in the section running along the west side of the street (Unit 1), to the south of Unit 4. The two most substantial structures were Structures 2 (Unit 12) and 3 (Units 13 and 14). The south wall had a doorway that had been blocked. A pit dug into the floor may have dated to a later period. Only the walls of Units 13 and 14, to the west of Unit 11, were excavated.

The north wall of Unit 10 blocked the doorway of Structure 2, and therefore must have been later in the construction sequence. A possible doorway between Units 4 and 10 may have provided access between the two units. The fact that they appear to have shared a wall supports the suggestion that they were part of the same structure, designated Structure 1a. Unfortunately a north-south wall in Unit 4, which we later realized belonged to Phase III, obscured the connection between the two rooms. The surface of Unit 10 was approximately 0.65 m higher than the surface of Unit 4.

As mentioned previously, Units 10 and 11 probably belonged to the same structure as Unit 4. The outer wall foundations of the two rooms ranged from 0.40 m to 0.60 m in thickness. A .30-m-wide curtain wall separated

Units 10 and 11, but the plaster floor of Unit 11 ran under the dividing wall, indicating that they initially formed one room. The floor of Unit 10 was replastered after the curtain wall was in place. A hearth was located toward the northern side of Unit 10. A shallow cobble-lined pit had been dug through the floor of Unit 10 in the southwest corner. Another shallow pit rested in the southern part of Unit 11, toward the center of the room. Architecture to the south of Units 10 and 11 dated to Phase III.

In Unit 4, a doorway provided access from the street. A bench of stones with a plastered surface, built against the exterior face of the southern wall of Unit 4, on the west side of the street, provided a link between Units 4 and 10, and between units in Trench B81 and the street. The east wall of Unit 10 was braced on the edge of the bench, and the platform may have been part of a buttressing system used in constructing terraced architecture.

Three phases were represented in Unit 4, two of which dated to Period IV. An earlier plaster floor ran under the stone feature along the southern wall. The doorway between Units 4 and 9 may have been open during this phase. A pot set 5 cm into the floor in the southwest corner may actually date to the later occupational surface in the room. Only the top part of the pot was intact, the lower part having been broken and the pieces scattered nearby. The badly disturbed bones of an infant were found in the fill inside the pot and surrounding fill. A freshwater pearl in the fill nearby may have originally been associated with the burial.

An upper plaster surface was contemporary with the stone feature running against the south wall and with the blocked doorway. The stone feature may be a bench rather than a wall foundation. Patches of white plaster coating the top surface of the stones support this interpretation. An oven base rested in the southeast corner of the room, next to the doorway. The edge of this feature partially rested on the eastern wall foundation. Although all the artifacts recovered dated to Period IV, it is possible that the oven was constructed in Period III, when the wall may not have been standing. Alternatively, if the oven did date to Period IV, the room may have been partially open or, more likely, another wall may have existed east of the one that was uncovered, as was the case with Unit 9. The west wall in Unit 4, shown in Figure 29, dated to Period III.

The northernmost extent of Structure 1b was not defined. Only the south side of Unit 9 (Structure 1b) was cleared. Unit 9 was probably added to Unit 4 after it was in use. Scattered patches of white plaster indicated there had been an upper surface of Unit 9 that was not preserved.

Unit 15, to the north of Unit 12, may have been a separate structure, judging from the comparatively thick wall foundation. A plaster floor was detected in the small portion of the room excavated. The earlier units (Units 17, 12, and possibly Unit 14) may have initially had associated courtyards but, if so, the areas were subsequently used for construction. By the end of the subperiod, the density of buildings was so high that the street was the only exterior space in the entire area. Perhaps house roofs replaced courtyards as the loci of outdoor activities.

From the limited evidence available, structures seem to have been larger in the earlier subphase than the later one. It appears that structures and individual rooms were subdivided to accommodate an increasing population. Perhaps families subdivided their houses as the extended family grew. The subdividing of space and absence of exterior space suggest that population density was high, at least in this part of the site, and that land was scarce.

The small size of the structures and the absence of exterior activity areas may be exceptional for domestic areas at small Near Eastern sites. Nonetheless, the artifacts indicate that most, if not all, of the structures were residential (Plates 20 and 21). Few artifacts of known function were unrelated to food preparation, cooking, and serving, or spinning and weaving. A small number of figurines and ornaments were recovered, including an imported Indo-Pacific shell (Reese 1990). There is no evidence for workshops, although a cluster of spindle whorls was found (see Chapter 5). All completely excavated rooms had hearths or ovens. The infant burial from Unit 11 also suggests the area was residential. The architecture appears to have been constructed in a relatively casual manner, and walls were fairly narrow. Overall, this site sector appears to have been one of the more modest residences.

AREA F: PHASES 13 AND 14

A half meter of collapse between Phases 12 and 13 probably resulted from the collapse of the Phase 12 building (Marfoe 1990a). The architecture in the 16-m^2 excavation area changed during this period, and it resembles Subperiod IV.1 architecture on the large mound. Although the overall layout of the area appears similar to earlier Area F phases, with two structures flanking a street, a new wall of the structure in the west part of the trench is somewhat smaller (1.00 m in width versus 1.20 m–1.40 m) and located 0.30 m to 0.40 m west of the earlier wall. The orientation is similar (ibid.). The new wall formed an outer wall for a structure. The floor of the room was not preserved, and only about 2 m^2 of the room were excavated.

Plate 20. Chariot wheel or spindle whorl from B81-0115/16-012 (Unit 11, fill above floor). Photograph courtesy of the Oriental Institute.

An exterior surface, probably a street, ran between the first wall and a second one. The surface consisted of flat-lying sherds and pebbles (Marfoe 1990a). The structure to the east continued in use from the previous phase. Even though the architecture may have been less massive than in the earlier phases, the wall was still relatively thick, and this area may have continued in use as an elite residential area. The quantity of artifacts was too small to inform about the function of the area or status of occupants.

Phase 14 is very similar to Phase 13 (Fig. 31), although the west wall was modified to one with a packed mud core lined with stone blocks on either side. No floor was found in association with the wall. The exterior surface east of the wall continued in use and in this phase consisted of pebbles with sherd scatters and ash patches (ibid.). Again, relatively few artifacts were recovered from this small exposure.

AREAS C AND C01: PHASE 16

The latest phase in Areas C and C01 (C01: Phase 16 and C: Phase 1) did not have preserved architecture and only scattered patches of surfaces and features were recovered (Fig. 32). However, on the basis of isolated features, we may assume that there was an occupation that postdated the major

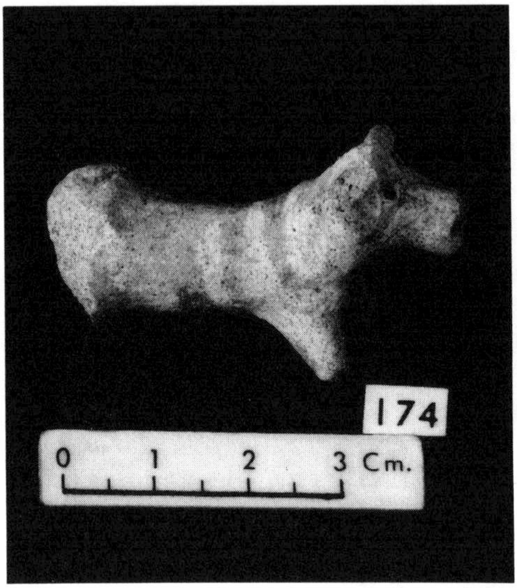

Plate 21. Dog figurine from Unit 3. Photograph courtesy of the Oriental Institute.

occupation in Area C. The remains were as little as approximately 0.10 m below the surface.

At first inspection, the Phase IV.1 remains suggest a lightly used activity area, rather than a more intensively used residential one. However, I attribute this appearance to the destruction of most surfaces and walls rather than to sporadic use of the area. Certainly, the large quantity of late Subperiod IV.1 pottery argues for substantial use of the area during this time (see Chapter 3).

In Trenches C35, C45, and C01, where preservation is relatively good, Area C01 Phase 16 and Area C Phase 1 features include two pebble platforms that probably served as oven bases, one poorly defined rocky feature of an unknown function, and three patches of stones and pottery, either exterior surfaces or Phase 1 wall collapse.

In Trenches C55/56, the Phase 2 (Subperiod IV.2) preservation of Period IV remains was uneven, so it is not surprising that no definite Phase 1 features were recovered. In C66 a sounding down to Period 2 remains yielded a pot on a Phase 1 plaster surface, but only a patch of the surface was uncovered.

AREA G

The Area G Phase IV.1 remains, like those in Area C, were very fragmentary. Again, I believe that the occupation during Subperiod IV.1 may have been

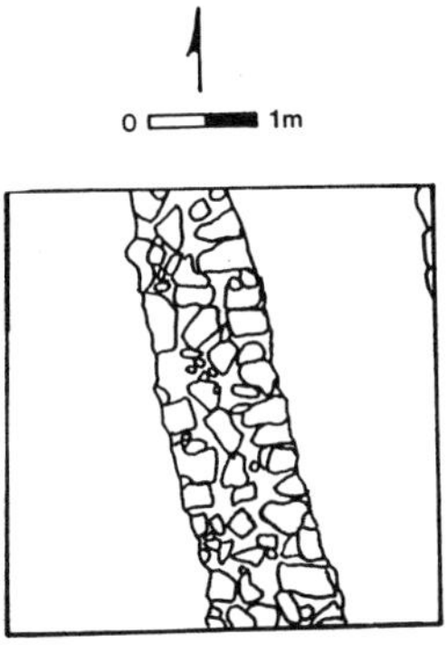

Figure 31. Plan of Area F Phase 13.

more substantial than the remains indicate, and attribute the disturbed Phase 2 remains to plowing, weathering, and stone robbing. Even some of the Phase 3 remains were fairly fragmentary and walls had been removed. The Phase 2 remains in Area G include four pits, a stone surface, probably an exterior area, and possibly part of a wall foundation.

Overall, Subperiod IV.1 remains suggest a trend toward increased settlement density and decreased residential interior and exterior space. The light evidence for occupation on the small mound has led to the conclusion that this period was characterized by settlement retrenchment (Marfoe and Algaze 1990, 429). However, it should be noted that the densely packed architecture contrasts with the more spacious, open settlement plan from the subsequent Period III village and suggests that population density was high, at least toward the center of the settlement. The artifact analyses in Chapters 5 and 6 show that the changes in residential structures during Subperiod IV.I were accompanied by economic reorganization, a decline in the range of economic activities carried out by households, and decreasing household economic autonomy.

PATTERNS OF SETTLEMENT EXPANSION AND DECLINE IN LATE-THIRD MILLENNIUM NORTH MESOPOTAMIA: EVIDENCE FROM KURBAN HÖYÜK AND OTHER SITES IN SOUTHEASTERN TURKEY

The pattern of urban development in the third millennium is much clearer than its cessation. Apparently, numerous third millennium centers contracted or were abandoned toward the end of the third millennium. For example, east of the Balikh valley, Chuera (Orthmann 1986, 62), Tell Leilan (Weiss et al. 1993), and Tell Taya (Reade 1968, 240) are among the sites abandoned.

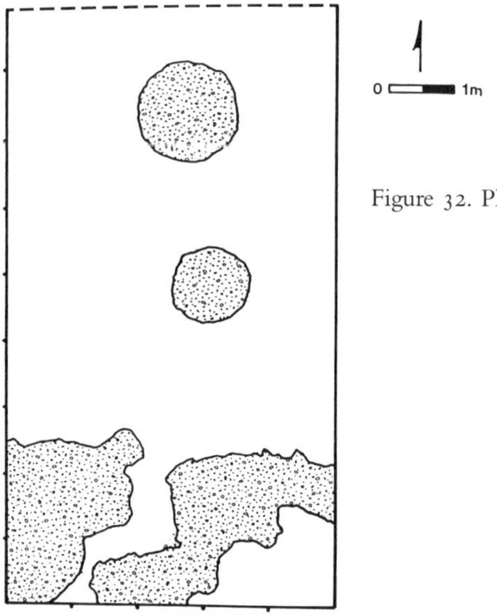

Figure 32. Plan of Area C01 Phase 16

At Tell Leilan, eight soundings at the site provided evidence for an occupational hiatus (Weiss et al. 1993, 999). At Kazane, located at the northern edge of the Balikh valley, settlement contracted but the site was not abandoned (Wattenmaker and Mısır 1994). To the west of the Balikh Valley, occupation at Selenkiheye (van Loon 1979) ceased toward the end of the third millennium. At Titriş Höyük, settlement actually expanded in the later part of the third millennium, but the lower town was abandoned at the end of the Early Bronze Age (Algaze et al. 1995).

The pattern of settlement retrenchment or abandonment at numerous sites has been interpreted as evidence for wide scale political and demographic collapse at approximately 2200 B.C., resulting from abrupt climatic change and desertification (Weiss et al. 1993, 996–1002). However, in the Carchemish region the number of sites increased and the aggregate settlement area expanded exponentially, suggesting regional variation in settlement trends toward the end of the third millennium (Algaze et al. 1994). Moreover, there is evidence for continued occupation, if not expansion, at Titriş Höyük toward the end of the third millennium. Houses were closely spaced in what appears to have been a highly urbanized settlement pattern (see Algaze et al. 1995, 19). Although a decline in settlement size and political disintegration has been posited for Kurban Höyük, an alternative scenario is also supported by the Kurban Period IV data.

Overall, the fragmentary nature of remains from Areas C and G suggest that settlement on the north mound became less dense toward the end of the third millennium. This find, combined with survey results indicating that large sites declined in size and new villages were established, has been interpreted as evidence for a decline in population and ruralization (Marfoe and Algaze 1990, 429; see also Wilkinson 1990, 104–5 and Algaze et al. 1992, 42–3, 47). However, exposures in Areas A and B on the main mound yielded buildings that were more closely spaced and had smaller rooms than architectural remains from earlier periods. The close spacing of buildings and limited number of exterior areas in both parts of the site suggests a highly urbanized settlement in which space was at a premium. Moreover, as will be discussed in the following section, the residents of the settlement had even stronger economic ties to specialists than they had in the preceding phases. Thus, it is possible that people at Kurban Höyük moved from the outer town to the inner town; increased population toward the centers of sites may have contributed to the apparent decline in site sizes during this time.

Given the absence of excavations at the center of the site, where public buildings may have been located, it is not known whether Kurban Höyük remained a socioeconomically diverse community. One hint that public buildings may have existed on the north mound comes from Area D, where a relatively massive gateway was found just below Period III (final third to early second millennium) remains (Marfoe and Algaze 1990, 430; Verhaaren 1989, 171). The wall foundations had apparently been reused in Period III, suggesting that the original building dated to the final phase of Period IV.

In summary, it is not clear whether centralized political control was maintained during this final phase of Period IV. Changes in site population and settlement size are equally unclear. The spatial organization of the community may have shifted from one in which houses were dispersed and exterior activity areas were interspersed among houses to a more spatially segregated system whereby houses were clustered on the south mound and open work areas were located on the north mound. It remains a possibility that a shift in settlement patterns (and increased nucleation), rather than an actual demographic or political decline, caused the apparent decrease in the size of urban centers at numerous sites in northern Mesopotamia. The increase in settlement in the Carchemish area suggests a political landscape in which centers of power shifted through time, rather than one characterized by synchronous political collapse and depopulation in various regions across north Mesopotamia. At Kurban Höyük, the pattern points to increased nucleation on the large mound, with more dispersed settlement on the small mound, but not necessarily a decline in population. As will be seen in the next chapter, the distribution of material remains reveals that a complex reconfiguration of economic and social relations occurred during this time, but this shift was not what we would expect during a period of pervasive economic disintegration.

5 CHANGING PATTERNS OF CRAFT PRODUCTION AND CONSUMPTION

In this chapter I examine the spatial distribution of craft goods and artifacts related to their manufacture in order to examine change through time in the organization of craft production. Determining the categories of craft goods produced by households and those produced by specialists provides the basis for examining reasons for increasing specialization of the economy (discussed in Chapter 7). I monitor change through time in patterns of production and consumption of pottery, stone tools, and textiles at Kurban Höyük and relate these changes to shifts in sociopolitical organization, pottery, chipped stone, and textiles. These three categories of goods represent important craft items in the ancient Near East.

In order to examine changing patterns of production and consumption during the process of urbanization, it was necessary to divide the mid-third millennium sequence at Kurban Höyük into relatively brief subperiods. This has, of course, resulted in smaller sample sizes from each subperiod than would be the case had I treated the four subperiods as one period. However, for the purposes of this study it is preferable to work with smaller sample sizes than to group artifacts from different subperiods, which would mask fine-scale changes through time. Ceramics and chipped stone were well represented in each room excavated, but some categories of artifacts examined in this chapter and the next, such as animal bones and ornaments, were not so abundant. This may well be in part a result of a relatively low rate of consumption of meat and certain craft goods among non-elites in early state society; if so, then exploration of the non-elites as participants in a changing social landscape may require that researchers sometimes work with smaller than ideal sample sizes.

Ceramics are well represented at most third millennium B.C. archaeological sites in the Near East, because pottery was widely used and broken (relatively easily) into highly durable sherds. Although their abundance has allowed archaeologists to use ceramics to study consumption patterns, it is more difficult to study ceramic production. Ceramic manufacturing evidence is generally rare archaeologically. Fortunately, in the Kurban case, some steps in the ceramic production process were so specialized that there were clues about the manufacturing context often not found in archaeological situations. This made it possible to consider the socioeconomic contexts of ceramic production. Textiles, however, are almost never preserved in the Near East, although evidence for production is more readily detectable archaeologically, because the tools were often made of materials that tend to preserve well (e.g., stone loom weights). In this case, we found few clues about either production or consumption patterns, but clay tablets from Ebla provided hypotheses on the organization of textile production as well as consumption patterns. Chipped stone production and use are both relatively easy to trace archaeologically because the manufacturing process generates a relative abundance of chipped stone debris. The debitage and tools are very durable. Both stone tools and manufacturing debris were well represented at Kurban Höyük.

Before interpreting the significance of the spatial distributions of these artifacts in terms of production patterns, it is necessary to consider the relationship between the locations in which they were used and the loci of their recovery. In general, damaged goods (e.g., broken ceramic vessels) and food remains might be discarded as trash in garbage pits, abandoned houses, streets and so on, whereas artifacts in good condition are more likely to have been used or stored where they were found. Very small artifacts, such as bone fragments, might have been discarded or inadvertently dropped where they were used. Streets appear to have been a common place for both the disposal of debris and loss of valuables.

With respect to ceramics, complete vessels found in situ were rare, and most sherds retrieved from Kurban Höyük probably represented vessels that had broken predepositionally. As is generally the case at Near Eastern sites, many sherds found on house floors probably derived from pots used elsewhere and discarded as trash after the house was abandoned. In this analysis I attempted to eliminate sherds that had been recycled from earlier deposits by excluding from the analysis sherds associated with floor leveling, building collapse, and architectural features (e.g., sherds used in wall foundations).

Because the ceramic analysis focuses on change through time rather than spatial variability, the inability to link ceramics to specific structures was not a problem. I considered ceramic assemblages from each site sector as representative of the households in that part of the site, although assemblages could not be linked to occupants of specific structures. Some differences in status of residents appear to have existed within the various neighborhoods but, judging from the architecture and objects, site sectors were internally relatively homogeneous compared with other contemporaneous parts of the site. For example, the houses in Area B are more similar to one another than they are to the "courtyard house" in Area A (Phase 15; see Figs. 28 and 29).

Stone tools were more likely to have been stored or used in the structures with which they were associated, because even broken pieces can be reworked. Small pieces of debitage might have been overlooked when rooms were cleaned. Larger pieces of debitage may have been stored for future use or discarded as trash after structures were abandoned. Even if some debitage was discarded in structures where flint knapping had not occurred, it is reasonable to expect that widespread flint working would result in a ubiquitous distribution of debitage and that specialized flint working would result in a more limited distribution.

Clay spindle whorls, used here to determine whether spinning thread was a household activity, might be found in the rooms in which they were stored or used, unless they were broken and discarded as trash. Spindle whorls might not be recovered from every house in which spinning occurred, but if thread was spun in many or all households, spindle whorls should have a fairly wide distribution (unless they were made of wood).

THE PRODUCTIVE CONTEXT OF THE KURBAN CERAMICS

Ceramics were the best represented class of artifact at Kurban Höyük, used in all parts of the settlement in all phases. They provided one of the primary sources of information on changing production and consumption patterns. Even in the earlier village phases, wheel-thrown pottery produced by specialists was used, along with ceramics thought to be domestically produced.

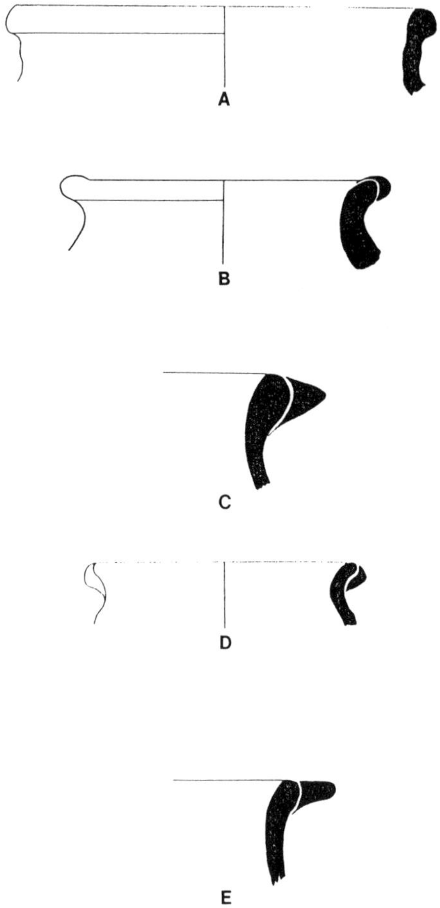

Figure 33. Variation in Handmade Closed Forms (from Algaze 1990b; scale 2 : 5).

However, the relative proportion of specialist-produced pottery increased through time. The majority of the Kurban ceramics can be divided into two groups. *Wheel-made pottery* forms the first group. Vessels in this category had very fine to medium grit temper and at least the rims were made on a wheel. This group of wares includes Plain Simple ware and the related Painted Band, Horizontal Reserve Slip, and Combed Wash ware variants, and Stone ware (sometimes called Metallic ware) and the decorated subcategories of Stone ware. Examples from this subcategory appeared to be well made and highly standardized. Forms include pot stands, cups, and bowls and jars of all sizes (see Figs. 6–13).

The second ceramic group includes the coarse handmade grit- and quartz-tempered burnished ware, often referred to as *Cooking Pot ware,* and a related ware that has both grit and chaff temper (see Figs. 4–5; also Fig. 33). These handmade wares were used primarily for production of lugged hole-mouthed pots, identified as cooking pots because they are often found in hearths and sometimes have evidence of exposure to fire on the exterior (Algaze 1990b, 329). Some trays, andirons, medium and large bowls, and storage jars were also made of this ware.

Examples of Karababa Painted ware (see Fig. 14) were excluded from this consideration of ceramic production organization, because it was not always possible to determine how the examples were manufactured (see Algaze 1990b versus Hauptmann 1982, 17; and Thissen 1982, 19). At least some of the sherds appeared to have marks from a slow wheel, but others may have been handmade. The casual, relatively carelessly painted designs on the pots suggest that this category of pot was produced comparatively informally. The Cooking Pot and Karababa Painted wares are the only major Kurban ware categories not included in the list of wares associated with kilns excavated from the nearby site of Lidar Höyük (Hauptmann 1982, 18), supporting the interpretation that the Karababa Painted ware sherds should not be grouped with those in the first category mentioned previously when organization of production is the main consideration.[1]

DIFFERENTIATING BETWEEN SPECIALIZED AND NONSPECIALIZED CERAMIC PRODUCTION

Three sources of information were used to determine which of the Kurban ceramics were produced by specialists: (1) the method of manufacture, (2) the recovery of a range of ceramics from a pottery workshop, and (3) the degree of standardization.

Ceramic technology is closely linked to the organization of ceramic production (Peacock 1982, 8–11; Rice 1987, 182). Kilns and potters' wheels allow one to produce large quantities of standardized products relatively quickly but require a high investment of labor and fuel resources. Ethnographically, the use of the wheel and kiln are always associated with production by specialists (Kramer 1985, 81; Rice 1987, 182). On the basis of ethnographic sources and consideration of the skills involved, Peacock (1982) has suggested that households producing their own pottery would not use a wheel or kiln, and that even a tournette would be unlikely. Thus, I interpreted evidence for use of a wheel or kiln as indicative of specialized production. Sherds with wheel marks were categorized as specialist-produced.

Many of the grit-tempered, wheel-made ceramic types at Kurban Höyük appeared superficially to be identical to those found in association with the Lidar kilns. The larger kilns were used for Plain Simple ware storage jars, finer plain and decorated wares and figurines, and the smaller kilns were used for the decorated and fine wares (Hauptmann 1982, 18). The only Kurban examples of potters' marks were from sherds in this category. Without chemical analyses of the ceramics it is not possible to determine if the Kurban pots were in fact produced at Lidar Höyük.[2] Regardless of where the Kurban pots were manufactured, it is reasonable to assume that similar kiln-firing practices were employed. Because of the evidence for use of the potter's wheel (and indirect evidence for kiln use) as well as the overall standardization in the assemblage (discussed later), I interpreted these wares as the products of specialists.

A small number of ceramics exhibited potters' marks, generally on the interior of the rim or just above the base on the exterior (see Fig. 8b and c). Ethnographically, these marks are sometimes used when several potters share a kiln to economize on fuel (Donnan 1971; Kramer 1985, 82).[3] This documented association between potters' marks and kiln use by specialists, combined with a high proportion of potters' marks on sherds associated with the Lidar kilns (Hauptmann 1982, 18), and similarities between the Lidar and Kurban pots in terms of the types of pots with marks, the specific symbols used, and the locations of the marks all suggest that in this case the potters' marks were used in the context of mass production.

As discussed in Chapter 1, goods produced by specialists are often more uniform than those produced by nonspecialists. Ceramics produced by individual households or extended families should be less standardized than those produced by specialists.

One recent ethnoarchaeological study of pots produced in the Philippines provided support for the expectation that ceramics produced by specialists would be more uniform than those produced by individual households (Longacre, Kramme, and Kobayashi 1988). The relative standardization of specialist-produced pottery was apparent in the range of measurements for height, width, and diameters of vessels analyzed. However, the authors question the utility of metric analysis for determining the degree of standardization in archaeological assemblages as a result of the problem in identifying ceramic types when the emic categories are not known (ibid., 106). Combining different size categories, for example, would mask the uniformity within each of the size categories. In their study, only complete vessels are used. The problem is even greater when sherds rather than

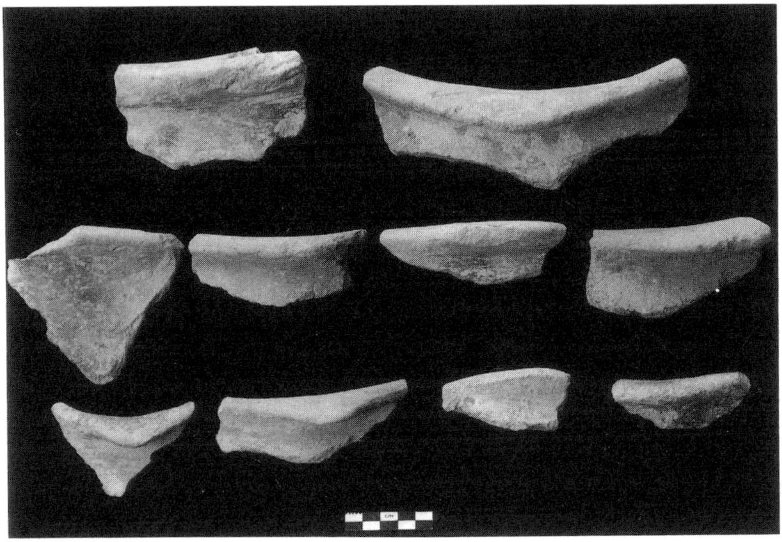

Plate 22. Examples of cooking pot lugs from Areas B and G.

complete vessels are used, because a single category might actually include sherds from a range of complete vessel forms. For example, a group of similar rim sherds might include several base forms.

Metric and chemical analyses of mid-third-millennium kiln wasters from Tell Leilan in Syria revealed a high degree of standardization among vessels from the same workshop (Blackman, Stein, and Vandiver 1993). Although sherds recovered from non-workshop contexts were less standardized, because they most likely came from multiple workshops, they were still relatively standardized compared to vessels produced by nonspecialists (ibid., 77).

In the Kurban Höyük case, the variability within categories of the handmade coarse ware forms is apparent even without metric analyses (see Figs. 5 and 33; Plate 22); each diagnostic sherd appeared to be unique (Algaze 1990b, 331). A comparison of measurements of sherds from both groups also supports the interpretation that a greater number of producers were involved in making the handmade vessels than the wheel-thrown ones.

Lugged cooking pots were not ideal for a metric analysis, because the rim dimensions varied depending on distance from the lug. Moreover, the uneven shape of the rim (resulting from both casual manufacturing and variability in the profile with distance from the lug) often made it difficult to estimate diameters. Nonetheless, the metric analysis supported impressions that the lugged handmade pots were more variable. I compared

Table 3

Diameters of Handmade and Beaded-Rim Jars

	Mean	Standard	Percentage coefficient of deviation
Handmade Vessels (n = 47)	25.17	7.63	25.2
Beaded-Rim Jars (n = 33)	18.90	3.92	20.8

Note: F-ratio = 2.60; p <.01.

the diameters of lugged handmade vessels with those of beaded rim jars, a wheel-thrown Plain Simple ware type in a similar size range (a Horizontal Reserve Slip ware example of the beaded rim jars is shown in Fig. 10b). The diameters of the handmade closed vessels were significantly more variable (Table 3).

Because the more standardized beaded rim jars were shaped on a wheel and the lugged vessels were made by hand, it is possible that the differences between the two samples in the degree of standardization resulted from differences in manufacturing technology. However, the social context of production may be more important in determining the range of variability in products than the technology of production. Preliminary results of an ethnoarchaeological study comparing the uniformity of specialist-produced handmade versus wheel-made pots in Morocco suggested that the two types were equally standardized. Both categories were more standardized than pots produced by households (Benco 1989). The specialist-produced pottery from the Philippines was as uniform in diameter as a sample of specialist-produced Islamic pottery from Morocco, even though the former was handmade and the latter wheel-made (Benco 1988, 66).[4] Although handmade pots are often made by specialists, the greater variability in appearance and dimensions of the handmade examples compared with wheel-thrown pots at Kurban Höyük suggest that, in this case, production of the handmade pots was relatively unspecialized and decentralized (i.e., not produced in a large workshop).

Having categorized the wheel-thrown ceramics as specialist-produced and the handmade ceramics as having been produced in a less centralized manner, it is now possible to examine change throughout Period IV in the ceramic production organization and consumption patterns. There is a small but steady decrease through time in the proportion of handmade to wheel-thrown pottery (Table 4). Through time, the wheel-thrown pottery increased

Table 4
Percentage of Handmade Versus Wheel-Made Pottery by Subperiod

	Handmade		Wheel-made	
Subperiod	No.	%	No.	%
IV.4	547	46	652	54
V.3	1,807	43	2,398	57
IV.2	10,073	37	16,804	63
IV.1	3,287	32	7,118	68

Note: X^2 for Subperiods IV.4 and IV.3 = 2.6, .25 > p > .10; X^2 for Subperiods IV.4 and IV.1 = 95.6, p < .001; X^2 for Subperiods IV.3 and IV.1 = 170.4, p < .001; X^2 for Subperiods IV.2 and IV.1 = 114.4, p < .001.

from 54% to 68% of the ceramic assemblage. With the exception of Subperiods IV.4 and IV.3, differences between levels are statistically highly significant. A similar trend was noted at the contemporary north Syrian site of Tell Chuera (Orthmann 1986, 69).

If higher ranking families relied more heavily on wheel-thrown pottery than lower ranking families, this chronological trend would have been even stronger than the numbers suggest; most of the later (Subperiods IV.2 and IV.1) ceramic assemblages came from areas with modest architecture, whereas many of the earlier (Subperiod IV.3) ceramic samples came from areas with more substantial architecture. Although functional differences between the areas may contribute to the differing proportions of wheel-made to handmade pottery, current evidence does in fact suggest that a greater proportion of wheel-thrown ceramics were used in areas with more elaborate buildings than in areas with more modest structures. For example, there is a higher proportion of wheel-made pottery in Area A (Phase 14), which had elaborate architecture, than there is in the later deposits from Area G, a more modest sector of the settlement (Table 5). This observation is further supported by findings from the center of Kazane, where ceramics associated with monumental architecture included only a small percentage of cooking pots.

Nonetheless, the chronological trend toward increased reliance on wheel-thrown ceramics appears to cross-cut status differences. Subperiod IV.1 deposits had a significantly higher proportion of wheel-thrown pottery than did those from Subperiods IV.2 and IV.3, although the samples from the latter subperiods included materials from areas with elaborate architecture.

Table 5
Comparison of Percentage of Handmade Ceramics from Areas with Elaborate Architecture Versus Areas with Modest Architecture

	Modest architecture		Elaborate architecture	
Subperiod	No.	%	No.	%
IV.3	—	—	463	35
IV.2	1,034	42	732	26

Note: For Subperiod IV.3, Area A Phase 14 deposits were used. For Subperiod IV.2 Area G deposits provided data from an area with modest architecture and Area F (Phases 8–12) provided data from an area with more elaborate architecture.
—No data available for more modest structures.

The relative decrease in handmade sherds might also have resulted simply from an absolute increase in the use of wheel-made vessels, rather than an actual decline in the use of handmade vessels. For example, a shift from using a communal bowl to individual place settings might have resulted in increased consumption rates of smaller vessels, which were generally made on a wheel. To establish that the decreasing proportion of handmade pottery did in fact represent a decline in consumption, rather than simply an increase in the use of wheel-made ceramics, I examined changes in the density of sherds from each category, using a sample of loci from Subperiods IV.2 and IV.1 (Tables 6 and 7).[5] The density ratios indicate that the discard rates, and presumably consumption rates, of handmade pottery did in fact decline from Subperiods IV.2 to IV.1. Wheel-made ceramics increased in density with a corresponding decrease in the density of handmade pottery. Overall, however, there does not appear to have been a major change in the total density of pottery. In sum, the density data support the conclusion that through time, households became increasingly dependent on specialists for their pottery.

Changes in the proportions of forms within the handmade category were examined to determine which forms may have been replaced by wheel-thrown ceramics. The analysis suggested that handmade open vessels, possibly used for serving food, declined steadily in proportion to the number of handmade closed vessels probably used for food preparation (from 19% to 5%; see Table 8). For the earliest village phases, cooking pots made up 74% of

Table 6
Ceramic Densities

Area	Locus description	Subperiod IV.2		
		m^3	Handmade	Wheel-made
G64: 006	suprafloor,[a] floor	0.2	5	18
G64: 030	suprafloor, floor	2.9	75	89
G64: 034	suprafloor, floor	0.6	103	118
G65: 007	suprafloor, floor	0.1	44	102
G65: 009	exterior surface	0.3	76	113
A04: 052	floor, bench	0.1	6	1
A04: 053, 055–56	suprafloor	1.1	61	63
		Subperiod IV.1		
Area	Locus description	m^3	Handmade	Wheel-made
A07: 022	suprafloor, floor	1.8	139	419
A02: 032–033, 035	suprafloor, floor	1.1	16	54
A07: 023	pit	1.6	102	150
B02: 018	fill on street	0.3	25	84
B03: 018	fill on street	0.6	24	34
B81: 004	suprafloor, floor	0.7	16	38
B81: 005	suprafloor, floor	0.1	8	20

[a] *Suprafloor* refers to fill just above the floor.

Table 7
Sherd Density

	Subperiod IV.2	Subperiod IV.1
Total number of		
handmade sherds	369	330
wheel-made sherds	504	799
Total volume of deposits that yielded data on sherd densities	5.3 m^3	6.2 m^3
Number of		
handmade sherds/m^3	70	53
wheel-made sherds/m^3	95	129

Note: X^2 for handmade and wheel-made sherds/m^3 in each subperiod = 6.69, $p < .010$.

Table 8

Percentages of Open and Closed Handmade Vessels

	Open		Closed	
Subperiod	No.	%	No.	%
IV.4	8	19	35	81
IV.3	8	9	85	91
IV.2	47	7	652	93
IV.1	12	5	244	95

the handmade assemblage. In the final phases, cooking pots contributed 93% of the diagnostic handmade sherds that could be assigned a function (e.g., casserole, bowl, lid, pot).

Overall, the ceramic data suggest that households became increasingly reliant on ceramics produced by specialists, probably in nucleated workshops. In the earliest phases, a substantial proportion of the pots consumed were made either by the households that used them or by small-scale specialists who served only a small number of households. By the final phase of this period, the majority of pots used by households were manufactured in relatively centralized workshops that produced large quantities of pots. The only exceptions to this were cooking pots and the occasional bowl or storage jar.

Although I have suggested that the handmade pottery was produced by households, it is also possible that it was manufactured by small-scale informally organized specialists. Unfortunately, it is difficult to differentiate between household production and small-scale production systems such as "household industries" on the basis of the end products. However, even if the handmade pots were produced by informal specialists, the lack of uniformity indicates that they were made by a larger number of specialists organized more informally than were the wheel-thrown pots. The trend toward increased reliance on wheel-made pottery signifies an increased centralization (in terms of workshop locations and number of workers relative to producers) of the ceramic production process, and increased standardization (although not necessarily decreased diversity) of ceramic types consumed by households.

There is little evidence for loci of ceramic production at Kurban Höyük itself. Household production and casual "household industries" leave few archaeological traces (Rice 1987, 186–7), and no manufacturing locations of handmade pots were recognized at Kurban Höyük. It is also not clear how many households, if any, were involved in ceramic production for exchange. As mentioned earlier, no workshops were found at Kurban Höyük, but the distribution of ceramic slag suggests that workshops for wheel-made pottery were concentrated in the saddle and the center of the small mound. From the deep soundings, a total of 14 samples of vitrified kiln material were found in Areas F and C01. Although the total volume excavated from Area A was more than twice that of C01 and F combined, only one vitrified kiln sample was recovered from Area A, and that sample came from an unreliable collapse layer. From the horizontal exposures, a total of 18 samples were scattered throughout the two building phases from approximately 450 m^2 of Area C (Subperiod IV.2) on the summit of the small mound. This contrasts with Area G (Subperiod IV.2) on the edge of the small mound and Area B (Subperiod IV.1) on the large mound. Combining Areas B and G, two building phases from roughly 350 m^2 were cleared, but not a single sample of vitrified kiln material was found in either sector.

The density of Period IV vitrified material on the small mound at Kurban Höyük is much lighter than we would expect from an actual pottery production area, but the spatial distribution of kiln wasters suggests proximity of Areas C and F to a ceramic workshop. It is also possible that the vitrified clay came from smelting furnaces (furnaces may be dug into the ground so dirt lining can be vitrified, or a furnace may be built of clay); a crucible found in the plow zone of Area C, just above the Period IV occupational layer (Yener 1990), indicates that metal working did occur in this part of the site. Given current evidence, little can be said conclusively about ceramic production at Kurban Höyük. However, available data do suggest that although all households at the settlement used some wheel-made pottery, only one part of the community may have been involved in the production process. It appears that the residents of the excavated areas on the large mound and east side of the small mound were consumers, but not producers, of pottery manufactured by specialists.

STONE TOOL PRODUCTION

Chipped stone provides the second data source on craft production. Although this period is referred to as the Early Bronze Age, chipped stone was second only to pottery in its abundance in Period IV levels at Kurban Höyük; more than 177 kg of chipped stone was recovered from 330 m^2 in Area C alone (MacDonald 1986, 61). The chipped stone assemblage was studied to determine whether stone tools may also have been manufactured by specialists. Most of the data comes from Areas G and B.[6] Preliminary results of an independent study of a large sample (ca. 5,000 pieces) of the Area C assemblage, and a smaller sample from Area A, have already been published (MacDonald 1986). The preliminary findings from these areas will be compared with those from Areas G and B. Although only Areas G and B are discussed in detail, available findings from all areas suggest spatial and chronological uniformity in the chipped stone assemblage, indicating that assemblages from Areas G and B are probably broadly representative of the entire Period IV settlement. Both areas are non-elite residential sectors toward the edge of the settlement. In this respect the results complement the study of chipped stone from Area C, located in what appears to have been a higher status part of the settlement on the summit of the small mound. Because Area G predates Area B, it is also possible to examine evidence for change through time.

To assess the patterns of stone tool production and distribution, two lines of evidence were used. First, the locations of manufacturing debris and finished products were examined to determine if households were manufacturing their own tools and if they produced a surplus for export. The presence of cores, waste flakes, and unretouched flakes or blades in houses, combined with the recovery of retouched pieces, would indicate household manufacturing and consumption. High concentrations of cores, waste flakes, and unretouched pieces would suggest surplus production for exchange. Finally, high densities of specific tool types might indicate other kinds of craft work (e.g., drills in bead manufacturing areas).

The spatial distributions of both debitage and finished products of different raw materials provided an additional source of information on the organization of stone tool production. The presence of finished tools and the absence of related debitage of the same raw material might indicate that the tools had been manufactured elsewhere and imported.

A total of 964 pieces of chipped stone were recorded: 527 from Area B and 437 from Area G. The majority of floor deposits from both areas were analyzed. Assemblages from the two areas were very similar, and both, together with the chipped stone from Area C (MacDonald 1986), can be characterized as an informal ad hoc or expedient flake industry, which could not be subdivided into formal tool types. Tools probably used for similar purposes (e.g., scrapers) varied in blank forms (including flakes, chunks, and blades), location of working edge, and direction of retouch (ibid., 62). The

Table 9
Raw Material Categories for Chipped Stone (from Stein 1986)

Area	Unknown	Nodular	Tabular	Cobble	Scavenged Paleolithic	Total
B	287	39	55	88	7	476
G	195	22	14	55	1	287

informal nature of the assemblage suggests an expedient, unspecialized production system.

The chipped stone assemblage was made entirely from flint, with the exception of two obsidian bladelets. A subsample of the chipped stone from Areas B and G was studied to determine the raw material sources (Table 9; Stein 1986). Most of the flint could have been collected from the immediate vicinity of the site. Of the 281 chipped stone pieces whose source could be identified, 51% were from river/wadi cobbles, which could be collected from the nearby Euphrates River. Of the remainder, 25% were of low-quality, locally available tabular chert, and 22% were of high-quality nodular flint, available in the limestone hills less than 2 km from the site. Colors included red-brown, brown, grey, purple, and pink. Areas G and B were similar in terms of material sources.

Flakes were much more prevalent than blades, making up 46% of the debitage category and 60% of the tool component of the assemblage from Areas B and G. In contrast, blades contributed only 3% of debitage and 9% to the tools. The Kurban Period IV assemblage is similar to that from the nearby and partially contemporaneous village site of Gritille Hoyuk in being a predominantly flake industry (Kurtz 1985).

The densities of chipped stone artifacts in a sample of deposits from Areas G and B did not indicate a major change in the importance of chipped stone through time (Tables 10 and 11). Although Area B had a higher density of chipped stone when raw counts were considered, the total weight of chipped stone per cubic meter was greater for Area G. To eliminate possible differences resulting from different types of deposits, I compared density ratios for interior floor deposits of the two areas. Area G had a higher density ratio when weights were used, but the two areas were identical when densities were calculated on the basis of counts. There is no strong evidence for a change through time in the importance of chipped stone.

Areas B and G are similar in the relative proportions of tool and debitage

Table 10
Density Data for Chipped Stone[a]

Area	Locus Description	Volume (m^3)	Weight[a] (total grams)	Count
G54: 004	pit	2.2	1,033	75
G55: 003	fill	0.25	—	18
G64: 002	suprafloor/floor	0.3	199	3
G64: 006	suprafloor/floor	0.1	—	2
G64: 011	suprafloor	1.32	—	22
G64: 012	suprafloor/floor	0.93	1,053	46
G64: 030	suprafloor/floor	2.9	248	28
G64: 034	suprafloor/floor (possible exterior)	0.6	167	16
G65: 007	suprafloor/floor	0.57	—	18
G65:009	exterior surface	0.3	1,570	36
Total for all deposits		7.24; 9.38[b]	4,270	204; 264
Total for interior contexts only		4.13; 6.12	1,500	77; 119
Density ratio for counts		$28/m^3$; $28/m^3$		
Density ratio for weights		587 g/m^3		
Density ratio for counts, interior contexts only		$19/m^3$		
Density ratio for weights, interior contexts only		363 g/m^3		

Continued on next page

categories, perhaps indicating that a similar range of activities was carried out in households from both parts of the site (Table 12). The areas are almost identical in the ratios of retouched (28% for Area B and 29% for Area G) to debitage pieces. One difference is the higher percentage of core fragments (21%) in Area B than in Area G (13%). Some of the core fragments from Area B were recovered from the street surface, where they may have been reused as paving. The presence of large cores in some Area A Period IV walls (M. MacDonald, 1990, personal communication), combined with an overall low concentration of cores in other Period IV deposits (MacDonald 1986, 64), suggests that larger cores may have been reused as construction material. Therefore, differences between Areas B and G in percentages of cores may reflect the types of deposits sampled (e.g., street versus courtyard) rather than differences between the two areas in stone tool production.

Whereas Area B has a higher percentage of cores, Area G has a higher

Table 10 *(continued)*

Area	Locus Description	Volume (m^3)	Weight[a] (total grams)	Count
B01: 032	suprafloor/floor	0.05	87	4
B01: 033	floor	0.27	165	23
B01: 036	suprafloor/floor	0.6	65	13
B02: 018	street	2.4	2,476	194
B02: 037	suprafloor	0.52	31	10
B02: 038	floor/suprafloor	0.5	46	8
B02: 041	doorway/street fill	0.03	18	2
B81: 013	floor/suprafloor	1.5	148	7
Total for all deposits		5.87	3,036	261
Total for interior contexts only		3.47	542	65
Density ratio for counts		$44/m^3$		
Density ratio for weights		$517\ g/m^3$		
Density ratio for counts, interior contexts only		$19/m^3$		
Density ratio for weights, interior contexts only		$156\ g/m^3$		

[a]Because weights were only recorded for a sample of the chipped stone analyzed, total weights are not known for chipped stone samples from several loci.

[b]The first number excludes loci for which total weights were not known and the second number includes all loci.

[c]Volumes given for certain loci may vary between Tables 6 and 10. In the field, volumes were calculated on a daily basis, as portions of each locus were excavated. For larger loci, it was sometimes necessary to limit analysis to only a sample of the artifacts. In these cases, only the volume for that part of the locus yielding material that was completely analyzed was considered in calculating densities. In some cases the proportions of the locus completely analyzed differed for ceramics and chipped stone. Therefore, the densities of the utilized portion of the locus also differed.

proportion of sickle blades and similar blades with trapezoidal cross-sections but without the characteristic sickle sheen that results when the blade comes in contact with plants and particles of silica adhere to it (see Table 12). This difference will be discussed in Chapter 6, when I consider evidence for agricultural production.

The spatial distribution of debitage and retouched pieces suggests that tools were produced on a household basis in both Areas G and B. Roughly 70% of all chipped stone in both areas represent manufacturing debris (see Table 12). For both areas, debitage was present in every room as well as in

Table 11
Chipped Stone Densities

Area	Count (No./m^3)	Weight (grams^3)
G	28	587
B	44	517

exterior deposits (Tables 13 and 14). This ubiquitous distribution of debris, combined with the informal nature of the industry, suggests that production occurred throughout the residential areas.

Although every household seems to have engaged in stone tool manufacture, it is possible that a few tool types may have been made by specialists. In particular, larger blades and sickle blades may have been an exception to this pattern of household production. No larger blade cores were found in Areas B or G. An absence of larger blade cores was also reported for Area C, where it was interpreted as evidence that blades were imported to the area (MacDonald 1986, 64). As mentioned previously, the absence of large blade cores may also have resulted from their reuse in construction. However, a heavy concentration of large blade cores was observed on the outskirts of Titris Höyük, providing compelling evidence for specialized production of flint blades (Algaze et al. 1995, 26).

Available data indicate that, in general, the organization of stone tool production did not vary spatially or chronologically. The results from Area G are consistent with those from the contemporaneous but possibly higher status sector of the site, Area C. In the latter area, 87% of the 5,000 analyzed pieces were not retouched (MacDonald 1986, 62–4), indicating that tools were produced there (ibid., 64), as well as in Area G. Results from Area B indicate that the pattern of household production of stone tools continued through the final subperiod (IV.1). The trend toward increased dependence by households on specialist-produced ceramics does not seem to have been paralleled in the patterns of stone tool production.

TEXTILE AND GARMENT PRODUCTION

In contrast to pots and stone tools, which were ubiquitous at Kurban Höyük but absent from third millennium B.C. economic records, textiles were archaeologically invisible, but written records attest to their economic im-

Table 12

Chipped Stone from Areas B and G

Category	Production Stage	Area B		Area G	
		No.	%	No.	%
Debitage	Waste	94	17.8	85	19.4
	Nodule with removals	2	.4	1	.2
	Flake core	48	9.1	16	3.6
	Blade core	5	.9	1	.2
	Core/core fragment	59	11.2	41	9.4
	Flake	158	30.0	162	37.0
	Blade	13	2.5	4	.9
	Crested blade	1	.2	0	0.0
	TOTAL	380	72.1	310	70.8
Retouched					
	Rejuvination flake	8	1.5	4	0.9
	Scraper	13	2.5	9	2.0
	Burin	2	0.4	2	0.5
	Piercer	6	1.1	6	1.4
	Notch	5	.9	3	0.7
	Pick	0	0.0	1	0.2
	Denticulate	2	0.4	2	0.5
	Flake, heavy retouch	0	0.0	13	3.0
	Truncated blade	1	0.2	0	0.0
	Sickle form blade (no sheen)	2	0.4	4	0.9
	Utilized flake	79	15.0	59	13.5
	Utilized blade	4	0.8	2	0.5
	Retouched blade	1	0.2	0	0.0
	Backed blade	2	0.4	0	0.0
	Multiple tool	7	1.3	2	0.5
	Handaxe	2	0.4	0	0.0
	Other	13	2.4	13	3.0
	TOTAL RETOUCH	147	27.9	128	29.2
	TOTALS	527	100.0	438	100.0

Table 13
Area G Chipped Stone Types and Spatial Distributions

	RM 1	RM 2	Exterior Trash	Exterior Surface Unit 4	Suprafloor
			Debitage/unretouched		
Waste	28	11	16	18	8
Nodule with removals	1	1	—	—	—
Flake core	2	1	4	5	1
Blade core	—	—	—	—	—
Core fragment	22	2	5	9	5
Flake	57	5	28	56	22
Blade	2	—	1	—	—
Micro blade	—	—	—	—	—
Crested blade	—	—	—	—	—
			Retouched		
Rejuvenation flake	1	—	—	—	2
Side scraper	—	—	3	—	1
Scraper	2	1	—	1	—
End scraper	—	—	1	1	—
Burin	—	—	—	1	1
Piercer	—	—	2	—	3
Notch	1	—	1	1	—
Pick	—	—	—	1	—
Denticulate	—	—	1	2	—
Flake (heavy retouch)	3	—	5	3	2
Sickle form blade (no sheen)	4	—	—	1	—
Sickle blade	5	3	—	1	—
Utilized flake	15	1	16	17	6
Utilized blade	—	—	1	—	—
Retouched blade	—	—	—	—	—
Backed blade	—	—	—	—	—
Multiple tool	—	—	—	—	—
Handaxe	—	—	—	—	—
Other	4	—	1	3	2

Table 14

Area B Chipped Stone Types and Spatial Distribution

	Street	RM 3	RM 4	RM 10	RM 11	RM 12
			Debitage/unretouched			
Waste	62	7	9	7	2	—
Nodule with removals	—	—	—	—	—	—
Flake core	39	4	2	1	—	1
Blade core	2	—	—	—	—	—
Core fragment	46	5	4	1	1	—
Flake	100	25	9	6	6	1
Blade	8	3	—	—	—	—
Micro blade	1	—	—	—	—	—
Crested blade						
			Retouched			
Rejuvenation flake	3	1	—	—	—	—
Side scraper	4	—	—	—	1	—
Scraper	5	2	—	—	—	—
End scraper	1	—	—	—	—	—
Burin	1	—	1	—	—	—
Piercer	5	1	—	—	—	—
Notch	4	—	1	—	—	—
Pick	—	—	—	—	—	—
Denticulate	—	1	—	—	—	—
Flake (heavy retouch)	1	—	—	—	—	—
Truncated blade	1	—	—	—	—	—
Sickle form blade (no sheen)	—	—	—	—	—	—
Sickle blade	1	—	—	—	—	1
Utilized flake	55	10	4	2	1	1
Utilized blade	3	—	—	1	—	—
Retouched blade	1	—	—	—	—	—
Backed blade	2	—	—	—	—	—
Multiple tool	6	—	1	—	—	—
Handaxe	2	—	—	—	—	—
Other	9	1	2	—	—	—

portance during this time. For this reason the organization of textile production is briefly considered here, in spite of the limited archaeological evidence at Kurban Höyük.

The recovered and published tablets from Ebla may represent only one subset of a broader range of economic transactions recorded by scribes (see Michalowski 1992, 243). If so, the apparent importance of those aspects of the economy recorded in the tablets, such as textile production and exchange, may be exaggerated. Moreover, it is likely that some kinds of economic activities or transactions involving specific types of materials may not have been recorded. For example, excavators found a large quantity of imported semiprecious stones in the Ebla palace, particularly lapis lazuli, but the analyzed texts found in the palace do not reveal that semiprecious stones played much of a role in the Ebla economy (Pinnock 1984, 20, 25). Despite these caveats, available data indicate that garments and textiles were perhaps the most frequently listed items in economic texts from the Ebla Palace (Gelb 1989, 158; Pinnock 1984, 22; see also, for example, Archi 1982, 211; 1987, 125). Weaving appears to have been among the most important manufacturing activities at the center. There are records of woven goods being delivered to the palace, as well as of exports to individuals. Detailed categories, which included both the type of clothing, type and quality of material, design (number of bands), and color, served to describe the garments. For example, one text listing goods received by the palace has been translated as follows:

> 6 E.-fabrics with two (woof) threads, 22 Gs.-fabrics, 4 best quality A.-fabrics; 428 A-fabrics, 130 Gs.-fabrics, 700 A.-fabrics, 100 fabrics of ordinary linens, 1410 top-quality fabrics, 3 turbans, 4 colored veils, 6 white turbans, 10 white veils, 7 veils in various colors, 2 multicolored dresses, 350 best-quality multicolored dresses, 10 sashes and tassels, 1 variegated braid for the head, 136 coarse braids, 8 hosiery, 2030 multicolored dresses; total 2800 items. (Pettinato 1991, 247)

Gold or silver swords or daggers, when listed in texts, were frequently mentioned in connection with garments (Pinnock 1984, 20–7).

In the archaeological record, spindle whorls, used to spin fibers into yarn, provide one indicator of textile production. Spindle whorls recovered from sites in the Near East have been fairly uniform in shape and made of ground stone or clay, although they are made of wood in the Near East today (Watson 1979, 179). The presence of stone spindle whorls in Area B, which dates to the final subperiod, suggests that at least some stone spindle whorls were still in use during the mid-late third millennium B.C. (see Table 15).

Table 15
Spindle Whorls and Related Artifacts

Subperiod	Type	Location	No.
IV.4/3	"Chariot wheel"	A	2
IV.3	"Chariot wheel"	C01 (Phase 12)	1
IV.2	"Chariot wheel"	F (Phase 12)	1
IV.2	"Chariot wheel"	C, Unit 13	1
IV.1	"Chariot wheel"	B, Unit 3	1
IV.1	Baked clay spool	B, Unit 3	1
IV.1	"Chariot wheel"	B, Unit 11	2
IV.1	Sandstone spindle whorl	B, Unit 11/13	1
IV.1	Limestone spindle whorl	B, Unit 11	1

Note: Following Hole et al. (1969) and Yener (1990), I suggest that these could instead be loom weights.

If households manufactured at least some of their own textiles, it is reasonable to expect that spindle whorls would be recovered from domestic contexts. For example, at the Neolithic site of Hajji Firuz in Iran spindle whorls were the most common find (Voigt 1983, 257). Spindle whorls might also be found in association with loom weights in workshops (cf. De Vries 1980, 39; Rothman 1988, 21). Concentrations of loom weights would suggest more intensive weaving by specialists.

The number of spindle whorls in Kurban Period IV levels is surprisingly low; only two could be definitively identified. It is possible that other pierced artifacts not immediately recognizable as spindle whorls were used to spin fibers. As long as the hole for the spindle is placed in the center of the spindle whorl, the latter need not be perfectly round; even an apple will suffice (Barber 1994, 37–8). Eight artifacts identified as clay "chariot wheels" might actually have been used as spindle whorls (Plate 19; cf. Hole, Flannery, and Neely 1969, 206; Yener 1990, 402). No models (chariots, figurines, etc.) with holes for wheel axles were found at the site. Moreover, "chariot wheels" were found in association with spindle whorls and a spool in Area B (see Table 15). Therefore, in the following analysis I maintain that the model wheels were actually used as spindle whorls.

The significance of the low number of spindle whorls from Subperiods IV.4 and IV.3 is not clear, given the relatively small clearances from these phases. Their absence from the more extensively sampled Subperiod IV.3 buildings might indicate that relatively high-status households did not spin their own thread and perhaps obtained textiles from specialized weavers. The recovery of only one spindle whorl from secure Subperiod IV.2 contexts is surprising given the broad clearances in Areas C and G of both elite and non-elite areas. It suggests that either yarn or textiles were imported to these areas.

In Subperiod IV.1, the concentration of spindle whorls in Area B signifies thread production for household use, and perhaps for exchange as well. Four perforated stones from this area may have served as loom weights (see Wright 1981, 148–9), but such stones were found elsewhere in the settlement as well as during all subphases. In the absence of information on wear marks indicating the function of these artifacts, it is not possible to determine which, if any, of these might have served as loom weights. It is also possible that horizontal ground looms, rather than warp-weighted looms, were used; the former do not generally leave archaeological traces (Barber 1994, 80–81). However, the exclusive presence of spindle whorls in one of the four exposures from Subperiod IV.1 suggests that textile production continued to be a specialized activity during this time. Because of the low density of spindle whorls in general, it is not possible to determine if households became increasingly reliant on textiles produced by specialists during this period. It is possible that a shift away from household production had occurred by Subperiod IV.3, or even earlier.

According to the Ebla texts, materials used for textiles included flax, felt, material with gold thread (ibid., 22), and wool (see Archi, 1980, 4). Flax *(linum)* seeds were found in Halaf and Chalcolithic levels at Kurban Höyük, but were absent from the Period IV deposits examined (Miller 1986, 120). Animal fibers would probably have been readily available from family herds during the first three subperiods (IV.4–IV.2; see Chapter 6), unless tribute payments included large amounts of wool or goat hair. However, during Period IV.1, when animal production may have become specialized (see Chapter 6), it may have been necessary for families to obtain animal fibers through exchange. If flax was grown by residents during this period, the plant remains may have been discarded in or near areas where the plant was processed into fibers. The absence of linseed at Kurban Höyük during Period IV supports inferences based on the scarcity of spindle whorls that textile production was not a major activity in the excavated areas at Kurban Höyük, although the ethnobotanical findings could only be a result of chance or lack of preservation (Miller 1986, 88).

The Ebla archives reveal aspects of the elite economy, and are not directly relevant to an understanding of non-elite households. Nor can it be assumed that economic organization in the regions of Ebla and Kurban Höyük were similar. However, the texts do highlight the value of textiles in ancient Near Eastern economic systems; although textile production in the non-elite sector may have been organized very differently, textiles were probably highly valued. The low density of spindle whorls at Kurban Höyük suggests that even non-elite households may have relied on specialized weavers throughout most of this period. Given the evidence cited previously for textile production at Ebla, and the curious near absence of evidence for thread production at Kurban Höyük, it is possible that most weaving activities were focused at local or regional centers, or perhaps in herding communities. Alternatively, the workshops of weavers may have been located closer to the center of the large mound at Kurban Höyük, an area that was not sampled. Results from the ancient city at Kazane do provide some support for the hypothesis that weaving was a specialized urban craft in southeast Anatolia. Excavation of 100 m^2 of an exterior workshop area yielded several large model chariot wheels and copper alloy needles. The workshop was located outside of a massive building, and numerous samples of sealing clay were collected from the workshop area, leaving open the possibility that the workshop was used by attached specialists (see Brumfiel and Earle 1987). Ongoing excavations at the regional centers of Titriş Höyük (Algaze et al. 1992) and Kazane (Wattenmaker and Mısır 1994) should provide additional information on the social contexts of weaving in this region during the third millennium.

We have thus far considered production organization for three crafts: ceramics, stone tools, and woven goods. Households relied on specialists for some types of pottery, and probably textiles as well, during Period IV. It is not possible to determine if the increased reliance through time in specialist-produced ceramics was paralleled by an increased reliance on textiles obtained through exchange. However, by Subperiod IV.2, if not before, some households may have abandoned spinning altogether. Textiles and ceramics contrast with chipped stone, which was clearly produced in each of the three areas studied, probably on a household basis. Together, these three sources of information on craft production suggest that some, but not all, aspects of the economy were reorganized as the society increased in complexity. I now turn to evidence for the organization of food production, to determine whether that aspect of the economy became increasingly specialized through time.

SHIFTING PATTERNS OF FOOD PRODUCTION AT KURBAN HÖYÜK 6

Archaeologists have assumed that although the political elites of early state societies may have received food as tribute, most households in the countryside produced their own food. This assumption of a stable, uniform food production strategy among non-elite households has not been systematically investigated in the Near East. In this chapter, I examine evidence for the organization of food production in each of the mid-late third millennium B.C. subperiods.

The predominant artifacts providing data on food production include flint sickle blades and animal bones. Flint sickle blades informed about agricultural production. Animal bones were used to study the organization of meat production as well as patterns of meat consumption.

AGRICULTURAL PRODUCTION

Evidence for involvement by households in agricultural production came from the distribution of sickle blades, believed to have been used in harvesting wheat and barley. These are prismatic blades with silica gloss on at least one edge. Because agricultural tools would not be used in domestic areas, and might only be brought to houses for repair and storage, the absence of such tools in a specific domestic structure would not indicate that the residents were *not* involved in agriculture. This is particularly true for Areas A and C, because not all chipped stone samples from secure contexts (e.g., floors) were analyzed. However, I expected that where large exposures were made, the degree to which inhabitants of the area were involved in agriculture would be clear. The distribution of sickle blades indicates that this was in fact the case. In areas where sickle blades were present, they were generally found in most structures for which reasonable exposures were obtained. The numerous blades recovered from streets may have been discarded as trash.

As with the other chipped-stone artifacts, the sickle blade spatial distributions are only available for some subperiods and areas. For the earlier periods, a sample of Area A chipped stone from Subperiod IV.3 was examined. Areas C and G provide data on Subperiod IV.2, and Area B provides the best documentation for Subperiod IV.1.

Conclusions are based only on the distribution of blades with clearly visible sickle sheen. However, Tables 16 and 17 include blades that did not exhibit sheen but that were of the same form as those with gloss. Although it is not possible to demonstrate that the latter category were in fact agricultural tools, their association with the sickle blades was statistically significant (see Table 17). They may, at least in some cases, represent agricultural tools that were not used enough to create a glossy silica coating.

The distribution of sickle blades in each subperiod suggests that in Subperiods IV.3 and IV.2 most, if not all, households included farmers, but that by Subperiod IV.1 some non-elite households had become divorced from agricultural production (see Table 16). Although the counts and percentages support this suggested trend, it is the spatial distribution of sickle blades, rather than their numbers, that provide the strongest evidence for a reorganization of agricultural production.

For Period IV.2, only a sample of the Area A Phase 13 chipped stone was analyzed. However, even with the small number of analyzed artifacts, the importance of farming is clear. As discussed in Chapter 4, Area A during Phase 13 may be interpreted either as a large elite residence or as three separate domestic units, at least one of which appears to have been elite (Structure 1). If the first interpretation is correct, then the presence of sickle blades in Unit 2 suggests that residents of this fairly elaborate structure were involved in agricultural activities.

If the alternative view is correct, then we can conclude only that the inhabitants of Structure 2 were farmers. Units 13.5 and 13.2 yielded a

Table 16
Sickle Blade Distributions

Period/Area	Sample	Sickle Blades	Prismatic Blades	% Sickle Blades	Total Blades
IV.3/A	182	3	7	1.6	5.5
IV.2/C	4,933	29	11	0.6	0.8
IV.2/G	437	9	4	2.1	3.0
IV.1/B	527	—	2	0.0	0.4

Note: Fisher Exact = 0.00085, $p < .001$ (excluding prismatic blades). Sample size represents total chipped stone sample.

concentration of sickle and prismatic blades. The relatively high proportion of the blades cannot be attributed to a chance find, because they were scattered throughout three loci (two floor levels) of Unit 13.2 and two loci of Unit 13.5. Rather, the high proportion probably reflects the fact that Units 13.2 and 13.5 were the most extensively excavated rooms of Phase 13.

Because no sickle blades were recovered from Structure 1, it is not clear that the residents were farmers, although the presence of prismatic blades without sheen suggests that they were. As discussed in Chapter 4, Structure 1 appears to have been an elite residence. Therefore, the presence of agricultural tools in this building would suggest the involvement of elite households in food production during this period. The significance of the lack of blades in Structure 3 is not clear; because of the limited excavation of that structure, combined with the generally low density of blades, it is probable that harvesting tools would not have been recovered even if the residents had been farmers.

Evaluating the significance of the results from Subperiod IV.3 is hampered by difficulties in interpreting architectural remains and by the limited exposure of individual rooms. However, they clearly show that at least one, and probably two, households were engaged in harvesting activities. Regardless of whether the remains represent one or three separate structures, the findings suggest that elite households, as well as lower status households, may have been involved in agriculture during this period.

Agricultural production continued to be an important household economic activity in Subperiod IV.2. For this subperiod, Area G provides data from a low-ranking residential sector, and Area C represents a higher ranking part of the settlement.

Table 17
Spatial Distributions of Sickle and Prismatic Blades

Period/Area	Context	Unit Number	Blades Recovered
IV.3 Area A	Structure 1	13.1	1P[a]
	Structure 1	13.4	1P
	Structure 2	13.5	4P, 1S
	Structure 2	13.2	2P, 1S
IV.2 Area C[b]	Structure 1	6	3S
	Structure 2	14	1S
	Structure 2	15	1S
	Structure 3	13	1S
	Structure 4	7	2S
	Structure 4	9	2S
	Structure 4	10	5S
	Street	1	3S
	Street	1 or 2	11S
IV.2 Area G	Structure 1	1	4P, 5S
	Structure 2	4	1S
	Structure 1 or 2	2	3S
IV.1 Area B	Structure 1a, 1b	9	1P
	Structure 2	12	1P
	Street	2	2P

[a]S = sickle blade; P = prismatic blade without visible sickle sheen; R = .69, using structures (rather than units) as the unit of analysis. Degrees of freedom = 7, $.02 < p < .05$.

[b]Proveniences for prismatic blades were not available for Area C. Area C distributions are based on project drawing records and personal communications from Mary MacDonald (1990).

In Area C, sickle blades were scattered throughout the excavated area, although the overall density was low. Agricultural tools were found in association with at least three of the four excavated structures. Structure 3 was the only exception; a blade was recovered from the pebble surface (Unit 11) directly adjacent to the structure, but it is not clear that this surface is associated with Structure 3. Given the limited excavation of this structure, the absence of sickle blades is not surprising.

The presence of sickle blades in Area C is significant. The ceramic slag and crucible from this area suggest that at least some residents may have been involved in craft production. Structure 1 was relatively substantial and was associated with some of the few metal objects found at the site. It was suggested in Chapter 4 that the building may have been occupied by a high-ranking family involved in, or even controlling, craft production. However, the occupants of this structure were also involved in agriculture. Overall, the results from Area C suggest that most households, including higher ranking ones, participated in farming activities, at least to a limited extent.

Results from Area G paralleled those from Area C. For Structure 1, sickle blades came from four different loci representing two floor levels. This widespread distribution demonstrates that the relatively high occurrence of sickle blades is not a result of chance discovery. Sickle blades were also found in a second room, which may have represented a second structure. Whether we interpret the architecture from Area G as representing one or two structures, it is clear that the relatively low-status occupants of this area participated in harvest activities.

The final subperiod, that of site nucleation (Subperiod IV.1), represented by Area B, contrasts sharply with that of the earlier subperiods. Although the 1984 exposures of Period IV material were roughly similar for Areas B and G, and the sample size for analyzed chipped stone was greater for Area B, no sickle blades were recovered from Area B, whereas nine were recorded from Area G. Although these differences are statistically significant, the actual number of blades is less important than the spatial distributions; sickle blades were found on three of four excavated floors in Area G (two floor levels of Unit 1 and one level of Unit 2); none of the five floors (three of which had two floor levels) in Area B yielded sickle blades. Of the three prismatic blades without sickle sheen from Area B, two came from the street and a third was retrieved from one of the earliest structures in this part of the site. The occurrence of the prismatic blade in an early floor level, combined with the recovery of a sickle blade in an Area B sounding beneath a Subperiod IV.1 floor, suggests that Area B had at one time been occupied by farmers. However, the absence of sickle blades and low occurrence of prismatic blades from the subperiod of increased nucleation (Subperiod IV.1) suggests that through time at least some of the inhabitants of this area became divorced from agricultural activities. It is perhaps relevant that Area B had a relatively high proportion of storage vessels, possibly used to store grains imported to the area. If households were involved in agriculture, we might expect exterior work spaces for processing grains. The lack of exterior work areas in Area B is also consistent with the absence of sickle blades.

These results are particularly significant because Area B was almost certainly occupied by low-ranking members of this community. It appears that non-elite households became involved in a specialized subsistence economy during this period.

Although no detailed information is available on the distribution of sickle blades in Subperiod IV.1 deposits in Area A, one sickle blade was associated with Unit 15.1. This suggests that some parts of the community maintained an involvement in farming.

One might suppose that a decreased density of flint sickle blades could indicate their replacement by metal sickles. However, this is unlikely, because flint sickle blades continued to be used at the site in the subsequent Period III (MacDonald 1986, table 1), and at least one example was recovered from a Period III deposit of Area B.

MEAT PRODUCTION

Animal bones were examined to determine whether households raised their own animals or whether meat production was a specialized activity. Although bones were widely distributed at the site, they were not as well represented as ceramics and chipped stone. In general, the density of animal bones was relatively low (in terms of number/m^3). However, zooarchaeological and textual studies concur on the importance of domestic animals in ancient Near Eastern ritual and economic systems.

In this section, I first provide a general discussion of the nature of the Period IV faunal assemblage and consider reasons for the fairly low density of bones. I then examine three main categories of data to determine if meat production was specialized on the household level: (1) the range of species present, (2) the ages of animals represented, and (3) the distribution of skeletal elements.

The relatively modest size of the Period IV faunal sample is partially a result of the exclusion from the analysis of samples from uncertain contexts. Some Period IV loci were excluded from this analysis because they could not be assigned to a subperiod or they came from tertiary fill (e.g., wash layers, subfoundation fill). Many of these contained large amounts of bone, which probably included faunal remains from a number of occupational surfaces that could no longer be differentiated. Although the faunal sample size was relatively small, almost all bones were from four species (*Ovis aries*—sheep, *Capra hircus*—goat, *Bos taurus*—cattle, and *Sus scrofa*—pig; see Tables 18 and 19).

Therefore, a relatively small total sample size was needed for reliable information on species frequencies, kill-off patterns, and body part distributions.

In contrast to objects such as stone tools, which would have been stored in structures, the animal bones represent butchering or meal remains that would not have been intentionally left on house floors. When large numbers of bones are found on house floors, they probably represent trash accumulated after the house was abandoned, either by carnivores or neighbors. Courtyards may be less carefully cleaned than interiors, but it is unlikely that sufficiently large quantities of bone for a complete study of household production would accumulate. The exception to this is when garbage pits in courtyards of, or in proximity to, houses are recovered. At Kurban Höyük, pits were occasionally found adjacent to (or in the courtyards of) houses, but the sample sizes were never large enough for a study of household production and consumption patterns.

Exterior areas, such as middens and streets, often have the highest concentrations of bones. Because these were public areas, it is usually not possible to draw conclusions about individual households using faunal remains from these areas. An exception may be street areas just beyond doorways. However, because bones disposed in streets would be vulnerable to destruction from trampling, or might be removed by carnivores, bone densities in streets would probably be low. Moreover, it would be risky to attribute refuse in a public area to the occupants of specific buildings. For these reasons, I used areas, rather than structures, as the unit of study, and then compared assemblages from different areas. I used the entire assemblage from each area to make inferences about household production, as was done with ceramics.

Several factors contributed to a relatively low density of animal bones at the site. Many of the excavated loci represented room interiors, where bones are less likely to accumulate (see Meadow 1978). The continuous occupation of most of the excavated structures probably afforded little opportunity for bones to accumulate. Dog bones in Period IV levels provide evidence of resident scavengers, and many bones exhibited signs of carnivore gnawing. In some areas, such as Area B, bone preservation appeared to be good, as indicated by the survival of relatively fragile bones such as caprine limb bone epiphyses. However, carnivore gnawing marks on bones were common, suggesting that even where preservation was relatively good, some bones had been destroyed by scavengers. In Areas C and G, proximity to the surface undoubtedly resulted in some bone destruction from plowing and weathering. For the deep soundings, meters of overburden afforded protection for bones in most levels. However, bone densities tended to be low in interior

Table 18

Summary of Identified Bones by Subperiod

		IV.4		IV.3		IV.2		IV.1[a]		IV.1	
Identification	Common name	No.	%	No.	%	No.	%	No.	%	No.	%
Ovis/Capra	Sheep/goat	28	50	140	60.34	294	50.95	145	58.23	915	82.58
Ovis aries	Domestic sheep	4	7.14	20	8.62	32	5.54	12	4.82	30	2.71
Capra hircus hircus	Domestic goat			9	3.9	7	1.21	9	3.61	74	6.68
Gazella sp.	Gazelle			1	0.43						
Bos taurus	Domestic cattle	13	23.21	39	16.81	70	12.13	50	20.08	52	4.69
Cervidae	Deer	3	5.36	11	4.74	17	2.95	1	0.4	1	6.09
Sus scrofa	Domestic pig	3	5.36	2	0.86	141	24.43	16	6.43	17	1.53
Sus scrofa	Wild pig			1	0.43						
Equus spp.	Equid	1	1.79			2	0.36	2	0.8	2	0.18
Carnivore	Carnivore	4	7.14	4	1.72	4	0.69	4	1.61	6	0.54
Felis sp.	Cat			1	0.43						
Canis spp.	Canid					1	0.17	5	2.01	6	0.54
Vulpes sp.	Fox					5	0.87				
Lepus sp.	Hare			4	1.72	2	0.36	2	0.8	2	0.18
Aves	Bird					1	0.17	2	0.8	2	0.18
Osteichthyes	Fish					1	0.17	1	0.4	1	0.09
TOTAL		56		232		577		249		1108	

[a]Numbers in these two columns exclude bones from Locus A08: 050, a well containing numerous bones from the same individuals.

spaces, which were well represented in the soundings. These preservation differences will be considered in the discussion of results. Finally, most of the houses sampled at Kurban Höyük had been occupied by low-ranking families who may have consumed meat infrequently.

SPECIES DIVERSITY AND EVENNESS

The diversity and evenness of the faunal assemblage provides one indicator of household involvement in animal husbandry, hunting, and fishing. In general, the types and range of species can be expected to vary, depending on the organization of production (e.g., see Zeder 1988, 1991), as well as other factors, such as ecological conditions and social context. If households produced their own meat, we would expect a relatively high diversity of species as a result of the need to minimize risk and the differential preferences among households for various kinds of meat. If meat was produced by specialists, we would expect a greater emphasis on animals that could be easily managed in large numbers.

In this examination of species diversity, I consider both species richness (the number of species) and evenness (the relative frequency of different species; Odum 1971, 148–9; see also Grayson 1984, 145 and Cruz-Uribe 1988, 179). Two measures of diversity are used: the Shannon-Wiener Information Function, which considers both the variety and evenness components of diversity, and a richness index, which considers variety alone (see Odum 1971, tabs. 6–1, a and c). If households raised their own animals, a greater variety of meat sources would probably have been exploited. The primary aim of a household raising its own animals would be to ensure a reliable supply of meat, as well as secondary products such as milk, wool or hair, dung (for fuel and fertilizer), and hides. Because species differ in their vulnerability to disease and environmental conditions, a wider range of species would provide greater security.

In particular, pigs are well suited to household production. They breed rapidly, provide a high meat yield, and can either feed on household garbage or forage (e.g., see Cronon 1983; Voigt 1983, 288–9; Zeder 1991, 30–1). Pig raising requires little effort when adequate wild food resources exist, because with minimal human encouragement they will forage on their own and return to their managers periodically (Voigt 1983, 288–9). Because pigs provide only meat and hides, we would expect households also to raise sheep, goat or cattle for milk. Sheep and goat would be exploited for fibers as well.

Table 19

Animal Bones by Subperiod and Area

	IV.4						IV.3								IV.2			
	A 11/12		F 1-7		Total		A 13		A 14		C01 11-14		Total		C/01 15		A 16/17	
Identification	No.	%	No.	%	No.	%	No.	%	No.	%	No.	%	No.	%	No.	%	No.	%
Ovis/Capra (domestic)	25	58.14	3	23.08	28	50.00	60	65.22	37	61.67	43	54.43	140	60.61	169	49.56	25	45.45
Ovis (domestic sheep)	1	2.33	3	23.08	4	7.14	9	9.78	3	5.00	8	10.13	20	8.66	15	4.40	5	9.09
Capra (domestic goat)							3	3.26	4	6.67	2	2.53	9	3.90	3	0.88		
Gazella (gazelle)									1	1.67			1	0.43				
Bos (domestic cattle)	10	23.26	3	23.08	13	23.21	11	11.96	14	23.33	14	17.72	39	16.88	44	12.90	8	14.55
Cervidae (deer)	2	4.65	1	7.69	3	5.36	5	5.43			6	7.59	11	4.76	9	2.64	1	1.82
Sus (domestic pig)	2	4.65	1	7.69	3	5.36					1	1.27	1	0.43	95	27.86	11	20.00
Sus (wild pig)							1	1.09					1	0.43				
Equus (ass/onager)	1	2.33			1	1.79									2	0.59		
Carnivora (carnivore)	2	4.65	2	15.38	4	7.14	1	1.09			3	3.80	4	1.73	3	0.88		
Felis (cat)											1	1.27	1	0.43				
Canis (dog)															1	0.29		
Vulpes (fox)																	5	9.09
Rodentia (rodent)																		
Lepus (hare)							2	2.17	1	1.67	1	1.27	4	1.73				
Aves (bird)																		
Pisces (fish)																		
TOTAL	43		13		56		92		60		79		231		341		55	

Continued on next page

Table 19 *(continued)*

	IV.2 (continued)						IV.1													
	G		F 8-12		Total		A15		A18/20		B		F 13/14		A 15 (L. 050)[a]			Total[b]	
Identification	No.	%	No.	%	No.	%	No.	%	No.	%	No.	%	No.	%	No.	MNI	%	No.	%
Ovis/Capra (domestic)	27	38.03	73	66.97	294	51.04	30	46.88	48	68.57	60	58.82	7	70.00	770	3	89.64	148	56.27
Ovis (domestic sheep)	3	4.23	9	8.26	32	5.56	3	4.69	2	2.86	6	5.88	1	10.00	18	2	2.10	14	5.32
Capra (domestic goat)	2	2.82	2	1.83	7	1.22			4	5.71	5	4.90			65	7	7.57	16	6.08
Gazella (gazelle)																			
Bos (domestic cattle)	13	18.31	5	4.59	70	12.15	15	23.44	9	12.86	23	22.55	2	20.00	2	1	0.23	50	19.01
Cervidae (deer)			7	6.42	17	2.95	1	1.56										1	0.38
Sus (domestic pig)	22	30.99	13	11.93	141	24.48	12	18.75	2	2.86	2	1.96			1	1	0.12	17	6.46
Sus (wild pig)																			
Equus (ass/onager)					2	.35													
Carnivora (carnivore)	1	1.41			4	.69	1	1.56	3	4.29					2	1	0.23	5	1.90
Felis (cat)																		1	0.38
Canis (dog)					1	.17	2	3.13			3	2.94			1	1	0.12	6	2.28
Vulpes (fox)					5	.87													
Rodentia (rodent)																			
Lepus (hare)									2	2.86								2	0.76
Aves (bird)	2	2.82			2	.35					2	1.96						2	0.76
Pisces (fish)	1	1.41			1	.17					1	0.98						1	0.38
TOTAL	71		109		576		64		70		102		10		859	16		263	

[a]This locus (AO8 1.050) represents a well in which bones were exceptionally well preserved., Due to the strong possibility that multiple bones from the same individuals preserved, the minimum number of individuals (MNI), as well as bone counts, are presented.

[b]For Area A, Phase 15, locus A08-050, the minimum number of individuals, rather than bone counts, were used in calculating the totals.

Sheep and goats are usually raised in tandem, although their ratios will vary, depending on factors such as environment and production organization (Redding 1981b). Both species provide milk and meat, as well as fibers used for weaving textiles. Sheep are generally more highly valued than goats in the Near East today, because their meat is considered tastier and because they provide wool. Although sheep require better pasture and more water, both species can be herded together, so that not much additional effort is required to raise both species rather than just one. Moreover, in some cases in which sheep and goat are herded together, the more mobile goats may stimulate sheep to move over greater distances than they would in a flock comprised exclusively of sheep (ibid., 119–21). There are also many advantages to raising both species in terms of herd security and product yields. Sheep are better adapted to cold, but goats are better able to survive high temperatures and drought. Whereas goats have a higher reproductive rate than sheep (ibid., 70), the meat of sheep has a higher caloric and fat content (ibid., table V-10). Sheep milk is superior to goat milk in terms of nutritional content, but goats have a longer lactation period, resulting in overall higher yields (ibid., 110) and availability of milk over a longer span of time. Sheep and goat are susceptible to different diseases, so that if one species in a herd is decimated in an epidemic, it is likely that the other species will survive (ibid., 131–2). Thus, in many ways, sheep and goat are complementary, and it is likely that households would raise both of them.

Cattle provide meat, milk, and hides, and serve as draft animals. Although they have more stringent water and grazing requirements than caprines, they would be raised as a source of labor and because of their exceptionally high meat and milk yields (Flannery 1969, table 3). Raising cattle is more efficient than caprine production in terms of labor input versus product yields (Galvin 1987, 127), although their lower suitability to arid conditions and high feed and water needs might limit their numbers and make them more of a risk than caprines.

Finally, tributary demands might have played a role in production choices. Economic texts document the movement of large numbers of caprines and cattle to the third millennium B.C. center of Ebla. The scale of the deliveries from such a large number of settlements (Pettinato 1981, 162–5, 202) suggests that the animals were sent as tribute payment from surrounding communities.

In summary, households might rely on sheep and cattle for milk, wool, meat, and labor, with pigs and goats maintained to minimize risk. Supplemental hunting might further increase the range of species exploited. Economic circumstances of families, individual preferences for wild resources, and variation in hunting or fishing skill may introduce even more variability into the assemblage. Economic stress might result in exploitation of animals not consumed under better conditions. This flexible strategy of non-elite household production should be manifested in an assemblage characterized by a relatively high degree of evenness (because of heavy reliance on several species of domestic animals), as well as richness (because of exploitation of wild resources along with several species of domestic animals).

Whereas households would employ a strategy of flexibility, efficiency would generally be a major consideration of specialized producers. Producers would be constrained in their choice of animals by the need to produce large surpluses of animals. Domestic animals relatively easy to manage in large numbers would be the likely focus of production. Pigs would not be a good choice, because they are difficult to manage in large numbers. When raised in large numbers, their high feed requirements (e.g., see Rappaport 1968, 59–68) and potential for disturbing cultivated land (Cronon 1983) might necessitate moving them beyond agricultural zones to more distant woodlands. Although they can be moved considerable distances (see Parsons 1962, 218), they are notoriously difficult to manage (Zeuner 1963, 260), and the labor costs of moving them are relatively high. In contrast, caprines and cattle can be herded in large numbers to pasture or water much more easily. Because of their differing water and feed requirements, caprines and pigs would not be herded together (Voigt 1983, 292). In terms of domestic animals, we would expect specialists to focus on the three herd animals: sheep, goats, and cattle. The role of wild resources would probably be minimal, because it would be difficult to procure a surplus of animals, particularly at a time when settlement density was relatively high and presumably the associated cultivated area was extensive (Wilkinson 1986, fig. 7).

Even with household production, elite households might use a more even range of species than non-elite households. The ability to provide animals with good grazing land and to replace lost animals might result in a heavier reliance on the high-risk but high-energy category of sheep and goats. Hunted animals might play an even higher role in the diet of elite households than of non-elite households if access to hunting grounds or hunted animals was restricted, or if animals inhabited areas far from the site. This strategy might result in high variety but overall lower diversity because of a focus on a relatively small number of domestic animals.

With specialized production, we would expect assemblages associated with non-elite residential architecture to be low in richness and high in evenness of species. As discussed previously, we would expect a strong focus on caprines and cattle, with the relative importance of each species depending on the availability of grazing land and demand for wool. Non-elite households may have received the less desirable goats, with most sheep and cattle reserved for the elite. Hunting would probably be of minimal importance, because a surplus of hunted animals would be relatively difficult to procure, and therefore hunted animals procured by specialists would be more costly.

Elite households receiving meat from specialists might have used an even more uniform range of domestic animals, with only sheep and cattle—which provide the highest quality meat—represented. However, the assemblage might be richer than that of non-elite households, if hunted animals with high quality meat, such as gazelle and deer, were either available from specialists or hunted as sport. The assemblages from elite households might not differ (in terms of richness and overall diversity) under conditions of either household or specialized production. However, the age curves of animals should vary depending on the organization of production, as will be discussed later.

These expectations outline differences between household and specialized animal production systems for both non-elite and elite contexts. Zeder (1988, 1991), working primarily with assemblages from public buildings and workshops at the urban site of Malyan in Iran, used the degree of diversity (among other criteria) to distinguish between faunal assemblages resulting from direct (transactions directly between consumer and producers) and indirect distribution systems. In addition to the need for reliance on efficiency with specialized production, indirect distribution systems minimize variability due to individual preferences. Although uniformity should be more pronounced in indirect than direct distribution systems, as Zeder has demonstrated (ibid.), a major split in subsistence strategies should have arisen with a shift from household to specialized production, even when distribution was direct. The reasons for this expectation were presented previously.

Because Subperiod IV.4 (village phases) had fewer than 100 bones, diversity and richness indices were not computed. However, the assemblage does appear to have been diverse, with caprines, cattle, domestic pig, and deer all contributing to diet (Table 18). Subperiod IV.3 (town foundation phases) represents the earliest deposits for which substantial faunal samples exist. At least two assemblages (Area C01 Phases 11–14 and Area A Phase 14), if not all of them, come from areas with relatively massive architecture. The animal bones indicate an emphasis on higher risk herd animals, with lower risk pig being of minimal importance. Game animals were well represented (see Table 18). The species exploited are consistent with expectations for faunal assemblages from elite

Table 20
Species Diversity Indices in the Kurban Faunal Assemblages[a]

Period	General Diversity	Richness
IV.3	0.38	3.80
IV.2	0.44	2.19
IV.1[b]	0.35	3.00
IV.1[c]	0.33	2.54

[a]Statistics used for diversity ($\bar{H}$) and richness (d) are those presented in Odum (1971, tabs. 6-1c, 1 and 3). Carnivores and equids were excluded from calculations, because they may not have been exploited for meat. Rodents were also excluded, because they were probably intrusive.

[b]Bones from Locus A08: 050 are excluded from calculations.

[c]Bones from Locus A08: 50 are included. However, MNIs were used for Locus A08: 050 instead of bone counts.

contexts. The relatively low diversity and high richness compared with that of assemblages from more modest site sectors dating to the following Subperiod IV.2 match expectations for assemblages from elite contexts (Table 20). The somewhat higher diversity and richness indices than those from the final subperiod, when food production appears to have been specialized, may indicate that the occupants of these structures procured their own meat. This possibility will be further examined using age curves in the following section. Alternatively, the high diversity index may result from the greater importance of high-status hunted animals, such as deer, in higher ranking households.

Subperiods IV.2 and IV.1 provided the best faunal data on change through time in meat production, because the broad excavations made it possible to consider socioeconomic and functional context. Overall, the remains from Subperiod IV.2 (town development) indicate a combined reliance on cattle, goat, sheep, and pig. Hunted animals played a minor role. The combined reliance on four species of domestic animals suggests household meat production; in particular, the importance of pig points to nonspecialized production.

Differences between elite and non-elite assemblages of Subperiod IV.2 are evident (Tables 21 and 22). As expected, the assemblages from the elite areas in Subperiod IV.2 (C35, C45, C01, F) have a greater focus on caprines at the expense of pigs. This is reflected is the lower diversity index. The

Table 21
Measurements of Diversity and Richness of Faunal Assemblages from High- and Low-Ranking Contexts from Subperiod IV.2

Area	General Diversity	Richness
Higher Ranking (C35/45, C01, F)	0.35	1.62
Lower Ranking (C55/56/66, G, A16/17)	0.50	2.58

results may indicate that caprines were preferred and that higher ranking households were able to pursue a higher risk strategy of animal husbandry than non-elite households. Alternatively, the focus on herd animals may indicate that higher ranking households did not raise their own animals and obtained meat from specialized herders. These possibilities will be explored further.

Deposits from Subperiod IV.1 (nucleation phases) appear to come from non-elite contexts. Whereas non-elite assemblages in Subperiod IV.2 indicated reliance on a wide range of species, those from Subperiod IV.1 suggested a focus on caprines and cattle, with pig and deer only occasionally exploited (see Tables 19, 22). The proportion of caprine bones increased from 58.5% (43% in non-elite assemblages) in Subperiod IV.2 to 66.6% in Subperiod IV.1, and cattle increased from 12.15% (roughly the same in non-elite contexts) to 20.08%. Pig bones decreased from 24.8% to 7%.[1] They were rare enough in Subperiod IV.1 loci to have been redeposited from earlier and later levels, and tended to occur in the least secure contexts of Subperiod IV.1. Deer also appear to have declined in importance. The more narrow focus on herd animals in this subperiod suggests a shift toward specialized production and exchange on the non-elite household level.

This change is reflected in the diversity indices of the two subperiods (see Table 20). The diversity index for the Subperiod IV.1 assemblage, based on faunal remains retrieved from non-elite contexts, closely approximates that of the elite assemblage from the preceding period (Tables 20 and 21). Large sample sizes tend to decrease the richness index (Grayson 1984, 145) and the lower richness index of Subperiod IV.2 may be related to the larger sample size. The almost exclusive emphasis on herd animals (86.2% of the assemblage) during Subperiod IV.1 suggests a specialized economy. This

Table 22
Subperiod IV.2 Faunal Remains by Context[a]

	Loci Associated with Relatively Elaborate Architecture (A03, C01, C35/45)		Loci Associated with Relatively Modest Architecture (A16/17, C55/56, G)	
Species	No.	%	No.	%
Ovis-Capra	190	64.85	104	39.55
Ovis	21	7.17	11	4.18
Capra	3	1.02	4	1.52
Bos	36	12.29	32	12.17
Cervidae	2	.68	8	3.04
Sus	41	13.99	101	38.40
Equus			2	
Carnivore			1	
Canis			4	
Vulpes			5	
Aves			2	.76
Pisces			1	.38
TOTAL	293		275	

[a]Counts of Carnivore, Canid, and Equus were eliminated when percentages were calculated, because bones from these animals may not represent meal remains.

interpretation will be further evaluated below through an examination of animal kill-off patterns and body part distributions. However, the findings are consistent with those from the study of sickle blade distributions. Together, the two lines of evidence suggest that non-elite households became increasingly dependent on specialists for animals and grain during the final subperiod of town nucleation.

It is possible that the decline in pig use resulted from changing ecological conditions rather than a change in production organization. During this period, population density was higher than in the past, and the amount of cultivated land would have been relatively high. There are some signs that deforestation of the surrounding oak-pistachio woodlands began in this period (Miller 1986, 89). There is also evidence for erosion, which often results from deforestation, by the end of the third millennium B.C. (Wilkinson 1986, 46). The disappearance of the woodlands, an ideal feeding ground for pigs, combined with an increase in cultivated area, may have made pig raising increasingly difficult. However, pig use increases in the subsequent Period III, in spite of the evidence for intensive cultivation and deforestation during this time (Wattenmaker 1987). This suggests that the environment was suitable for pig raising and supports the suggestion that their declining importance resulted from reorganization of the economy. Density ratios (bones of each species/m^3) were examined to establish that the apparent decline in pigs was not simply a result of an increase in the importance of caprines and cattle (see Redding 1981a). The density ratios of caprines and pigs, based on a sample of deposits for which volume information was available, support the conclusion (based on percentages) that pig exploitation did decline in importance (Tables 23 and 24). Densities for pig are clearly higher in Areas C and G (Subperiod IV.2) than those in Area B (Subperiod IV.1), demonstrating that pig use declined. Differences cannot be attributed to archaeological context. We might expect pig bones to be better represented in exterior deposits (see Meadow 1978), but the density of pigs is low in the Area B street deposits (Table 25). Preservation conditions also cannot account for the significant decline in the density of pig bones, because Area B had better preservation conditions but a lower density of pig bones (Table 24). At the same time that the density of pig bones declined, the density ratios of caprines based on both count and weight increased in Subperiod IV.1.

Better preservation conditions in Area B may have contributed to the increased density of caprines in Subperiod IV.1 levels; it is possible that caprines were not well preserved in Areas C55/56 and G, and that caprine exploitation did not increase.[2] However, archaeological context is not responsible for the apparent increase in caprines, which we would expect to be better represented in interior loci (ibid.); both interior and exterior deposits from Areas C and G had a lower density of caprine bones than similar deposits of Area B (see Table 23).

A pig provides almost three times the amount of meat as a caprine and a cow may yield 3.5 times as much meat as a pig (Flannery 1969, 83, table 2). Given the major differences in meat yield of caprines versus pigs, the difficulty in translating bone counts into meat yield, and the ambiguous data regarding a possible increase in the role of cattle in Subperiod IV.1, it is not clear if the proposed increase in consumption of caprine meat in Subperiod IV.1 compensated for a decrease in consumption of pig meat.

As mentioned previously, preservation conditions were considerably worse in Areas G and C than in Area B, and this difference is reflected in architectural remains from the three areas. It is reasonable to expect that, all factors being equal, Area B would have a higher density of bone than Area G and non-elite sections of Area C, because of the better preservation conditions.

Table 23

Raw Data on Bone Densities

Context	Volume (m)^3	Cattle No.	Cattle Weight (gms)	Goat No.	Goat Weight	Sheep No.	Sheep Weight	Sheep/goat No.	Sheep/goat Weight	Pig No.	Pig Weight	Other No.	Other Weight
Area G Suprafloor, Floors													
G64: 002	3.6	3	20										
G64: 006	0.2							1	7				
G64: 012	0.8			1	22			3	5	1	5	19	4
G64: 030	2.9							1	1			1	4
G65: 007	1					1	5					4	3
Area G Exterior Surfaces													
G65: 002	0.27											3	4
G65: 005	0.56											2	32
G65: 009	0.3	1	65	1	3			3	12	14	107	15	14
Area G Pit													
G54: 004	2.2	3	27					3	7			1	1
Area G Fill Above Surfaces													
G64: 034	0.6									2	5	1	2
G65: 003	0.4	3	46			2	3	5	10	1	5	22	15
G64: 022	0.1											1	1
Area G Totals	12.93	10	158	2	25	2	3	17	47	18	122	69	81

Continued on next page

Table 23 *(continued)*

Context	Volume $(m)^3$	Cattle No.	Cattle Weight (gms)	Goat No.	Goat Weight	Sheep No.	Sheep Weight	Sheep/goat No.	Sheep/goat Weight	Pig No.	Pig Weight	Other No.	Other Weight
C55, 56, 66 (lower-status section of C)													
Courtyard or Interior Surfaces													
C56: 010	0.4											5	
C56: 029	0.72											1	
C66: 007	1.6	1								2			
Area C Street													
C55: 011	1.64							3		4		11	
C55: 016	0.72					1		2		7		38	
C56: 024	0.24							1				7	
C66: 003	0.12							1				3	
Area C Fill													
C55: 008	0.04											1	
C55: 010	0.3											2	
C55: 024	.34											1	
C55: 028	1.01									1		10	
C56: 003	0.15							1					
C56: 007	0.35											1	
C56: 017	1.8					1		1		9		8	
C56: 016	0.25	1								1		9	
C56: 020	0.4									2		5	
C56: 025	0.3							1		1		2	
C56: 027	50.54											4	
Area C totals	10.92	2				2		10		2		108	

Continued on next page

Table 23 *(continued)*

Context	Volume $(m)^3$	Cattle		Goat		Sheep		Sheep/goat		Pig		Other	
		No.	Weight (gms)	No.	Weight	No.	Weight	No.	Weight	No.	Weight	No.	Weight
Area B Floor/suprafloor													
B01: 024	0.25	1	14					1	8			1	5
B01: 033	0.27							2	3			3	2
B01: 036	0.12	1	5										
B02: 037	0.53	1	6							1	3		
B02: 038	0.53							2	24			3	4
B81: 012	0.15							3	12	1	2	1	6
Area B Ovens/hearths													
B01: 025, 030	0.4	1	4					2	9			1	1
B02: 040	0.06											3	6
Street													
B01: 018	2.75	2	19			2	17	5	23			16	27
B02: 018	2.4	3	38					15	72			46	41
B02: 041	0.03											3	9
B03: 017, 018	1.8							1	9			2	18
Area B totals	9.19	9	86			2	17	31	16	1	2	80	122

Table 24

Bone Density Ratios for Horizontal Exposures of Subperiods IV.2 (Areas C and G) and IV.1 (Area B)

	Cattle		Ovis/Capra		Pig		Total[a]	+
Area/Subperiod	No.	gm	No.	gm	No.	gm	No.	gm
C (IV.2)	.2[b]	—[c]	1.1	—	2.5	—	13.6	—
G (IV.2)	.8	12.2	1.6	5.8	1.4	9.4	9.1	38.4
B (IV.1)	1.0	9.4	3.6	17	.1	.2	13.4	42.1

[a] Totals include both identified and unidentified fragments.

[b] The first density ratio (column a) is based on counts and the second (column b) on weights.

[c] Bones from some Area C faunal samples were recorded before I joined the project. Bones from these samples were counted but not weighed (Mary Evins, personal communication, 1982). For this reason, weights were not available for bones from this area.

In fact, the density based on counts was equal for Areas C and B (see Table 24). Although the density based on counts was lower for Area G than for Area B, the densities based on weights were fairly close. A higher proportion of the Area B deposits represent exterior areas, which tend to have a higher density of bone. Whereas 73% of the total volume of Area B deposits used to calculate density ratios are from exterior areas, only 28% of the total volume of Area C loci, and 9% from Area G were derived from exterior contexts. In spite of better preservation in Area B, Area C streets actually had a higher density of bone (based on counts) than Area B (see Table 25). Given available evidence, the shift to specialized meat production did not lead to increased consumption of meat, and may have resulted in an actual decline in meat use.

KILL-OFF PATTERNS AND MEAT DISTRIBUTION

In this section, I examine kill-off patterns to determine if animals were raised by the consumers, or whether they were raised by specialists and procured through exchange. Mortality data for domestic sheep and goat have also been used to investigate other problems. These include, for example, determining the goals of the herders (e.g., meat or milk production; Payne 1973; Redding 1981a; Stein 1988), establishing whether meat was distributed through indirect channels, rather than through direct transactions between

Table 25

Bone Density Ratios Based on Bone Counts for Street Deposits

Area	Volume (m^3)	Cattle	Ovis-Capra	Pig	Unidentified	Total[a]
C	2.72	0	2.9	4	21.8	28.7
B	6.38	.8	3.6	0	10.5	14.9

[a] Totals include both identified and unidentified bone fragments.

herders and consumers (Zeder 1988), or monitoring urban-rural animal exchange (Mudar 1982).

In the study of kill-off patterns, I will focus on caprines, because they are the most likely to have been raised by specialists, and they were relatively abundant in the Kurban assemblage. If herders aim for either energy optimization or herd security, the prime age for slaughter of male caprines is between nine months and three years (Payne 1973; Redding 1981a, 204). By the age of three, animals are approaching or have reached their maximum size, so that it is no longer advantageous to maintain them for meat alone (Payne 1973). The greater appeal of lamb meat might also encourage selection for young animals in their first year of life, particularly for elite consumption, to the extent that this did not interfere with herd security. If animals are raised for meat, and winter feed is not a problem, most male caprines will be slaughtered between the ages of two and three, with only a small number kept alive for breeding (Payne 1973, 282). Female caprines are generally kept alive for milk and breeding until they became infertile or ill.

If animals were raised by households, we would expect to find a wider range of age categories represented. Ideally, these should include very young animals that died of natural causes, animals of prime age (two to three years) for slaughter, and an older breeding population, although the first category is often underrepresented archaeologically because of the fragility of bones of young animals (Brain 1976). If households consumed animals produced by specialists, we would expect most animals to be in the prime-age category. Very young animals that probably died of natural causes, and very old animals culled from the breeding population, would be poorly represented.

The approximate ages of caprines at death can be determined from mandibular tooth eruption and tooth wear data (Payne 1973). An alternative approach used data on epiphyseal fusion of long bones to determine the proportion of the population slaughtered in an age group (Hole, Flannery, and Neely 1969, 284). Because the approximate ages at which caprine bones fuse are known (Silver 1970), the kill-off pattern can be constructed by computing the proportion of bones fused for each age category.

Tooth data provide the most precise estimates of the age of animals at death and are therefore most useful when trying to determine if a particular age group is represented in the assemblage. One major shortcoming of this approach is that different slaughtering practices may have been employed for sheep and goat; because of the difficulty in distinguishing between the permanent teeth of sheep and goat, different slaughtering practices for the two species would not be recognized. Moreover, teeth may be underrepresented in an assemblage for a variety of reasons. These include the use of mandibles of mature animals in bone tool manufacture, or the disposal of low-meat-yield body parts, including heads, in an unexcavated part of the site or wherever slaughtering occurred.

Long bones provide a second set of data with which to cross-check findings based on tooth eruption and wear patterns. The primary advantage of fusion data is that, with large sample sizes, it is possible to construct separate kill-off patterns for sheep and goat. Moreover, because a large number of skeletal elements are used, selection against one skeletal part (e.g., use of fused metapodia for tools) should not seriously affect the results. However, this approach has serious limitations. Because, as mentioned previously, bones of immature animals are relatively fragile (see Brain 1976), young animals will often be underrepresented, unless preservation is exceptional. Fusion data provide estimates of the proportion of the population surviving beyond a certain age category but do not indicate the ages at which the animals were killed. Because all long bones are fused by the time an individual reaches the age of four years, fusion data do not reveal kill-off patterns for older animals. Given the limitations of both techniques, both tooth wear and long bone fusion data should both be used to cross-check results.

Data from Subperiod IV.4 (village phases) were not adequate for a study of kill-off patterns. Because of the small sample sizes, results for Subperiods IV.3 and IV.2 were combined, although data are presented for each subperiod separately. Thus far in this analysis these two subperiods have looked similar in terms of production organization, and they appear similar with respect to kill-off patterns as well.

Mandibular data for Subperiods IV.3 and IV.2 document the exploitation of older animals probably kept alive for breeding. This suggests that caprines were produced at Kurban Höyük. Most animals represented were killed between the ages of three and eight years, beyond the prime-age range (Fig.

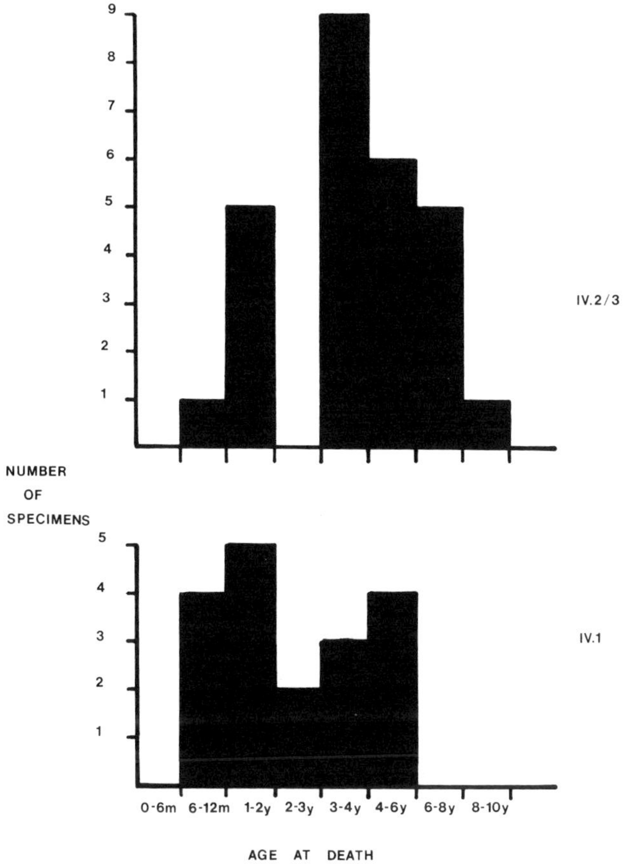

Figure 34. Caprine Mortality from Mandibles ($z = 1.28$, $.05 > p > .01$).

34). Although some younger animals were consumed, there is a conspicuous absence of animals killed between the ages of two to three years, the age group we would expect to be best represented if animals were raised for meat and consumed in the parts of the site from which faunal samples were obtained. Five of the six mandibles of animals killed before the age of three all come from the elite, possibly administrative, Phase 14 building in Area A and the poorly preserved and little understood building constructed directly above it. Because of the small sample, it is not possible to say if these site sectors were supplied with meat. However, the absence of prime-age animals in other excavated parts of the site suggests that households in those areas were consuming only their older animals and sending the prime-age animals elsewhere, perhaps as tribute payments.

Table 26

Fusion Scores for Period IV[a]

Age category	Survival Score			
	Subperiods IV.2/3 (%, sample size)		Subperiod IV.1 (%, sample size)	
6-10 months	100	15	89	9
13-16 months	73	15	36	11
18-28 months	81	27	70	10
30-36 months	84	13	60	10
36-42 months	50	4	38	4

[a]Scores are calculated following Redding (1981).

Herd animals are an ideal tributary item, because they can be moved on hoof, and they provide the recipients with a range of products. Because animals can be kept alive until their meat is needed, spoilage is not a problem. The Ebla archives document the delivery of large numbers of animals to the palace (Archi 1981, 2–3), perhaps as tribute. The Kurban data provide some evidence for the intrasite or intersite transport of animals as tribute in the Karababa Basin as well.

The mandibles indicate that during Subperiods IV.3 and IV.2 both non-elite and elite households were raising their own animals. Although it is risky to use faunal data to infer individual household production strategies, it is clear from the results of both mandibular and fusion data that many households were involved in pastoral production. Animals that died after reaching four years of age were represented in all areas examined, with the exception of the two structures mentioned previously. The debris of two houses that may have been elite (one in Area C01 and a second in Area F) contained mandibles of animals at least six years of age.

Fusion data (Table 26) for Subperiods IV.3 and IV.2 support findings based on mandibular data. Unfortunately, the sample size was too small to permit construction of separate age-curves for each subperiod area, or for sheep and goat. It was, however, large enough to provide an overview of kill-off patterns for the site as a whole. As with mandibular evidence, fusion data from both subperiods indicate that approximately one fourth of the population did not survive beyond two years of age, that few animals represented were slaughtered between the ages of two and three, and that some animals lived longer than three years. The mandibular data suggest that 44% survived beyond three to four years of age and the fusion data indicate that 50% survived beyond 3 years. These data provide support for the interpretation that the breeding population was well represented at the site and that prime-age animals were exported, either to another part of the site or to other settlements.

In the discussion of species use, the concentration on caprines in elite assemblages was noted. It was not clear whether this emphasis resulted from the procurement of animals from specialized producers or from a preference for caprines, and from the ability of elite households to pursue a high-risk production strategy. The evidence for widespread involvement of households in pastoral production suggests that differences in faunal remains from elite and non-elite houses result from two alternative household production strategies, rather than differences between households in their involvement in specialized animal production. The data suggest that some elite households did raise their own animals, but that they were able to focus on relatively high-risk animals that must have been highly valued. In contrast, non-elite households pursued a lower risk strategy of exploiting a wider range of animals, which included caprines and cattle but also pigs, which served as a safety net.

Mandibular and fusion data suggest that a major change in caprine production took place during the final subperiod of nucleation (see Fig. 34 and Table 26). Although some older animals are represented, there is a greater concentration of mandibles from younger animals slaughtered between the ages of six months and three years. No animals in the sample lived beyond six years. Although the difference between mandibular data from Subperiods IV.2 and IV.3 and IV.1 is significant only at the .10 level ($z = 1.28$), fusion data also indicate the slaughter of animals in the prime-age category (see Table 26).

The shift in exploitation from older to younger animals, combined with a trend toward increased reliance on caprines, suggests a trend away from household production. All areas sampled for this subperiod, with the possible exception of the well, appeared to be non-elite. Although with this sample size it is not possible to say that specific households did not raise their own animals, the data indicate that some non-elite households became divorced from pastoral production and procured their animals from specialists.

It is possible that Kurban relied on nomads or transhumant specialists for some caprines and pastoral products during this period. Intensified cultivation (see section on tribute that follows) may have limited available summer pasturage and decreased its quality, creating a need for the movement of animals to highland pastures. Alternatively, animal products may have been obtained from herders at nearby settlements. In summary, the data on kill-off patterns parallel conclusions based on the low species diversity that meat production became specialized on the non-elite level during this period.

A shift to specialized pastoral production would have implications for the availability of goat hair and wool, important in cloth production. Households would have to obtain either the raw materials or finished products from specialists. As discussed in Chapter 5, textile production may have been a specialized activity during Period IV, even prior to specialized animal production.

BODY PART FREQUENCIES

The final aspect of pastoral production examined—the relative frequencies of different skeletal parts—indicates whether meat was obtained from specialized herders or butchers. If animals were produced by households, we would expect them to be butchered or at least processed and consumed in the vicinity of residential structures. In such cases, all or most parts of the skeleton should be represented. The relative frequencies of different body parts should reflect their relative abundance in a skeleton (e.g., one atlas versus two scapulae) and their durability. With surplus production and exchange, animals may be distributed to consumers as cuts of meat (Scott 1981; Zeder 1985). This might be reflected in a disproportionate number of skeletal elements from specific sections of the carcass. High proportions of low-meat-yield body parts, in particular lower limb and skull bones, should be found in areas in which butchering occurred. High-meat-yield bones from the upper limbs and axial part of the skeleton should be disproportionately well-represented in areas in which meat was imported. The following analysis focuses on caprines, the only category well enough represented at Kurban Höyük for a study of body part distributions.

The skeletal elements represented in an assemblage reflect not only the bones originally deposited but also the relative durability of the bones discarded. Factors such as the density of a bone, the age at fusion, and the

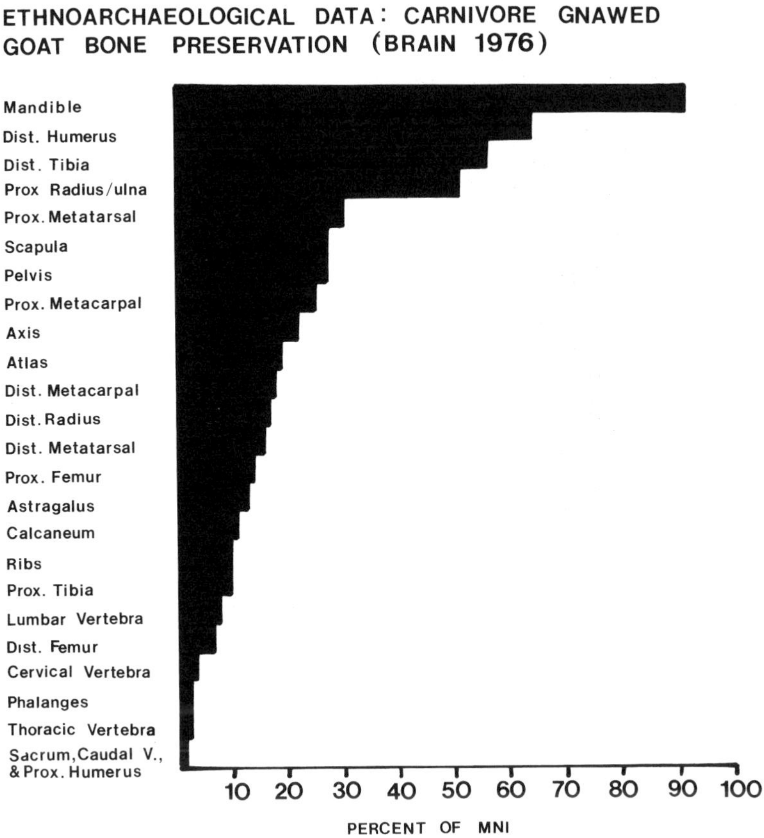

Figure 35. Ethnoarchaeological Data: Carnivore-Gnawed Goat Bone Preservation.

bone's appeal to dogs determine the probability that a bone will be preserved (Binford 1978; Brain 1976). This makes it necessary to control for differential preservation of skeletal parts when interpreting the significance of body part frequencies. The method used compares the relative frequencies from an archaeological assemblage with the relative frequencies of various goat bones collected from Hottentot villages (Brain 1976; Klein 1976; see Fig. 35). Because ethnographic documentation of Hottentot cooking, butchery, and bone disposal established that all bones of the animals were discarded in the study area, variation in the MNIs of different skeletal parts can be attributed to differential durability. For this reason, the modern data provide a useful baseline for comparison with archaeological data.

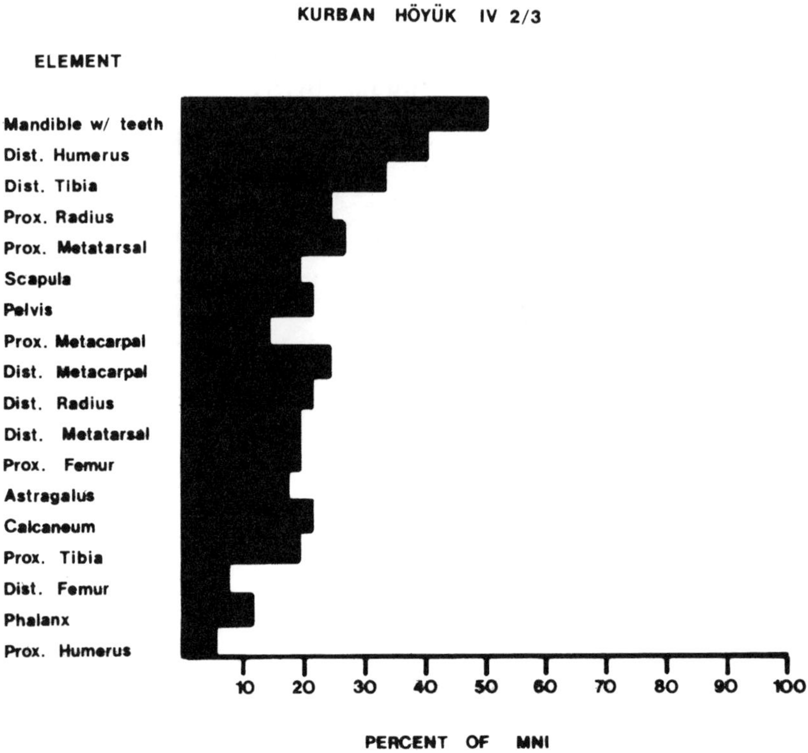

Figure 36. Caprine Skeletal Part Representation for Subperiods IV.3 and IV.2.

Figure 36 lists the body parts from Subperiods IV.3 and IV.2, with the ordering based on their ranking in the Hottentot assemblage. Figure 37 summarizes the data from Subperiod IV.1. For both the Hottentot and Kurban assemblages, the frequency was expressed as the percentage of the expected number actually observed, with the expected number calculated on the basis of the MNI.

Ideally, this method would be used to analyze body part distributions for each part of the site separately. Unfortunately, it was necessary to combine different areas because of the small sample size. Viewing the site as a whole, body part distributions from Subperiods IV.3 and IV.2 appear to result largely from the relative durability of different skeletal parts. Butchering clearly took place at Kurban Höyük, and there is no evidence that specific meat cuts were systematically and differentially removed from those parts of the site excavated. Although the low-meat-yield proximal metacarpals were significantly less frequent than we would expect, this does not appear to result from meat distribution patterns, because other low-meat-yield bones

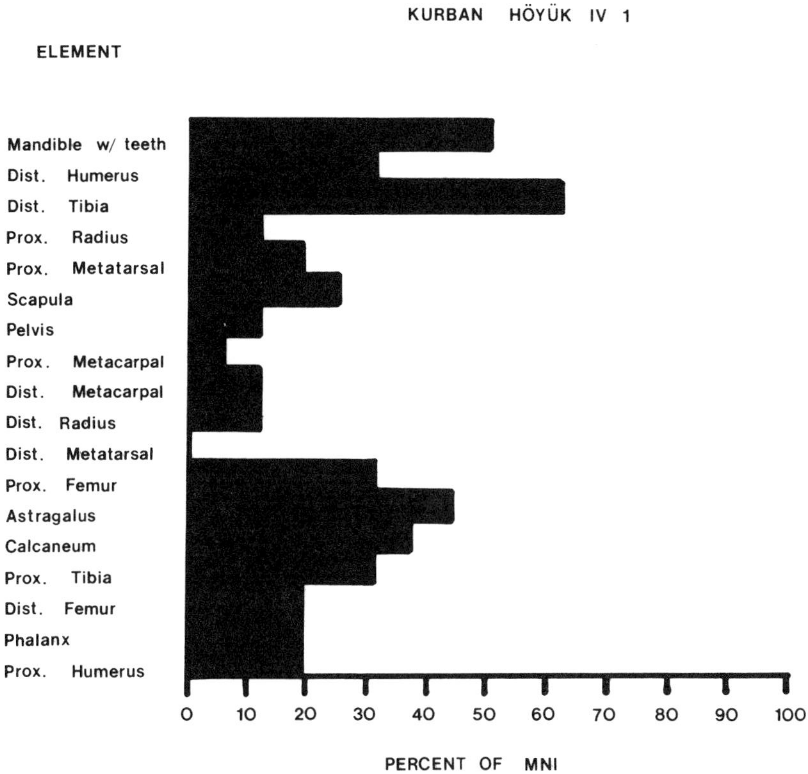

Figure 37. Caprine Skeletal Part Representation for Subperiod IV.1.

were well represented (e.g., astragali, mandibles). Because other skeletal parts from the forelimb were well represented, including the distal metacarpal and distal radius, it is unlikely that the low frequency of the proximal metacarpal points to the removal of caprine forelimbs from the area. Many bone awls recovered from the site appear to have been made from the proximal metapodia of caprine-size bovids, and perhaps the use of metapodia in bone-tool manufacture resulted in their lower than expected occurrence amid assemblages representing meal remains.

In spite of small samples from some areas, the proportion of high- (forelimb and hindlimb) to low- (skull, lower limbs, and feet) meat-yield body parts is remarkably uniform both between different areas and subperiods, for Subperiods IV.4, IV.3, and IV.2 (Table 27). High-meat-yield parts contributed between 18% to 25% of the assemblage in each subperiod (Table 28). For the five areas that have more than fifty bones (IV.3: Area A, Phase 13; IV.2: C55/56/56, C01, C35/45, F: Levels 8–2), the percentage of high-meat-yield bones ranges from 19% to 25%. Potentially high-status areas

Table 27
Caprine Body Part Frequencies[a]

Subperiod	Area, phases	Head No.	Head %[b]	Forelimb, scapula No.	Forelimb, scapula %	Hindlimb, pelvis No.	Hindlimb, pelvis %	Metapodia, feet No.	Metapodia, feet %
IV.4	A, 11-12	15	60	5	20	0	0	5	20
	F, 1-7	4	45	1	11	2	22	2	22
	Total count for subperiod	19		6		2		7	
IV.4, A and F	Percent of all body parts for subperiod		56		18		6		20
IV.3	A, 13	38	55	8	12	8	12	15	21
	A, 14	34	81	3	7	0	0	5	12
	C01, 11-14	36	57	6	9	6	9	16	25
	Total count for subperiod	108		17		14		36	
	Percent of all body parts for subperiod		62		10		8		20
IV.2	A, 16-17	13	42	5	16	3	10	10	32
	C55/56/66, C01, 15	38	46	4	5	13	16	27	33
	C35/45	74	57	17	13	16	12	24	18
	A03, 8-12	51	61	7	8	10	12	16	19
	G	8	29	8	29	3	10	9	32
	Total count for subperiod	184	52	41		45		86	
	Percent of all body parts for subperiod				12		12		24
IV.1[c]	A, 18-20	12	21	7	13	17	30	20	36
	A, 15	31	76	3	7	1	2	6	15
	B	18	31	12	21	16	27	12	21
	C01, 16	5	63	0	0	0	0	3	37
	F13, 14	0	0	0	0	3	6	2	4
	Total count for subperiod	67		22		37		43	
	Percent of all body parts for subperiod		40		13		22		25

[a]Vertebra and ribs are not included in this summary chart, because they were almost always coded as "medium mammal."

[b]Percentages represent the percent of bones of a specific body part from the designated phases and area or subperiod. For example, this number indicates that 60% of bones from Area A, Phases 11 and 12, represent skull bones and teeth.

(A, F, C01) had roughly the same proportion of low-meat-yield bones as did the lower status area (C55/56/66). The exception to this was the Phase 14 administrative building from Area A that, contrary to expectations, contained mostly low-meat-yield skull elements. Given the small sample size of bones from this building, it is difficult to interpret the significance of this pattern. In general, the fairly even representation of low- and high-meat-yield parts suggests that animals were butchered in every part of the site. If animals were exported from these areas, as I suggested earlier, they were probably exported on the hoof, rather than as cuts of meat. The evidence supports previous lines of faunal data indicating household production of animals.

For Subperiod IV.1, the relative frequency of different caprine body parts does not follow the order expected if relative durability served as the primary factor leading to differential representation (see Fig. 37). Although the sample size is small, the higher than expected relative abundance of proximal and distal tibiae, proximal femora, astragali, and calcanea might indicate that hindlimbs were more heavily used in these areas than other bones. This suggests that some meat cuts were obtained through exchange.

The relative proportions of high to low-meat-yield body parts also suggest a divergence from the earlier pattern of meat production and distribution (see Table 28). The proportion of high-meat-yield parts increases from 25% in Subperiod IV.2 to 35%. For the two parts of the site containing more than fifty bones, Areas A and B, high-meat-content bones made up 43% and 47% of the assemblages, respectively. This percentage is high not only for Kurban Höyük but in comparison with that found at the nearby third millennium B.C. village at Gritille Höyük, where there was no evidence for specialized pastoralism. Assemblages from two different sectors of that settlement each contained approximately 20% high-meat-yield bones (Stein 1988, 167).

Given the small sample size from this period, the results are not conclusive. The disposal of foot bones in all parts of the site excavated suggests that butchering took place in a number of locations, perhaps on a household or otherwise informal basis. In addition, some meat may have been distributed as cuts of meat to parts of the site. It is much easier to transport live animals than butchered carcasses, and live animals do not pose a meat-storage problem. Therefore, specialized butchering prior to distribution may have been carried out primarily in administrative contexts, where institutions were responsible for supplying a large number of people of varying status on a regular basis, and in a limited number of locations (see Zeder 1988, 1991).

ANIMAL PRODUCTION AT OTHER SITES IN THE KARABABA BASIN

The animal bones are among the most comprehensively published data sets from the Karababa Basin at present. Contemporaneous assemblages from three other sites, Hayaz, Gritille, and Lidar, have been published to date (Buitenhuis 1985; Kussinger 1988; Stein 1987, 1988). At these sites, as well as at Kurban Höyük, sheep, goat, cattle, and pig made up the bulk of the third millennium B.C. faunal material. These data from other sites are not, at present, directly comparable to those presented here, because they combine faunal remains contemporary with Kurban Period IV with material that predates or postdates Period IV. For Gritille Höyük, the material was subdivided into three subperiods, but the earliest predates Period IV, and the latest includes remains contemporary with Kurban Period III. At present it is not possible to link the middle subperiod with a specific subperiod of Kurban IV, although this may be possible in the future.

The Kurban evidence from Subperiods IV.3 and IV.2 for household involvement in animal husbandry matches the conclusion that animal production at Gritille Höyük represented a generalized low-risk, subsistence-oriented strategy (Stein 1988, 225). However, some important differences between the two assemblages do exist. In his examination of kill-off patterns for caprines, pig, and cattle, Stein found that all age groups were present, suggesting that Gritille Höyük did not export animals. Contrary to the findings for Kurban Subperiods IV.3 and IV.2 he did not find evidence indicating surplus production and export of caprines. Nor did Stein find indicators such as those from Kurban Period IV.1 of specialized animal production (1988, 215–31). He suggested (1988, 228) that differences between the two sites may reflect greater integration between towns and centers than between villages and towns.[3]

If, as I suggested previously, the low proportion of prime-age caprines in most areas at Kurban Höyük during Period IV.2 resulted from the provisioning of the political elite as part of a tributary economy, it is also conceivable that the contradictory data from the two sites stem from a tributary system in which the goods extracted from various settlements differed. Gritille may have supplied the political elite with other commodities, such as grain, or labor, rather than animals.

The use of different chronological units in the two studies may also have led to divergent findings. Age-curve data are often very sensitive to the chronological and spatial units (e.g., elite versus non-elite sectors) employed, and kill-off

Table 28

High- Versus Low-Meat-Yield Body Parts by Area and Subperiod

Subperiod	Area								
		A		F		Total			
IV.4	High	5[a]	20%	3	33%	8	24%		
	Low	20	80%	6	67%	26	76%		
		A Phase 13		A Phase 14		C01		Total	
IV.3	High	16	23%	3	7%	12	19%	12	18%
	Low	53	77%	39	93%	52	81%	52	82%
		A Phase 16/17		C55/56		C01/C35/C45			
IV.2	High	8	26%	17	21%	33	25%		
	Low	23	74%	65	79%	98	75%		
		F		G		Total			
	High	17	22%	11	39%	86	25%		
	Low	67	78%	17	61%	350	75%		
		A Phases 18–20		A Phase 15		Area B			
IV.1	High	24	43%	4	11%	28	47%		
	Low	32	57%	37	89%	30	53%		
		C01		F		Total			
	High	0	0	3	60%	59	35%		
	Low	8	100%	2	40%	111	65%		

[a]First number represents the total number of bones in this category (high-meat yield bones from Area A deposits dating to subperiod IV.4). The second number represents the percentage of bones that fall into this category from a given area and subperiod that are categorized as high-meat yield or low-meat yield (e.g., 20% of bones from Subperiod IV.4 loci in Area A represent high meat yield body parts).

patterns generated using different chronological units of analysis may not be directly comparable. By combining data from periods (or parts of a settlement) in which two different kill-off patterns were employed, it is possible to obtain results suggesting that yet a third pattern was used. For example, if in one period prime-age animals were imported, and in the following period prime-age animals were exported, the resulting combined age-curve would include animals from all age groups, indicating generalized production for consumption only. Numerous other possible explanations for differences between the sites exist. These include the nature of the site sectors sampled, the possible absence of deposits contemporary with Kurban Subperiod IV.2 and IV.1 at Gritille Höyük, and differences in economic organization on the north bank of the river, where Gritille Höyük is located, and the south side, where Kurban Höyük and the regional center of Titriş are located.

The data for animal production from Kurban Höyük echo that for agricultural production. Both lines of study suggest that during this period of early state development, most households at this town site were producing their own food. There is no evidence for specialized agricultural and animal production on the non-elite household level from the first three subperiods of the mid-third-millennium B.C. deposits. Both low- and fairly high-ranking households appear to have raised their own crops and animals, although higher status households may have pursued higher risk pastoral production strategies focusing on fewer species. It is likely that some surplus caprines were produced by households for export, possibly to the political elite residing either at Kurban Höyük or higher order sites nearby. This suggestion cannot currently be adequately tested, because of the lack of excavations from the central part of the larger mound at Kurban Höyük, where massive public architecture may have been located. However, there was some evidence that the massive building on the slope of the large mound, closer to the center of the large mound than other excavated areas, may have been supplied with caprines.

During the final occupational phases of the mid-late third millennium B.C., both agricultural and animal production appear to have become specialized activities, with even non-elite households procuring comestibles through exchange networks. The absence of sickle blades from some structures and an overall decreased density suggest that some households no longer harvested crops. The decreased density of pigs, the almost exclusive reliance on herd animals, and the decreased proportion of older animals, all suggest that fewer households raised their own animals. Because of the difficulty in linking animal bones to specific households, it is not possible to say if some households were entirely divorced from food production, or if some households farmed and others raised animals. However, the near absence of prismatic blades from Area B, combined with evidence for a disproportionate number of high-meat-yield bones, suggests that households in this part of the site may have obtained both agricultural and animal products from specialists. It is perhaps significant that the house from Area A Phase 15, which produced a sickle blade and may have been occupied by farmers, appears more similar to the earlier houses from Areas C and G in having a courtyard area. In contrast, the structures in Area B probably did not have courtyards. This difference, as well as evidence for decreasing house size in Area B, may be related to the need for greater space in houses of farmers or herders, for processing of agricultural goods, and for sheltering animals.

FOOD PRODUCTION AND TRIBUTE

Increasing political centralization and escalating tribute demands may have affected household economies (Blanton et al. 1982). The analysis of the spatial distribution and sizes of settlements, combined with assessment of the amount of land needed to support each settlement, provides an indirect measure of the tributary economy (Brumfiel 1976; Steponaitis 1982). In situations in which centers did not have enough arable land to support its population, but small settlements had enough land to produce a surplus, it can be inferred that the outlying sites provided the center with agricultural surpluses. Ideally, we would like to measure changes through time within Period IV in the availability of, versus the need for, arable land, but this is presently not possible because sites could not be dated to subperiods within Period IV (Wilkinson 1990).

Results of an intensive foot survey in a 75-km^2 area surrounding Kurban Höyük, combined with adjacent surveys and excavations, provide an overview of settlement and land use for an area of approximately 1000 km^2 (Wilkinson 1990). Assuming a population density of 100 people per ha of settlement, and a minimum requirement of .5 ha of cultivated land per person, cropped annually, Wilkinson found that the area surrounding Kurban Höyük was sufficient to support the estimated population, even with a one-year fallow system (1990, fig. 4.4). The figure of 1 ha per person (with a fallow system), derived from modern statistics on caloric intake and land productivity (see Wilkinson 1990) falls at the low end of estimates for land needed per person. It is less than average for irrigation-based agriculture (see Adams 1981, 87; Kramer 1982, 67), which is more productive per ha than dry farming. Given the conclusion that settlements were capable of being self-supporting with a nonintensive agricultural system, it is noteworthy that the earliest evidence of fertilization using settlement-derived debris, interpreted as an indication of a shift to annual cropping, dates to this period (see Wilkinson 1986, 45–46; 1989, fig. 8, and 1990). Other signs of agricultural expansion and intensification during this period include a shift from wood as a fuel source to animal dung, perhaps indicating deforestation

(Miller 1986, 89) and the onset of gully erosion and alluvial aggradation (Wilkinson 1986, 46). These converging lines of evidence for intensified land use during Period IV suggest that smaller sites such as Kurban Höyük may in fact have been supplying others with surpluses,[4] or that sites were producing surpluses for export to other regions.

Findings from Titriş Höyük support the view that smaller sites were supplying the center with surpluses. A survey of the Titriş hinterland revealed that the center did not have enough land to support its population and most likely imported agricultural surpluses (Algaze et al. 1992). Moreover, the botanical remains from a slightly later phase of the mid-late third millennium B.C. indicated that clean grain was imported to the excavated parts of the site; parts of the plant removed in processing were underrepresented (Algaze et al. 1995). Surface collections from Titriş Höyük yielded a higher proportion of sherds from large storage vessels than did smaller sites in the region (Wilkinson 1994, 495). This pattern may have resulted from the storage at Titriş Höyük of surpluses extracted from sites in the countryside (ibid.).

It is also possible that agricultural surpluses were exported beyond the Euphrates Valley. The most likely candidate would be the Harran Plain, which was easily reached from the Karababa Basin along the Incesu Basin (Wilkinson 1990). Regional survey of the Harran Plain revealed a high density of Early Bronze Age settlement (see Yardımcı 1991), with Kazane Höyük reaching 100 ha (Wattenmaker and Mısır 1994). Texts indicate that Harran, only 35 km south of Kazane, was clearly a major regional center during the third millennium (see Pettinato 1991, 147–8), although the exact size of the site during this time is not known. This proposed relationship between the Karababa Basin and the Urfa Plain has historic parallels; during medieval times, the Samsat area sometimes sent surpluses to the heavily populated Urfa area (Redford 1986, 115). Although the Karababa Basin had a low density of sites, limited by geographical constraints, the area would have been of crucial importance to polities engaged in long-distance river trade, and may have been an extension of inland polities, rather than as an autonomous political unit. Available data suggest that agriculture was intensified during this period, most likely to support the large numbers of people residing in centers, as well as to meet the demands of the political elite.

The animal bones provided another source of support for the existence of a tribute system. I suggested previously that the low proportion of prime-age animals during Subperiods IV.3 and IV.2 indicated surplus production and export by households, perhaps to meet tribute payments. Because during Subperiod IV.1 residents of the excavated areas may have received animals through exchange, rather than produced surplus animals themselves, it is not possible to determine if some animals were exported as tribute during this time.

Current evidence is not adequate for a study of changing tributary systems. However, by Subperiod IV.2, the tribute economy may have had a major influence on the ages of animals consumed at the site, and by the end of Period IV, agricultural production was sufficiently intense to cause noticeable environmental changes in the area immediately surrounding Kurban Höyük. These findings are consistent with expectations that tribute pressures would escalate following political centralization. Having examined evidence for the reorganization of craft and food production, and changing consumption patterns, we can now consider reasons for the trend toward increasing specialization of the economy.

7 TOWARD UNDERSTANDING THE DEMAND FOR SPECIALIST-PRODUCED GOODS IN EARLY STATE SOCIETY: THE FINDINGS FROM KURBAN HÖYÜK

Thus far I have examined the range of goods produced by specialists and those produced by households as a first step in determining why specialization occurred. The results clearly suggest increasing involvement of households in a specialized economy following state formation in the area. Changes took place on the household level in both food and craft production. However, reorganization of these two components of the economy did not take place concurrently.

Most households seem to have engaged in agricultural and animal production until the final subperiod, when animal husbandry became a specialized activity and at least some households were no longer involved in agriculture. In the first three subperiods, even higher ranking households appear to have produced at least some of their own food. Most likely some administrators and craft specialists were not involved in subsistence production once state society formed, but these would appear to have been the exception, at least at the smaller sites such as Kurban Höyük.

Although households farmed and raised animals throughout most of the period, they were dependent on specialists for much of their pottery. This reliance on specialists increased through time. Pottery produced in workshops made up a steadily increasing proportion of the ceramic assemblage. By the end of the period, households obtained almost all ceramics other than cooking pots from specialists.

Evidence for textile production was less conclusive, but it is likely that many non-elite households no longer manufactured thread for cloth by Subperiod IV.2, toward the end of the period. Definitive evidence for thread manufacture was confined to one site sector (Area B) dating to Subperiod IV.1. It is perhaps significant that the residents of this area appeared to have obtained meat, and presumably wool as well, from specialists. Residents of areas that raised caprines (for example, Subperiod IV.2 deposits of Areas C and G) presumably had access to wool from sheep, but, surprisingly, there was no evidence that they produced thread.

Chipped stone was the only class of artifact examined that was clearly produced by households throughout the entire period. Most of the chipped stone recovered was probably made by non-specialists; only a few categories of chipped stone, such as sickle blades and obsidian points, may have been made by specialists. Overall, results indicate that following political centralization, households did become increasingly involved in a specialized economy and did not produce many of the goods they consumed.

Household production of surplus subsistence goods, perhaps for tribute, was suggested by the low proportion of prime-age domestic animals throughout most of this period, as well as the high proportion of storage vessels at Titriş Höyük. It was not possible to monitor changes in surplus production through time, although evidence for declining settlement density and environmental degradation by the subsequent period, Kurban Period III, might have been a result of production intensification toward the end of Period IV. Having examined change through time in food and craft production, we are now in a position to consider why increasing specialization of the economy occurred.

CENTRALIZATION, SCALE, AND SPECIALIZATION: THE SEQUENCE OF CHANGES

The Kurban data provide insight into the relationships among political centralization, increasing scale of the society, and increasing specialization. Available evidence from Kurban Höyük suggests that political reorganization occurred during Subperiod IV.3. During this time the fortification wall was constructed (Area A Phase 13) and, shortly afterward, the site grew to its maximum size and the administrative building was erected (Area A Phase 14). At the city of Kazane, the construction of monumental architecture and the major expansion of the settlement onto the outer town date to approximately this time period. Ceramic comparisons with Tell Mardikh suggest that the major reorganization at Kurban was contemporary with the main occupation of the Tell Mardikh palace (Phase IIB1; Mazzoni 1985, 9).[1] Available evidence indicates that changes in scale and sociopolitical complexity at Kurban Höyük may represent large-scale reorganization not only in the Karababa Basin but throughout northwest Syro-Mesopotamia.

If the changes in settlement organization at Kurban Höyük during Subperiod IV.3 do indeed mark the period of regional political centralization, then the ceramic analyses indicated that non-elite households used specialist-produced ceramics prior to state formation. However, their reliance on pottery produced in workshops increased in Subperiods IV.2 and IV.1, following political reorganization. Judging from the presence of model "chariot wheels" (which I interpret as possible spindle whorls) in the very small exposures of Subperiods IV.4 and IV.3, households may have spun their own thread prior to state emergence. Their lower densities for Subperiods IV.3 and IV.2 suggest that non-elite households seem to have relied on specialists for thread and probably some cloth by this time. Data indicate that this aspect of the economy may have become specialized at roughly the same time as, or shortly following, political reorganization. Specialized subsistence production on the non-elite-household level occurred subsequent to political centralization, during the final subperiod. In summary, available evidence indicates that specialized craft production intensified following higher level political reorganization but that most households continued to produce their own food for some time after a state society was formed. Having summarized the findings, it is now possible to evaluate evidence for the construct presented in Chapter 1, which relates specialization of the economy to the changing role of goods in an early state society.

THE ROLE OF EFFICIENCY IN EARLY STATE ECONOMY: EVIDENCE FROM THE KURBAN HOUSES

A number of researchers have argued that the greater efficiency of specialization motivated people to increase their reliance on specialists in antiquity (e.g., Blanton et al. 1982; Brumfiel 1980; Lees and Bates 1974). If households at Kurban Höyük increased their reliance on specialists because of the greater efficiency of specialized production, we would expect the products made by specialists to be those goods most frequently used, produced, and repaired. These would include food, ceramics (which have a high breakage rate), and stone tools, which were clearly used for a range of activities and which require frequent replacement or repair because of dulling and breakage through use. The high density of ceramics and chipped stone at Kurban Höyük supports the expectation that these were among the most regularly used categories of artifacts. In addition, we would expect the goods produced by specialists to be food and utilitarian goods already used by households, rather than new categories of prestige goods. Finally, we would expect some households to be surplus food producers and others to be engaged in craft production. Within the sphere of food production, we might find that some families focused on agricultural production and others on herding, as a result of overlap in the milking and harvesting seasons, and (if agriculture was intensified and cropping was annual) the need to take animals to the uplands to graze during the agricultural season.

For a number of reasons, it appears that productive efficiency was not the primary motivation behind increased specialization. Judging from the prevalence of chipped stone debitage throughout all excavated areas, stone tool manufacture and repair were carried out fairly regularly, and this remained a household activity. With the exception of ceramics, the categories of goods we would expect to have been specialist-produced if efficiency was the major consideration (animals, cultivated plants, and stone tools) continued to be produced by households.

If the primary goal of specialized production was to save time or effort, we might expect most ceramics to be undecorated. However, in the Area A deep sounding, where paint on pottery was best preserved, decorated ceramics increased from 3.4% in Subperiod IV.4, 3.0% in IV.3, and 3.9% in IV.2 to 7.4% of the assemblage in Subperiod IV.1, indicating that increasing specialization was not accompanied by a greater emphasis on effort minimization. The majority of decorated sherds were of the Horizontal Reserve Slip ware variety. This type of design represents an efficient means of decorating a pot with stripes, and indicates that efficiency may nevertheless have been a consideration. However, if effort minimization was the primary aim, we would not expect to see an increase in decorated sherds coincident with an increased reliance on specialists.

Available evidence indicates that the steadily increasing importance of craft specialization was not matched by a reorganization in food production. By Subperiod IV.2 households had increased their reliance on specialist-produced pottery and probably cloth. However, during this time, sickle blades were found in all structures for which we have data, and the skeletal remains of older caprines representing a breeding population were found throughout each part of the site. Admittedly, the sample of domestic architecture is small, and it is possible that had we looked elsewhere at the site, we would have encountered non-elite domestic structures without associated sickle blades or bones from older animals. However, the presence of older animals in association with relatively substantial architecture in Areas A (Phase 13), C/Co1, and F, as well as agricultural tools in two of those areas (no data were available from Area F) suggests that even relatively high-status families in rural settlements produced their own food.

Within the sphere of food production, households did not appear to engage in only agriculture or herding, as we might expect if production scheduling conflicts occurred. Rather, the mandibles of older animals and sickle blades, correlates of meat and plant production, respectively, were found in all areas of the site for which we have data. It was not until Subperiod IV.1, subsequent to increased reliance on specialist-produced crafts, that food production appears to have become specialized on the non-elite level.

Perhaps the efficiency of specialization became an important consideration following the increased demand for specialist-produced goods. The combination of tribute demands and desire for specialist-produced goods may have led to specialization in food production as well. However, available evidence does not indicate that time constraints and efficiency were *primary* considerations leading to the initial increase in specialized craft production.

Archaeologists tend to emphasize the role of efficiency specifically when contemplating specialization among non-elite households, in part because we have assumed non-elites were homogeneous in terms of social identities, activities they conducted, and the goods they used. It is assumed that consumers had little choice regarding consumption patterns. However, in viewing the archaeological record at Kurban Höyük, variability in household consumption patterns is more salient than similarities among households. When we view non-elite household members as active participants in a socioeconomically diverse society, it seems more obvious that non-elite households, like the political elites, probably had complex motives and goals when making choices about consumption. Some factors considered by consumers may have been conscious and others less so, but the choices probably resulted from the weighing of multiple, and sometimes conflicting, factors (such as time, cost in surpluses, quality, and appearance of a good).

In highlighting the role of efficiency in specialized production, archaeologists often assume that producers and consumers had the same goals. In some cases, manufacturing efficiency may have been a primary consideration of producers, whereas consumers may have valued characteristics of the products. As an example, potters may have shifted to the wheel and kiln in an effort to produce greater quantities of pottery in less time and with less effort. However, it does not necessarily follow that this more efficient production process would have led to lower "costs" for the consumer. Households may have valued those pots because they were obviously produced by specialists in workshops (and therefore looked a certain way) rather than because they were less costly to consumers.

The emphasis by archaeologists on the greater efficiency of specialization production may be out of proportion to its significance in at least some pre-industrial complex societies. In the following section, I consider another characteristic of specialized production that has been largely neglected by archaeologists—the ability to produce highly standardized goods that convey clear messages about the consumer.

INCREASING POLITICAL CENTRALIZATION, SOCIOECONOMIC COMPLEXITY AND SCALE, AND THE USE OF GOODS TO CONVEY SOCIAL MESSAGES

It was proposed in Chapter 1 that productive specialization intensified in response to the greater scale and degree of social differentiation in state societies. Greater standardization of specialist-produced goods would have facilitated communication of social information. The greater inaccessibility of specialist-produced goods would have increased their social value. The expectations were that (1) involvement in a specialized economy would increase in the non-elite sector following increasing demographic scale, (2) households would continue to produce their own subsistence products and low visibility goods and, (3) production of goods with high social visibility would increase as scale and sociopolitical complexity increased.

The Kurban evidence is consistent with these expectations. Major expansion at Kurban Höyük occurred during Subperiod IV.3; an increase in the proportion of specialist-produced ceramics is evident during this time, and the first statistically significant increase occurs in the subsequent Subperiod IV.2. The monotonic increase in the proportion of sherds representing cooking pots relative to those from handmade open vessels suggest that households increasingly relied on specialists for all ceramics other than cooking pots.

Vessels used for serving food have a high degree of social visibility. They are items of social display, used in serving guests, and therefore convey social messages (see Pollock 1983a). Ethnographically, food containers are often used as ethnic markers or items of competitive display (Hodder 1982, 56). Food serving and consumption often accompany religious rituals, adding another dimension to their social significance. Even when not used primarily in food serving, vessels are often used in social displays (see for example Cohen 1969, 67–68).

Garments, along with jewelry, often serve to convey information on ethnicity, status, and so forth, because of their portability and visibility. In addition, garments allow for flexibility in the messages conveyed, because they can be changed to signal specific messages, such as the occurrence of a social event (e.g., a wedding or funeral), much more rapidly and inexpensively than larger and more long-lived forms of material culture, such as houses. Because textiles are made of limited resources, their production is labor intensive, and they tend to wear out relatively quickly, they are useful markers of rank. The close attention paid by the Ebla Palace officials to the details of textile color and decoration, as indicated in the recording system for garments (see Chapter 5) suggests that such details were significant in third millennium B.C. north Syria, probably because of the information they conveyed.

In contrast to the public uses of serving vessels and cloth, stone tools, along with cooking pots, were probably used primarily inside the home or courtyard, and they were limited to viewing largely by relatives. By this time metal had become an important display item, and it may have replaced chipped stone as a medium for conveying social information such as status. Metal would have been produced by specialists, if only because of the skill involved in metallurgy.

To summarize, the goods examined can be divided into two categories: those used in social events and those used within the household. Stone tools and cooking pots, goods of low visibility, were produced informally, probably by households. Vessels used to serve food and textiles, both potentially of high visibility, were produced by specialists.

There were two exceptions to this general pattern. First, stone sickle blades, which would function as a work tool rather than object of social display, may have been made by specialists. Specialized production of sickle blades may have been a result of the difficulty in their manufacture. Similarly, storage jars with wheel-thrown rims were made by specialists (see Fig. 7) and, depending on where they were kept, may have been fairly inconspicuous. If kept in storerooms they would have low visibility, but, because of their size alone, would have been highly visible if kept in courtyards or living rooms. Again, specialization may have been in part a response to the difficulty in manufacturing large storage jars.

Most likely, visibility and social significance were not the only factors determining which goods were produced by specialists, although the data suggest that, with respect to craft production, they were the primary ones. As Hodder (1982, 55–6) pointed out, even less visible goods played a role in reinforcing cultural categories, and if exchange networks were reliable, perhaps all crafts would have been made by specialists in highly competitive complex societies. Prior to the establishment of reliable and predictable exchange systems, households may have tended to maintain autonomy in the goods most essential to survival, particularly food. Craft specialization at Kurban Höyük appears to have focused on goods of high visibility, and perhaps those difficult to manufacture, such as long flint blades. Some jars may have been used for transport of grain, oil, wine, and so forth, and, in situations where large quantities of goods were transported, vessels may have been mass-produced as a result of the need for large quantities.

It is not clear why food production became specialized in the final subperiod, following the major shift toward specialized craft production. Although the data do not support the role of efficiency as providing the major impetus to increased craft specialization (see later discussion), efficiency may have become a major consideration as the demand for specialist-produced craft goods intensified. It may be that by Subperiod IV.1, demand for specialist-produced goods was sufficiently high, and exchange networks, transport systems, and back-up strategies (e.g., state provisioning if harvests failed) were sufficiently reliable, that households were willing to sacrifice the security of household production in exchange for greater surpluses possible through specialized production. Alternatively, expanding agriculture in response to tribute demands, increasing population, surplus-oriented goals in a hierarchically organized society may have created conflicts between agricultural and pastoral production that necessitated specialized food production. For example, if a one-year fallow system was replaced with annual cropping, then animals that normally grazed on fallow fields between the fall planting and spring harvest might have to be taken a fair distance from settlements to graze, creating the need for specialized herders. Whatever the reasons leading to specialized food production, the results of this study suggest that the processes leading to specialized craft and food production were distinct, although they may have been closely interlinked. Moreover, unlike specialized craft production, the system of specialized food production appears to have been short-lived; faunal remains from the subsequent Period III suggest a return to household food production (Wattenmaker 1987).

One might question the conclusion that goods used by non-elite households functioned to convey social information and argue that mass-produced and simply decorated or plain utilitarian goods have been treated here as if they were prestige goods. Although I have argued that the highly standardized and skillfully made vessels carried social information, I am not proposing that they were important as markers of prestige (see later discussion). As David, Sterner, and Gavua (1988, 370) observed, pots that encode messages are not necessarily selected with an eye to aesthetics or care in execution. The fact that these goods were functional and used in non-elite houses does not negate the fact that they were also valued for their symbolic significance. The fact that pottery was used in agricultural societies on a daily basis for the transport, storage, and cooking of grains enhances its symbolic value (see Hall 1987, 7). Through their use in potentially emotion-laden activities, such as successful harvests, shared meals, and the payment of tribute, pots might become powerful symbols of these activities.

Household items serve not only to convey information to others, but also to reinforce information already known to the observers. The same messages broadcast to outsiders will be repeated within the household, with repetition serving to highlight and reinforce the messages (Hodder 1982, 54–7). The statement of David et al. with respect to designs on ceramics also applies to the overall appearance of ceramics: "Designs on pottery, far from being 'mere decoration,' art for art's sake, or messages consciously emblemic of ethnicity, are low-technology channels through which society implants its values in the individual—everyday at mealtimes" (1988, 379).

Grave goods are more widely recognized as having symbolic significance; Plain Simple wares and the related Combed Wash and Painted Band wares, well-represented in the Kurban household assemblages, were recovered in stone-lined graves from the neighboring site of Lidar Höyük (Hauptmann 1983, 96–110). The recovery of north Syrian Metallic wares (similar to those from domestic contexts at Kurban Höyük) in graves at Kültepe, in central Anatolia (Özgüç 1986, 34–8) suggests that household goods also served as long-distance trade items. This ware made up less than 2% of the ceramic assemblages from earlier Period IV domestic levels, but by the end of the period represented a significant component (3.7% in Area A18/20, 6.9% in Area A15, 8.1% in Area B, and 10% in Area F). The multiple use of goods as household items, burial, and trade goods suggests that the categories of "utilitarian" versus "sumptuary" goods are not as discrete as archaeologists have tended to view them, and perhaps should best be viewed as different ends of a continuum.

Attempts to distinguish between goods signifying rank and other kinds of information may be risky, because all goods probably carried multiple messages and most goods probably reflected ranking to some extent. The spatial distribution of specialist-produced decorated ceramics suggests that even mass-produced pottery varied with social context. At the center of Kazane, approximately 19% of the ceramics from a workshop area associated with monumental architecture were decorated, compared with 3% in the assemblages from the modest Kurban houses. In some assemblages recovered inside a second monumental building at Kazane Höyük, almost 50% of the sherds came from vessels that had been decorated. These differences in the proportion of decorated ceramics were immediately visible to the archaeologists and must have been obvious to the people who used them as well.

One implication of the findings from the ceramic analyses is that the material culture of non-elite households was dynamic, highly variable, and responsive to changes in political and socioeconomic organization, rather than static and invariable. The use of prestige symbols to verify status and power can only be effective if there is some recognition of goods symbolizing prestige, and demand for them, among the non-elite. For this reason, understanding changes among the non-elite that create such demand forms a critical part of research on the organizational dynamics of complex societies. The finding in southern Mesopotamia that in some cases the styles of grave goods of higher ranking groups were influenced by styles used by lower ranking groups (Pollock 1983b) underscores the fact that the non-elite were also active manipulators of status markers and active participants in the material component of the social system.

PATTERNS OF PRODUCTION ORGANIZATION

The construct examined in this book considers the reasons for an increased demand for specialist-produced goods among non-elite households in state societies, rather than the ways in which specialization might be organized. One view on this latter issue holds that specialized production was organized by the political elite. In examining craft specialization in the Susiana Plain during the fourth millennium B.C., Johnson (1987, 116–7, 121) has proposed that the political elite organized centralized craft production to increase the dependency of villagers on political centers.

Many data collected in the Kurban study were more useful for studying household production and consumption patterns, rather than for examining the organization of specialized production. However, when combined with textual data from northwest Syria, some patterns are evident. Production appears to have been organized on multiple levels, including household, centralized (involving large workshops but not administered; see Sinopoli 1988), and administered production. The Kurban results suggest that chipped stone was produced by households. Chipped stone is apparently not listed in published economic texts from Tell Mardikh or elsewhere in the Near East, indicating that they were not exchanged on the elite level or were not considered valuable enough to record (see later discussion).

Ceramics appear to have been manufactured in a number of places, judging from the extensive workshop on the western terrace of the large town of Lidar Höyük and a second one, of unknown extent, in association with a house on the north slope of the Lidar mound (Hauptmann 1983, 95–6; 1985, 204). Ceramic slag recovered from the lower mound at Kurban Höyük suggests a third ceramic production location near the excavated part of Areas C and F. Given the limited excavations in the Karababa Basin, it is surprising to have found any ceramic workshops at all. This evidence, combined with the near absence of references to ceramic production, collection, or distribution at the center of Tell Mardikh, suggest that ceramics were produced in centralized workshops, but that ceramic production was not administered by the political elite.

The absence of textual references does not necessarily mean that ceramics were not exchanged; textual records tend to be concerned with highly valued trade goods such as precious metals or essential provisions such as grain. As discussed previously, quantities of semiprecious stones found in the Ebla Palace were not accounted for in texts (Pinnock 1984, 25), perhaps as a result of chance (e.g., records were made but discarded prior to the destruction of the palace, or have not yet been studied) or the fact that these goods were produced in relatively small quantities for palace use and not valued enough to be recorded. However, the lack of attention to ceramics probably reflects the fact that the political elite were not concerned with their production and distribution. Potters are included among the craft specialists listed in the Ebla tablets (Pettinato 1991, 115) and pottery must have served as containers for oil, wine, and so forth, but descriptions in texts are of the contents, with minimal information provided about the containers (e.g., Archi 1982, 212, 216, 218).

Spinning does not appear to have been a household activity during most of Period IV; clear-cut evidence for spinning was only found in one part of Kurban Höyük. The evidence from Area B suggests that some spinning and weaving was carried out at relatively small sites. On the basis of the minimal evidence for spinning at Kurban Höyük, combined with textual references to textile production at Ebla, it was suggested that weaving may have been concentrated in workshops and at larger sites. The Ebla records mention textile factories (Archi 1982, 209), rations for state-supported weavers (ibid., 204), and inventories of large quantities of garments in storage (ibid., 211). References to garment expenditures indicate that substantial quantities were redistributed as gifts or payment, or were exported to other centers (ibid., 208, 219). The tablets also record the delivery of garments to palace officials (Archi 1981, 12; 1982, 218). Metallurgy also was at least partially administered, as indicated by the large quantities of unworked precious metals (and metal objects) delivered to the palace (Archi 1980, 2), records of metals in storage (1982, 211), metal objects produced in a workshop (Archi 1982, 216), and records of metal and metal objects distributed (Archi 1981, 3, 5; 1982, 209).

FACTORS GUIDING PRODUCTIVE ORGANIZATION IN COMPLEX SOCIETIES

On the basis of the patterns discussed previously, it is possible to propose some general statements about the organization of production in complex societies. The evidence presented previously suggests that the organization of production is guided by the social visibility of the goods being produced and the scarcity of the materials of which they were made.[2]

At Kurban Höyük, chipped stone, which was made from readily accessible river cobbles and of low social visibility, were produced on a household basis. This category was probably of minimal significance for communication systems beyond the household level. Cooking pots, made of widely available clay and of low social visibility, were also produced either by households or by informal specialists. There is some evidence that cooking pots varied between sites and neighborhoods, perhaps with ethnicity of the users. For example, within the site of Kazane, we see heavily burnished cooking pots associated with one site sector and unburnished cooking pots associated with a second sector. Ceramics of higher social visibility were made by specialists working in formal centralized workshops. The presence of multiple manufacturing sites in the area, combined with the lack of references from Near Eastern texts to ceramic production, suggests that ceramic production was not administered by the state. The lack of interest in ceramics on the part of the elite suggests that goods in this category (socially visible, but of readily accessible materials) may have served primarily to convey information on group affiliation or location of residence (e.g., town versus urban dweller; affiliated with the northwest Mesopotamian steppe rather than the Anatolian highlands) rather than ranking, at a time when the society became larger and more diverse. As discussed in Chapter 1, specialization may have served to increase standardization within categories of goods, thereby providing clear-cut messages about identity.

Finally, textiles are of high social visibility and would be scarcer than clay or chert, because their availability depended on the success of flax crops and of herding. Goods in this category would be used to express ranking as well as other kinds of information, would often be produced by specialists, and might be partially administered. Variability in quality of the raw materials, amount of labor involved, and skill of specialists would serve to restrict access and indicate rank. However, because textiles are made from self-renewing resources, they might not be as important for signifying rank as goods of even scarcer materials, such as metal.

Non-elite households appear to have manufactured their own goods that were not utilized in ritual and social contexts, such as eating meals, or in social interactions involving people other than household members. They apparently procured goods of higher social visibility through exchange. This interpretation does not negate the fact that all material culture communicates social information, but emphasizes that in large-scale, diverse societies, specialist-produced goods were particularly effective bearers of certain kinds of information about social identity. The display of specialist-produced goods might communicate, for example, participation in an urban economy, access to goods produced in specific workshops, the availability of surpluses with which to obtain specialist produced goods, or knowledge about elite consumption patterns. While I have argued that the ways in which goods were used had a major impact on the context in which they were manufactured (and vice versa), reasons for specialization were, of course, multifaceted. For example, the need for large quantities of goods, such as containers used by the political elites in the storage of goods, might encourage mass production by specialists as an efficient way to meet the high demand.

Subsistence specialization would follow a different pattern than craft production, on both the elite and non-elite levels. Subsistence specialization on the elite level served primarily to provision those involved in other activities (as proposed by Zeder 1991). On the non-elite level, we would expect households to remain largely independent in food production, unless very secure supply systems were in place and demand for surplus was high.

The meanings of goods will of course be different in each cultural context, but some general aspects of the hypothesis proposed here for increasing specialization have support beyond the Near East. For example, Sinopoli (1988, 586, 594–5) found that in the medieval empire of Vijayanagara in southern India, both pottery and textiles were produced by specialists. However, potters and pottery were rarely mentioned in texts, and production probably occurred in relatively small-scale workshops. In contrast, textile production, although not administered, was of great concern to the political elite, who tried to regulate it indirectly because of its importance in international trade and the symbolic importance of textiles (1988, 594). There is evidence that the elite had some involvement in metal working as well (ibid., 586).

The Aztec Empire provides a New World example. The distribution of artifacts at the local center of Hucxotla suggests household or small-scale specialized production of food, fibers, and chipped stone (Brumfiel 1987, 107). Documentary evidence from the early colonial period, believed to be relevant to the Aztec period, records the types and number of specialists in hinterland sites. Only 9% of the specialists produced elite goods (ibid., 104). In contrast, at the capital producers of elite crafts, such as metalsmiths, feather workers, and cloth manufacturers, were well represented in the list of specialists (ibid., 110). Garments and ornaments, goods of high social visibility, made up the bulk of the elite craft products (ibid., 111). These were largely made of relatively scarce materials imported from the tropical lowlands (ibid., 112). As least some aspects of procurement of the raw materials and production of the prestige goods entailed administrative support (ibid.). Although prestige goods were available on the market, sumptuary laws prohibited the display of these goods by the non-elite (see Chapter 1; Anawalt 1980).

Overall, the data support the expectations that more widely available raw materials, and goods of low social visibility, would not be used primarily as markers of ranking and would be made relatively informally. These variables (scarcity and social visibility) appear to have played an important role in determining whether goods were produced by households, specialists, or administered specialists. The results from Kurban Höyük suggest that the proposed relationship between social visibility of goods, scarcity of raw materials used to make them, and the context in which they were produced applies to the non-elite household as well as the political elite, although the quality of the goods, quantities, and so forth would be different. As we have seen, only small quantities of prestige goods would end up in low-ranking households at more rural sites.

HOUSEHOLDS AND GOODS IN EARLY STATE SOCIETY

Although economic specialization is widely recognized to be closely associated with state formation, the connections are poorly understood. The results of this study suggest that the relationship between state formation and increasing specialization on the non-elite level is an indirect one, resulting from a number of processes. I have proposed that the need for highly standardized goods to signify status in larger scale societies (characterized by greater diversity and increased anonymity) played a role. The increased importance of goods in signifying rank, specialized production as a means of restricting access to badges of rank, and emulation on the non-elite level appear to have been factors as well. Once demand for specialist-produced goods among the non-elite was high, efficiency of production may have been of greater consideration.

I have argued that increased sociopolitical complexity and scale led to critical changes in how goods were valued and used. These changes were more visible on the elite level, but they appear to have been profound on the non-elite household level as well. Most data encountered by archaeologists on survey or in excavations represent non-elite domestic debris, but the non-elite component of society has played a minor role in considerations of the structure of complex societies. Use of this abundant information to examine broad questions about the operation of complex societies would greatly enhance our investigative abilities. The household, the lifeblood of the state, may prove to be one of the best sources of information on the rise and organizational dynamics of complex societies.

APPENDIX: A CERAMIC SERIATION FOR KURBAN PERIOD IV

To date Kurban Period IV occupational phases relative to one another, the Period IV ceramics from Kurban Höyük were seriated using a multidimensional scaling program, MINISSA (of the OSIRIS.IV statistical package), which performs a smallest space analysis. This horseshoe method (Kendall 1971), labeled thus because of the shape of the resulting plot of variables, was selected for the seriation of occupational phases, because it provides a measure of the temporal distance between variables (occupational phases) in contrast to nonscaling methods that simply provide an ordering of variables. In this case I seriated occupational phases; MINISSA has also been used in archaeology to seriate ceramic attributes (Cowgill 1972; Minc n.d.; Pollock 1985; Steponaitis 1982) or loci (Drennan 1976).

To identify ceramic attributes useful as chronological indicators, cross-check their reliability, and establish the chronological relationships among levels from different parts of the site, I first examined data from the deep soundings, recorded by Guillermo Algaze. Because Area A had both the longest sequence and largest sample of analyzed ceramics, I examined data from that sounding to isolate the ceramic attributes most promising for establishing a relative chronology. Although changes in densities of ceramic types probably provide the most reliable data on chronological trends, relative frequencies of ceramic types is considered adequate for constructing a chronology (Marquardt 1978, 267). To identify possible chronological trends, I examined changing ware frequencies and percentages of most common forms (within ware and vessel size categories) after I eliminated clearly intrusive sherds.

I also eliminated samples from contexts described as "collapse/fall" by the excavators on the assumption that these deposits would contain ceramics from earlier phases that were incorporated into construction material, as well as later sherds discarded after an area was abandoned. Wherever samples were adequate, I limited the analysis to material from surfaces, features, and fill above floors.[1] In general, small sample sizes necessitated the inclusion of "fill/fall" deposits; I did so under the assumption that intrusive materials would be outnumbered by those discarded during or shortly after occupation of an area. Moreover, some material included in "fall" was probably contemporary with the surfaces they were associated with, representing ceramics used on roofs or stored in wall niches or on wall pegs. As walls and roofs of abandoned structures collapsed, these pots would be incorporated in the collapse.

Concerned that ceramic breaks might be different from stratigraphic breaks, I examined evidence for change in wares, using stratified occupational phases, rather than the stratigraphic/architectural subdivisions of IVC, B, and A, as the units of analysis (see Table 1). The Area A levels included Phases 11 to 20. The aim of the initial data screening was to identify obvious ceramic breaks, so that these relatively brief chronological units with small ceramic samples could be recombined without the loss of information on change through time. In general, I tried to combine the minimum number of phases possible, given available sample sizes. I combined Phases 11 and 12, the two levels from Period IVC, because samples from each of these phases were too small to work with alone, and both levels were very different from the others.

For Subperiod IVB, Phases 13 and 14 were analyzed separately, because Phase 14 may have represented a public building or elite residence, whereas most other deposits from Area A were domestic and non-elite (see Chapter 4). I wanted to eliminate Phase 14 ceramics from the analysis if the assemblage proved to be significantly different from other levels. Phase 16 and 17 were treated as one unit, because a large sample of sherds from these levels came from deposits that could only be assigned to "Phase 16/17," and the sample size from Phase 17 was very small. Moreover, preliminary data analysis did not indicate a break between the two levels. Although the sample of ceramics from Phase 18 was small, a noticeable break between ceramics from Phase 16/17 and those from Phase 18 led to the decision not to combine them. Because Phases 19 and 20 also had small sample sizes, ceramics from Phases 18, 19, and 20 were combined.

Following the grouping of Area A levels, I proceeded to search for good chronological indicators. The attributes examined include vessel form (e.g., beaded rim cup), ware (e.g., Combed Wash ware), and decoration (e.g., Horizontal Reserve Slip ware with thin bands versus thick bands). In selecting types to use in the seriation, I examined changes in percentages, using both total diagnostics and diagnostics within a particular vessel category (e.g., percentage of small beaded-rim open vessels among all small open vessels) to calculate percentages (Tables 29 and 30). The latter calculation was done to minimize the role of locus function as a factor contributing to ceramic variability (see Minc n.d.). For example, the building in Phase 14 may have been an administrative one, whereas most other structures included in the analysis were domestic. As a result, we might expect a lower proportion of cooking pots in Phase 14 deposits, although the proportions of different forms of cooking pots might be similar to those in domestic contexts. For the seriation, type frequencies were calculated as percentages within specific vessel categories, rather than as percentages of the total sample of diagnostics.

A few well-represented forms, such as beaded-rim cups, bowls, and jars made up the bulk of the assemblage, and these were included in the seriation. The remainder of the ceramic assemblage was very diverse, so that most of the diagnostic sherds were poorly represented, making it difficult to differentiate between variation as a result of chance and that as a result of changes through time in use of various ceramic forms. To minimize the likelihood that apparent chronological trends resulted from chance, only forms that made up at least 3% of the diagnostic sherds in at least one level were considered as possible chronological indicators. Only those types that increased or decreased more or less monotonically were used in the seriation. For each type, there was almost always one exception to the monotonic trend. For example, Painted Band wares were generally found only in the later deposits, but a few sherds were found in the earliest levels of the sounding. This probably resulted from contamination of deposits as a result of the sinking of pits, rodent activity, and so on, and was not significant enough to seriously affect results.

After types were selected in this manner, I added some types that I did not detect in the initial data screening but that I observed in the field to have limited distribution. Finally, some types were included because Algaze (1990b) suggested that they may be reliable chronological indicators, and plots of their

Table 29

Counts and Percentages for Area A Ceramics[a]

		Type											
Phase(s)	Sherd count	A	B	C	D	E	F	G	H	I	J	K	L
11–12	861 (157)	21; 13[a]	0; 0	2; 1	5; 3	0; 0	0; 0	1; .6	0; 0	0; 0	1; .6	0; 0	19; 12
13	869 (127)	20; 16	0; 0	0; 0	6; 5	1; .8	0; 0	0; 0	1; .8	0; 0	0; 0	0; 0	7; 6
14	1,324 (184)	44; 24	0; 0	0; 0	24; 13	1; .5	0; 0	0; 0	4; 2	0; 0	0; 0	0; 0	14; 8
16–17	2,420 (394)	60; 15	7; 2	16; 4	35; 9	4; 1	2; 1	0; 0	4; 1	3; .8	1; .2	6; 2	24; 6
18–20	1,397	13; 5	4; 2	13; 5	20; 8	6; 2	1; 1	0; 0	0; 0	1; .4	16; .6	4; 2	85; 32

Note: The first number represents the sherd count for a given type, and the second number represents the percentage of sherds of that type in a specified sample (in this case, Area A ceramics from Phases 11–12 that were categorized as Type A).

[a]For type descriptions, see Figure 38.

[b]Numbers in parentheses represent total number of "diagnostic" sherds (e.g., rims, bases, decorated wares).

[c]Percentages of types are based on the total number of diagnostic sherds to relevant phases.

Table 30

Ceramic Data Used in Seriation

	Type											
Area/phase	A[a]	B	C	D	E	F	G	H	I	J	K	Sherd sample
A11-1	56[b]	0	3	6	0	0	4	0	0	0.1	0.1	861
A13	72	0	0	12	2	0	0	14	0	0	.05	869
A14	62	0	0	33	2	0	0	33	0	0	0.2	1,324
A16-17	55	6	35	20	3	1	0	7	7	0.4	0.3	2,420
A18-20	30	7	47	15	6	2	0	0	7	1.3	0.5	1,397
A15	31	8	37	16	3	2	0	3	2	0.9	0.8	3,546
B	28	12	30	16	5	1	0	0	7	0.9	0.7	3,715
C01, 11-13	20	1	3	3	5	0	0	12	3	0	0	1,262
C01, 14	17	0	7	14	0	4	0	21	0	0	1	885
C01, 15	36	4	19	9	0	0	0	19	0	0.4	0.2	1,197
C01, 16	38	4	50	16	0	0	0	0	0	0.8	0.5	510
C2b	53	5	54	12	1	1	0	0	0.2	0.5	0.6	8,100
C2a	47	8	35	14	4	1	0	3	1	0.4	0.7	2,028
F1-7	69	0	0	12	12	0	0	0	0	0	0.9	476
F9-12	52	0	21	15	15	3	0	7	0	2	1	740
F13-14	27	0	60	12	12	8	0	0	0	0.4	0.8	691
G	65	0	38	28	2	0	0	5	0	0	—	2,530

Note: Total ceramic sample = 42,551.

[a]For type descriptions, see Figure 38.

[b]For Types A through I, numbers represent percentages of types within vessel categories (e.g., small open vessels, large closed vessels). Percentages for Type J repesent percentages of those ware categories among all diagnostic sherds. Percentages for Type K represent the proportion of that subtype relative to another subtype, Type L (Horizonal Reserve Slip ware with thin versus thick bands).

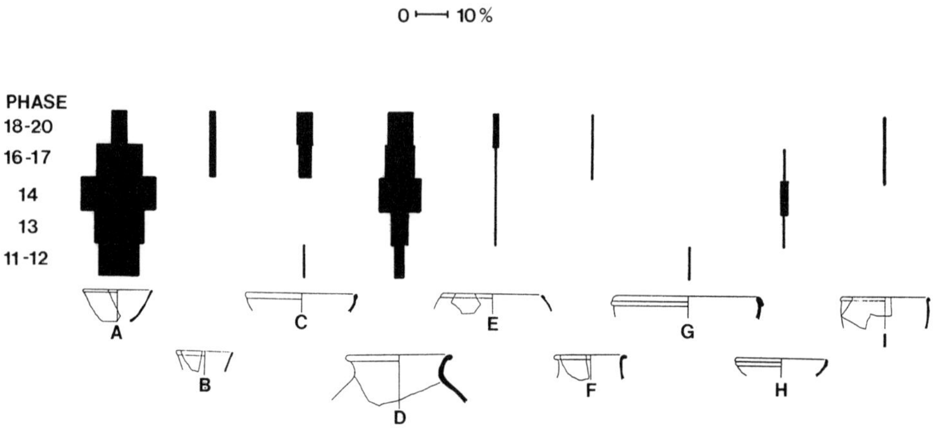

frequencies through time supported these observations. These included thin versus thick banded Horizontal Reserve Slip ware, band-rimmed bowls with in-curving upper walls versus clubbed rim bowls, and Metallic ware jars with everted rims (ibid.; see also Fig. 38). Horizontal Reserve Slip ware appeared to be a promising chronological indicator in Area A, where it increased steadily relative to other wares, but this determination was not useful in this particular analysis. The thin slip did not preserve well in deposits from the small mound; without the slip the ware was indistinguishable from Plain Simple ware. In some cases only traces of the wash were visible on sherds from the small mound, and many sherds that originally had a wash were probably recorded as Plain Simple wares. Because the actual percentage of Horizontal Reserve Slip ware could not be used as a diagnostic indicator, the ratios of the two subforms of this decoration (thin versus wide stripes) were used instead (see Algaze 1990b, 338).

To cross-check the utility of the chronological indicators selected, I first seriated the occupational phases from the Area A deep sounding, where the stratigraphic relations were known. Of the three soundings, Area A provided the best opportunity for establishing a relative chronology, because it had the most complete sequence and the largest ceramic sample (6,871 sherds). In conducting multidimensional scaling, the data are entered into the program in the form of correlation coefficients for the variables to be seriated (Table 31). To obtain the correct data configuration, it is necessary to specify the correct number of dimensions for a solution. The number of dimensions is guided by the Kruskal's stress value, which measures the "badness of fit" (Kruskal and Wish 1978, 27–30). In general, the fewer dimensions used, the less chance for error. A value of 0.15 or less is generally reliable; a higher

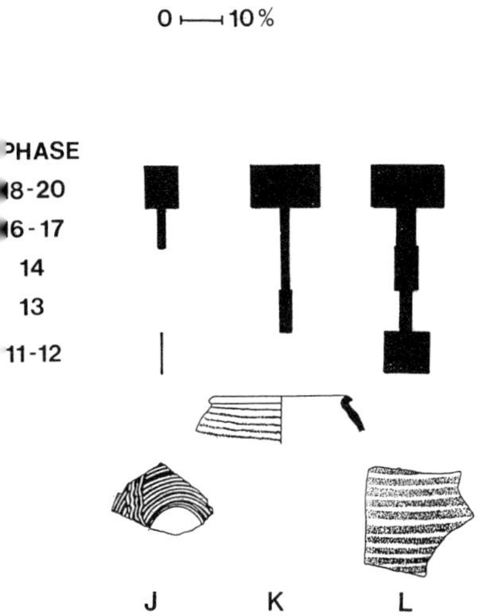

Figure 38. Ceramic Forms Used in Seriation: Relative Proportions in Area A.
Note: Percentages for A to I represent the proportion of each form within vessel categories. Percentages for J were calculated as the proportion among all diagnostics (because vessel class was not always known). The percentages for K were calculated as a relative proportion compared with L (because this category of decoration, Horizontal Reserve Slip ware did not always preserve well in all areas). (A) Plain Simple ware cup with *short* beaded rim. (B) Plain Simple ware cup with *long* beaded rim. (C) Plain Simple ware beaded incurving bowl. (D) Plain Simple ware high-necked everted beaded-rim jar. (E) Plain Simple ware incurving beaded-rim jar. (F) Stone ware everted beaded-rim jar. (G) Plain Simple ware band-rimmed (double-beaded brown with incurving upper walls). (H) Plain Simple ware everted multiple-beaded-rim bowl. (I) Plain Simple ware beaded bowl with slightly incurving wall. (J) Plain Simple ware and Combed Wash wares. (K) Horizontal Reserve Slip ware with thin horizontal reserve bands (less than 0.5 cm). (L) Horizontal Reserve Slip ware with wide horizontal reserve bands.

stress value would indicate the need to increase the number of dimensions (Drennan 1976, 50–2). One way to select the number of dimensions is to run the program specifying a range of dimension numbers, then plot the resulting stress values against the corresponding number of dimensions, and choose the dimension for which the stress value drops (Kruskal and Wish 1978). In the seriation of Area A levels, a two-dimensional solution was used, because the Kruskal stress value was 0.00, indicating an excellent fit. In addition, the small number of cases being seriated dictated a two-dimensional solution. A stress value of 0.00 sometimes indicates a degenerate solution, in which the points cluster in a small number of locations, rather than an excellent fit. However, examination of the scatter plot ruled out degeneracy in this case. The resulting configuration did indeed place the levels in the expected order, providing support for the assertion that the attributes selected varied primarily as a result of change through time, rather than other factors such as function or status. Results have been incorporated in Figure 39, which presents the ordering of all Period IV levels included in this analysis (see Fig. 39, V1–V5).

Table 31
Correlation Table

Variables (and associated areas and phases)

		V1	V2	V3	V4	V5	V6	V7	V8	V9	V10	V11	V12	V13	V14	V15	V16
		A11	A13	A14	A16	A18	C11	C14	C15	C16	C2A	2CB	A15	F1–7	F9–12	F13–14	B
A13	V2	0.97															
A14	V3	0.81	0.91														
A16	V4	0.83	0.81	0.73													
A18	V5	0.48	0.42	0.34	0.87												
C11	V6	0.82	0.91	0.9	0.75	0.39											
C14	V7	0.52	0.68	0.9	0.55	0.24	0.8										
C15	V8	0.8	0.85	0.84	0.91	0.69	0.9	0.77									
C16	V9	0.58	0.52	0.44	0.91	0.98	0.47	0.33	0.77								
C2A	V10	0.79	0.74	0.62	0.98	0.91	0.65	0.42	0.86	0.95							
2CB	V11	0.7	0.63	0.51	0.95	0.95	0.57	0.35	0.83	0.98	0.98						
A15	V12	0.6	0.56	0.5	0.93	0.98	0.52	0.4	0.8	0.99	0.96	0.98					
F1–7	V13	0.99	0.98	0.84	0.83	0.46	0.83	0.55	0.79	0.55	0.78	0.67	0.58				
F9–12	V14	0.92	0.91	0.82	0.97	0.74	0.83	0.62	0.92	0.82	0.94	0.88	0.84	0.92			
F13–14	V15	0.35	0.28	0.21	0.76	0.96	0.28	0.19	0.61	0.95	0.82	0.91	0.92	0.31	0.64		
B	V16	0.61	0.56	0.48	0.92	0.96	0.49	0.32	0.74	0.95	0.95	0.94	0.92	0.6	0.81	0.85	
G	V17	0.84	0.84	0.85	0.99	0.83	0.85	0.85	0.98	0.81	0.97	0.93	0.97	0.84	0.84	0.73	0.9

Variables (and associated areas and phases)

Note: V = variable.

The next step was to link up the deposits on the small mound with those on the large mound. I first had to determine the units of analysis in Area Co1. Six building phases had been identified by excavators: Phases 11 to 16. Because samples from each level of this narrow sounding were small, it was necessary to increase the sample sizes by combining phases. I examined data from each phase separately to determine whether any breaks could be ascertained. Phases 11 to 13 were combined because sample sizes in each level were small; they were all associated with the same wall, represented new floors in the same building, and the ceramics indicated that Phases 11 to 13 were homogeneous but that a major break occurred between Phases 14 and 15. Phase 14 had some types that only occurred in later levels in Area A and were not present in Phases 11 to 13. Phases 14 and 15 were not combined because there appeared to be major differences in the assemblages from these phases. Phases 15 and 16 were treated separately, because excavators reported that Phase 16 signaled a major break in the nature of occupation (Marfoe and Evins 1990, 137). Moreover, Phase 16 was just below the mound surface and poorly preserved, and the ceramic assemblage was probably somewhat mixed.

To further test the utility of the chronological indicators, I first seriated the Area Co1 phases. The phases from Co1 were plotted in the known stratigraphic order, providing additional confirmation that the ceramic attributes used in the analysis do in fact vary as a function of chronology (Fig. 39, v6–v9). I then seriated the phases from Areas A and Co1, using the longer Area A sequence as a stratigraphic anchor, in order to match up levels from the two mounds (see Table 4). The results differ slightly from the correlations proposed on the basis of architectural similarities. In both cases, no occupational remains on the small mound were assigned to the earliest phases (IVC). Whereas Marfoe and Algaze (1990, 422; see also Ingraham 1986, 51–2) placed Co1 Phases 11 through 15 with Area A Phases 13 and 14 (Period IVB), the seriation placed Phases 11 to 14 closest to Area A Phase 14[2] (Fig. 39, v6–v7, v3), and Phase 15 closest to Area A Phase 16/17 (Period IVA; Fig. 39, v8, v4). Area Co1 Phase 16, whose dating was left open in the earlier study, was linked with the final levels in Area A (Fig. 39, v9, v5). These results suggest that the small mound had been occupied in Subperiod IV.A (see Marfoe 1990b, 186 for an alternative view).

Finally, I seriated the levels from the sounding in the saddle, Area F. Because of small sample sizes, it was not possible to subdivide the three sets of occupational phases defined on the basis of stratigraphy (Marfoe 1990b, 176–7), Phases 2 to 7 (v13), Phases 8 to 12 (v14), and Phases 13 and 14

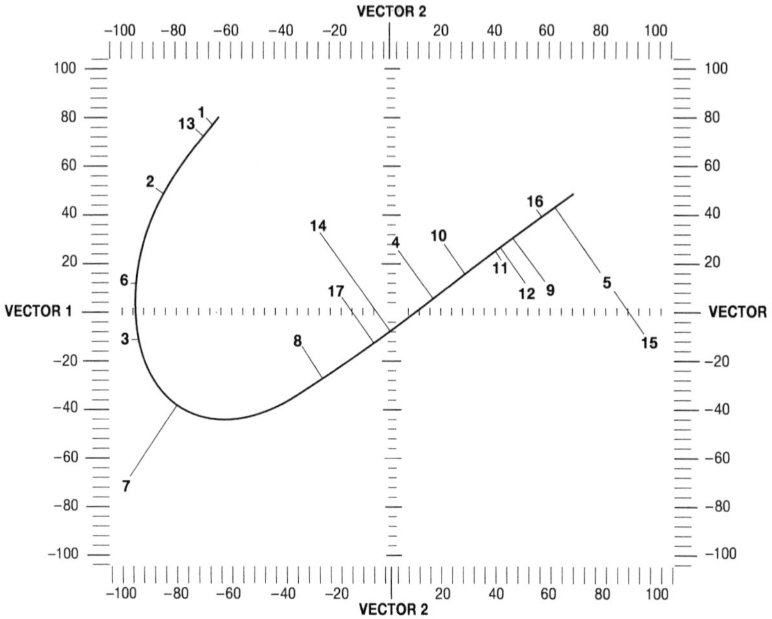

Figure 39. Multidimensional Scaling Results with a Two-Dimensional Solution (stress value = .05).
Note: Variable numbers refer to excavation areas and phases (see Tab. 31).

(v15). Once again, the phases were seriated in their correct stratigraphic order, with the earliest phases toward the left of the curve (Fig. 39; v13) and the latest phases toward the right of the curve (Fig. 39; v15).

The results suggest that the saddle was occupied at the beginning of Period IV, with the earliest phases contemporary with the earliest Period IV levels in Area A (Phases 11 and 12; Fig. 39, v13, v1). There appears to have been a gap in occupation, with the next set of phases correlated with Area A Phases 16/17 and Area C01 Phase 15 (Fig. 39, v14, v4, v8). Phases 13/14 of Area A, the subperiod in which the fortification wall was constructed and the settlement expanded (Area A, Phases 13/14; IVB), does not appear to be represented in this part of the site.

The final set of Area F phases, 13 and 14, were most closely linked with the final phases in Area A, as well as the final phase of Area C01 (Fig. 39, v15, v5, v9). The conclusions for Area F differ from those in Marfoe (1990b) only in respect to Phases 8 to 12, which were dated in the earlier report to Subperiod IV.B, the period of site expansion and large-scale construction of a wall system. Given the limited excavations in this part of the site (16 m^2), I would not argue on the basis of the seriation results that this part of the site was not occupied during the middle part of Period IV; it is possible that occupational deposits from this time would have been recovered in areas immediately adjacent to the excavation unit. Moreover, the sample size from Area F Phases 8 to 12 was only 740 ceramics, and it is possible that with larger samples Phases 8 to 12 would have been more closely related to Area A Phases 13 and 14 than with Phases 16/17.

The second part of the seriation was conducted to date the horizontal excavations relative to one another, as well as to the deep sounding levels. Although Area C was stratigraphically linked to the Area C01 sounding, Areas B and G were not stratigraphically linked to other Period IV deposits.[3] Again, a two-dimensional solution (with a stress value of .05259) was used to seriate all Period IV levels.

The seriation of the two Area C Phase II subphases yielded a slightly later date than that suggested in Marfoe (1990b, 190). In the earlier report Area C had been dated to Subperiod IV.B. In this analysis, Area C Phase II, which was stratigraphically linked to Phase 15 of C01, was most closely associated with early IVA levels of Area A (Phases 16/17), as was Area C01 Phase 15 (Table 1).

One potentially alarming result was that the earlier subphase of Area C fell slightly later in the sequence than did the later subphase (Fig. 39, v10 and v11). The reverse dating of the Area C Phase II subphase may have been a result of chance. These subphases are both stratigraphically linked with a single building phase, Area C01 Phase 15; there is no evidence that changes in the ceramic assemblages would have occurred over such a short time span. If changes did occur, it is unlikely that the chronological indicators used in this analysis are powerful enough to differentiate between such temporally close subphases. With the exception of Area C, where extensive excavations yielded ceramic samples large enough to attempt a seriation of subphases, the minimal chronological unit of analysis was the occupational phase; more often, a series of phases were used. Results from soundings suggest that the chronological indicators used are successful for seriating occupational phases, but they may not be useful for seriating subphases.

Some disturbance of Area C deposits occurred, as indicated by the removal or destruction of walls from Structures 3 and 4 (see Chapter 4). This may have been partially responsible for the reverse dating obtained in the results. Area C deposits were just below the plow zone, and surfaces tended to be poorly preserved and patchy, making it difficult to establish stratigraphic links between different deposits. It is therefore possible that disturbance of some loci led to the mixing of ceramic assemblages from different subphases, or that some subphase assignments were incorrect. In the analyses conducted in Chapters 5 and 6, the artifacts from the two subphases were combined because of uncertainties in phasing of some of the deposits.

It is surprising to note that both subphases were more closely correlated with the later Co1 Phase 16 than with Co1 Phase 15, although they were stratigraphically linked with the later phase. Moreover, Area C deposits were more closely correlated with Area A Phases 18 to 20, the final phases of the sequence, than was Area Co1 Phase 15. The slightly later-than-expected date may be a result of the fact that a badly disturbed occupational layer from the last phases of Period IV (Area C Phase I; Area Co1, Phase 16) overlaid the Area C Phase II deposits. Occasional features and patches of surfaces represented what must have originally been a more extensive Phase I occupation. As the surfaces of the uppermost phase were destroyed by plowing, weathering, and so on, the ceramics from this occupation may have been incorporated in the fill from Phase II deposits, resulting in a ceramic assemblage that appeared to be slightly later than it would have had mixing of ceramics from the two levels not occurred.

The seriation of Area G levels supported the initial conclusion prior to the excavations for this study that it was roughly contemporary with Area C (Table 30; Marfoe and Algaze 1990, 422). With respect to the sequence in Area A on the large mound, Area G was most similar to Phase 16/17 (early IVA), as was Area C (Fig. 39 v. 4, 17). Ceramics from Area G appeared more similar to those from Area Co1 Phase 15 than did the ceramics from Area C, which were more similar to those from Co1 Phase 16. This may be a result of the fact that in Area G fill deposits more than approximately 10 cm above surfaces were excavated as separate loci, and ceramics from these fill layers were generally not included in this analysis of the Area G ceramic assemblage in order to reduce the likelihood of contamination from the final occupation. Together, Areas C and G provided data from two contemporary areas toward the later part of the Period IV sequence, one from the center of the small mound and one toward the periphery.

Area B ceramics were most similar to those from the final level of Area A (Phases 18–20; Fig. 39, v5 and v16). This fits with stratigraphic findings; in both areas the occupational surfaces had at most .5 m of fill between the Period IV and Period III surfaces. There were also examples of Phase III deposits directly above Period IV remains in Area A, as well as reuse of Area B Period IV buildings during Period III (see Marfoe and Ingraham 1990 for relevant data from Area A). As mentioned in Chapter 2, when excavations for this study commenced, we thought that Area B deposits were contemporary with those from Area G and C. The results of the seriation supported the findings from excavations that Area B deposits postdated those from Areas C and G. Area B provided a fairly large data set with which to compare results from Areas C and G for a study of change through time in production and consumption patterns.

Finally, an effort was made to establish a chronological link between Area A Phase 15 and other Area A phases. Because the Phase 15 deposits were north of the fortification wall, whereas other excavated Area A deposits from Subperiods IVB and IVA were south of the wall, there was no stratigraphic connection between Phase 15 and other Area A deposits. Phase 15 could only be assigned to Subperiods IVB and IVA (Marfoe and Ingraham 1990, 45–6). The seriation results indicated that Phase 15 is contemporary with the final Area A phases of IVA (Phases 18–20; Fig. 39, v12, v5). This Period IVA date is consistent with the fact that Phase 15 architecture cuts into the Period IVB fortification wall (see Marfoe and Ingraham 1990, 46).

The seriation is viewed as a starting point, rather than a final ceramic chronology for the mid-third millennium B.C. in southeastern Turkey. Kurban Höyük remains the only site in the region to have yielded a sizable ceramic collection from the entire mid-third millennium. Titriş Höyük (Algaze et al. 1995) and Kazane Höyük have yielded large collections from specific phases within this period that will allow us to refine the chronology in the near future. The collections from broad exposures, it is hoped, will allow us to take into account factors such as function of deposit and status of consumers in our continued efforts to refine the ceramic chronology.

NOTES

CHAPTER 2

1. This increase is based on settlement data for the intensively surveyed 100 km^2 around Kurban Höyük (Wilkinson 1990). Additional survey data are available from the 1000-km^2 area around Kurban Höyük, although the territory beyond the 100-km^2 survey area has not been intensively surveyed by foot. The less intensive survey probably missed some early third millennium B.C. (Kurban Period V) sites, which tended to be small. In contrast, mid-late third millennium (Kurban Period IV) sites tended to be highly visible. Although it is important to keep this bias in mind, current evidence suggests an approximately tenfold increase in aggregate settled area in this more extensive region (see Wilkinson 1990, table 4.1).
2. The inscription was interpreted by Irving Finkel (Algaze 1990b).

CHAPTER 3

1. The possibility that the latest occupational layer on the small mound dates to Period III has been considered by Marfoe and Evins (1990, 139). However, as the authors note, no Period III pottery was found on the small mound. The similarity between ceramics from C01 Phase 16 and the final period IV phases

from Area A provides strong support for the interpretation that the uppermost level of the small mound dates to the final phases of Period IV.

CHAPTER 4

1. The major objective of this chapter is to present the primary data used in my interpretation of the function of each area excavated and status of its occupants before the significance of artifacts patterns can be interpreted in the following chapters. More detailed reports of the findings than I provide can be found in the published volumes on Kurban Höyük. The final reports on Areas A, C01, and F include stratigraphic sections, detailed plans, and discussions of the stratigraphic relationships between loci, architecture, and other data (Algaze 1990a).
2. These figures are calculated from the list of families in each category on p. 230 (Watson 1979), and from house plans in Watson 1979, figs. 5.7, 5.9–5.10, 5.15–5.16, 5.19–5.20, 5.22, 5.24.
3. When referring to findings reported in the final report on Kurban Höyük (Algaze 1990), I use the Period IV subdivisions as reported in that publication: Periods IVC, IVB, and IVA. As discussed previously, these subdivisions are based on changes in architecture. To minimize confusion caused by the introduction of a different relative chronology in this book, when referring to conclusions reported in the final report, I have provided the approximate corresponding subperiods suggested by my ceramic seriation in parentheses.
4. The grid system used in 1980 differed from that used in later seasons. Therefore, the 1980 excavation areas were designated B01–B04, and areas of expansion in 1984 are referred to as B62–B82.

CHAPTER 5

1. Karababa Painted ware was well represented at the Lidar cemetery, indicating that the absence of this ware in the kiln area is not a result of differences between Kurban Höyük and Lidar Höyük in use of this ware.
2. A neutron activation analysis of ceramics from Kurban Höyük and other sites in the region, including Lidar, is being carried out by M. Evins.
3. Because potters claim to be able to identify their own pots (Kramer 1985, 82), it is not clear why marks would be necessary. One reason for the use of marks may be to avoid disputes over ownership when pots break during firing.
4. The Philippine pots were classified according to emic vessel categories and measurements within classes were taken. In the Moroccan case, archaeological sherd samples were used, making it more likely that different native vessel cate-

gories were placed in the same group. The possibility that the handmade Philippine pots were more variable, but that lumping of different vessel categories created the appearance of greater variability in the Moroccan wheel-made ceramic assemblage, must be considered. It is also possible that the Moroccan material came from a greater number of workshops, resulting in a greater range of variability (see Sinopoli 1988). However, the overall low coefficient of variation for diameters within the Moroccan assemblage might suggest that neither the lumping of different subgroups or materials from numerous workshops were serious problems.

5. The analysis of density ratios was confined to these subperiods, because more data on excavated volumes were available. Even within these subperiods, artifact densities could only be calculated for a sample of deposits. For some loci, the volume excavated was not known; for other loci, not all ceramics had been analyzed. Because both the volume excavated and registration numbers of artifact samples collected were recorded daily, it was sometimes possible to calculate artifact densities for portions of loci even when not all ceramics had been analyzed.
6. Much of the chipped stone data from Areas G and B presented were recorded by Gil Stein and Kathy Ataman. Preliminary findings of a sample of the analyzed chipped stone were summarized in Stein (1986).

CHAPTER 6

1. These percentages were calculated after excluding bone counts from Well A08: 050. Almost all identified bones in this locus were caprines. Because of the exceptional preservation of material in the well, the assemblage was not directly comparable to other assemblages at the site, and the use of Number of Individual Specimens (NISPs) would provide misleading information on change through time. Because of the large sample size of this single locus and the likelihood that some bones came from the same individuals, inclusion of the bones in these calculations would exaggerate the importance of caprines during this period. However, incorporation of the well material would greatly strengthen the evidence for an increased reliance on caprines. When MNIs are used for Locus A08: 050, and NISPs are used for other deposits, the proportions of major food sources are almost identical to those calculated when bones from A08: 050 are excluded (73.6 versus 73.8 for caprines, 12.0% versus 12.4% for cattle, and 7.0 versus 7.1% for pig).
2. Area F also provided Period IV.2 occupational remains, which were much better preserved than those in Areas C and G and which yielded a reasonable faunal sample. Area F03 had a substantially higher density of caprines (28.1 bones/m^3) than did Areas C, G, and B. However, because the bones may have

been associated with an elite building, the high caprine density may reflect higher levels of consumption of sheep among the elite. Alternatively, they may indicate that the density of caprine bones in Subperiod IV.2 deposits was initially higher than suggested by the poorly preserved remains of Areas C and G. The pig and cattle density ratios (3.3 and 1.9 respectively) were only slightly higher than those in non-elite deposits of Subperiod IV.2.

3. Stein's comparison uses data from Kurban Höyük published in a preliminary report (Wattenmaker and Stein 1986). Because the report was published prior to the construction of the ceramic chronology employed in this book, and many bones included in this study had not been analyzed at the time, the results differ in some respects from those presented here. Nonetheless, the major similarities and differences between the Gritille and Kurban findings discussed by Stein still hold.
4. When the higher estimate of 1.5 ha per person is used, the estimated 2,000 ha of cultivable land surrounding Titriş Höyük (Wilkinson 1990, fig. 4.4) does not appear to have been sufficient to support the population of the regional center.

CHAPTER 7

1. Combed Wash wares postdate Subperiod IV.3, the time when the fortification wall was constructed. Combed Wash wares are present in deposits above the Ebla Palace (Mazzoni 1985, 9). This comparison rests on the unlikely assumptions that ceramics types appeared in different regions at the same time, and that similar ceramics were used contemporaneously in elite and household contexts. Regardless of the precise sequence of use of different ceramic types in each area, the assemblages are roughly contemporary. Mazzoni places the palace assemblage in Phase I of the Amuq sequence (1985, 10), the phase most closely related to Kurban IV. Many ceramic types from the palace, such as corrugated cups, are similar to those found in Kurban Period III (see Algaze 1990b). It may be that these did not become widely used in the Karababa Basin until after the destruction of the mid-late third millennium B.C. Ebla Palace, and that the Combed Wash ware in the Karababa Basin predates that in northwest Syria. If so, then the Ebla Palace would be roughly contemporary with Subperiods IV.2 and IV.1 at Kurban Hoyuk. It is also possible that these forms were used in elite contexts prior to their use in non-elite domestic areas. Because excavations of Period III deposits at Kurban Höyük yielded only low-status domestic areas, this would account for their seemingly later occurrence in Kurban Period III.
2. When specialization plays a limited role in the economy, some goods signifying rank may be made of widely available materials (e.g., clay), because the

amounts produced by specialists are limited, even if the raw materials are widely accessible. In general, once specialized production becomes the norm, and specialization is not, in itself, an effective means of restricting access, the organization of production appears to be guided by the social visibility of the goods and the scarcity of the materials of which they were made.

APPENDIX

1. Differences in data presented by Algaze and those presented here may be partially a result of the fact that some deposits included in Algaze's analysis were excluded from the present one. Algaze included more than 12,000 sherds from Area A in his analysis (1990b), whereas this analysis was based on 6,871 sherds from Area A. One reason for differences in interpretation may be that Algaze attempted to find differences between each of the three subperiods (IVC, IVB, and IVA), whereas I examined evidence for changes between sets of occupational phases (including phases belonging to different subperiods). Another difference in the approaches is that Algaze tended to look for attributes that were absent from one subperiod but present in another; In this study I looked for trends in relative percentages, rather than the presence or absence of forms or wares.
2. Phase 14 was almost mid-way between Area A Phases 14 (IVB) and Phase 16/17 (IVA).
3. Ceramics from the 1980 excavations of Area B were analyzed by G. Algaze, who recorded ceramics from all Period IV deposits, excluding those excavated in Area B and G in 1984; I coded ceramics from the 1984 excavations. To avoid introducing variability resulting from inconsistencies in the two recording systems, I used only ceramic data recorded by Algaze for the relative dating of Area B, because material from the soundings had also been recorded by him. For Area G, it was necessary to use the data I had recorded from 1984 excavations, because earlier excavations did not yield much material for Algaze to record.

BIBLIOGRAPHY

Adams, Robert McCormick

1981 Heartland of Cities. Chicago: Aldine.

Algaze, G.

1986 The Ceramic Sequence. Anatolica 13: 54–60.

(Ed.) 1990a Town and Country in Southeastern Anatolia, Volume II: The Stratigraphic Sequence at Kurban Höyük. Chicago: Oriental Institute Publications.

1990b Period IV: The Middle-Late Part of the Early Bronze Age. *In* Town and Country in Southeast Anatolia, Vol. II, Guillermo Algaze, ed., pp. 311–43. Chicago: Oriental Institute Publications.

Algaze, G., Adnan Mısır, and Tony Wilkinson (with contributions by Elizabeth Carter and Ronald Gorny)

1992 Şanlıurfa Museum/University of California Excavations and Surveys at Titris Höyük, 1991: A Preliminary Report. Anatolica 18: 33–53.

Algaze, G., K. Ataman, M. Ingraham, L. Marfoe, M. McDonald, N. Miller, C. Snow, G. Stein, B. Verharen, P. Wattenmaker, T. Wilkinson, and A. Yener

1986 The Chicago Euphrates Archaelogical Project 1980–84: An Interim Report. Anatolica 13: 37–148.

Algaze, G., Ray Breuninger, and James Knudstad

1994 The Tigris-Euphrates Archaeological Reconnaissance Project: Final Report of the Birecik and Carchemish Dam Survey Areas. Anatolica 20: 1–96.

Algaze, G., et al.

1986 The Chicago Euphrates Archaelogical Project 1980–84: An Interim Report. Anatolica 13: 37–148.

1995 Titris Höyük, A Small EBA Urban Center in SE Anatolia: The 1994 Season. Anatolica 21: 13–64.

Anawalt, Patricia

1980 Costume and Control: Aztec Sumptuary Laws. Archaeology 33: 33–43.

Appadurai, Arjun (ed.)

1986 The Social Life of Things. Cambridge: Cambridge University Press.

Archi, Alfonso

1980 Notes on Eblaite Geography. Studi Eblaiti 2/1: 1–17.

1981 Notes on Eblaite Geography II. Studi Eblaiti 4: 1–17.

1982 About the Organization of the Eblaite State. Studi Eblaiti V: 201–220.

1987 More on Ebla and Kish. *In* Essays on the Ebla Archives and the Eblaite Language, Vol. 1, Cyrus H. Gordon, Gary A. Rendsburg, and Nathan H. Winter, eds., pp. 125–140. Winona Lake, Ind.: Eisenbrauns.

1988 Harran in the III Millennium B.C. Ugarit Forschungen 20: 1–8.

Balfet, H.

1965 Ethnographical Observations in North Africa and Archaeological Interpretation. *In* Ceramics and Man, F. R. Matson, ed., pp. 161–77. Chicago: Aldine.

Barber, E.

1994 Women's Work: The First 20,000 Years. New York: W. W. Norton.

Behm-Blancke, Manfred R., et al.

1984 Hassek Höyük. Vorläufiger Bericht über die Ausgrabungen in den Jahren 1981–1983. Instanbuler Mitteilungen 34: 31–150.

(Ed.) 1992 Hassek Höyük. Naturwissenschaftliche untersuchungen und lithische Industrie. Istabuler Forschungen Band 38. Tubingen, Germany: Ernst Wasmuth Verlag.

Benco, Nancy L.

1988 Morphological Standardization: An Approach to the Study of Craft Specialization. *In* A Pot for all Reasons: Ceramic Ecology Revisited, C. Kolb and L. Lackey, ed., pp. 57–72. Philadelphia: Temple University.

1989 Organization and Technology of Traditional Pottery Production in Morocco. Paper presented at the American Anthropological Association, Washington D.C.

Binford, Lewis

1972 Archeology as Anthropology. *In* An Archaeological Perspective, pp. 20–32. New York: Seminar Press.

1978 Nunamiut Ethnoarchaeology. New York: Academic Press.

Blackman, J., G. Stein, and P. Vandiver

1993 The Standardization Hypothesis and Ceramic Mass Production: Compositional, Technological and Metric Indices of Craft Specialization at Tell Leilan (Syria). American Antiquity 58: 60–80.

Blanton, Richard

1994 Houses and Households: A Comparative Study. New York: Plenum Press.

Blanton, Richard E., et al.

1982 Monte Alban's Hinterland, Part I: The Prehispanic Settlement Patterns of the Central and Southern Parts of the Valley of Oaxaco. Memoirs of the Museum of Anthropology, University of Michigan, No. 15. Ann Arbor.

Blau, Peter M.

1977 Inequality and Heterogeneity: A Primitive Theory of Social Structure. New York: Free Press.

Braidwood, R. J., and L. Braidwood

1960 Excavations in the Plain of Antioch I. Oriental Institute Publications 61. Chicago: University of Chicago Press.

Brain, C. K.

1967 Hottentot Food Remains and Their Bearing on the Interpretation of Fossil Assemblages. Scientific Papers of the Namib Desert Research Station 32: 1–11.

1976 Some Principles in the Interpretation of Bone Accumulations Associated with Man. *In* Human Origins, G. Isaac, and E. McCown, eds., pp. 121–38. Menlo Park: W. A. Benjamin.

Bretschneider, J., and Annemarie Dietrich

1994 Beydar: Mitteilungen über die Erforschung eines urbanen Zentrums im Norden Alt-Syriens 1. Münster: Selbstverlag des ördervereins Tell Beydar e.V.

Brumfiel, Elizabeth M.

1976 Regional Growth in the Eastern Valley of Mexico: A Test Case of the "Population Pressure" Hypothesis. *In* The Early Mesoamerican Village, Kent V. Flannery, ed., pp. 234–49. New York. Academic Press.

1980 Specialization, Market and Exchange, and the Aztec State: A View from Huexotla. Current Anthropology 21: 459–478.

1987 Elite and Utilitarian Crafts in the Aztec State. *In* Specialization, Exchange and Complex Societies, E. Brumfiel and T. Earle, eds., pp. 102–18. Cambridge: Cambridge University Press.

1994 Introduction. *In* The Economic Anthropology of the State, E. Brumfiel ed. Lanham, Md.. University Press of America.

Brumfiel, Elizabeth M., and Timothy K. Earle (eds.)

1987 Specialization, Exchange and Complex Societies. Cambridge: Cambridge University Press.

Buitenhuis, H.

1985 Preliminary Report on the Faunal Remains of Hayaz Höyük from the 1979–1983 Seasons. Anatolica 12: 61–74.

Carneiro, Robert

1967 On the Relationship between Size of Population and Complexity of Social Organization. Southwestern Journal of Anthropology 23: 234–43.

Clark, J., and W. Parry

1990 Craft Specialization and Cultural Complexity, B. Isaac, ed., pp. 289–346. *In* Research in Economic Anthropology, Vol. 12. Greenwich, Conn.: JAI Press.

Cohen, Abner

1969 Customs and Politics in Urban Africa: A Study of Hausa Migrants in Yoruba Towns. Berkeley: University of California Press.

Costin, C. L.

1991 Craft Specialization: Issues in Defining, Documenting, and Explaining the Organization of Production. Archaeological Method and Theory 3: 1–56.

Cowgill, George

1972 Models, Methods, and Techniques for Seriation. In Models in Archaeology, David L. Clarke, ed., pp. 381–424. London: Methuen.

Crawford, Harriet

1977 The Architecture of Iraq in the Third Millennium B.C. Copenhagen: Akademisk Forlag.

1991 Sumer and the Sumerians. Cambridge: Cambridge University Press.

Cronon, William

1983 Changes in the Land. New York: Hill and Wang.

Cruz-Uribe, Kathryn

1988 The Use and Meaning of Species Diversity and Richness in Archaeological Faunas. Journal of Archaeological Science 5: 179–96.

Davenport, William H.

1986 Two Kinds of Value in the Eastern Solomon Islands. *In* The Social Life of Things, Arjun Apadurai, ed., pp. 95–109. Cambridge: Cambridge University Press.

David, Nicholas, Judy Sterner, and Kodzo Gavua

1988 Why Pots Are Decorated. Current Anthropology 29: 365–389.

De Vries, K.

1980 The Greeks and Phrygians in the Early Iron Age. *In* From Athens to Gordion: The Papers of a Memorial Symposium for Rodney S. Young, K. De Vries ed., pp. 33–49. Philadelphia: University Museum, University of Pennsylvania.

Donnan, Christopher

1971 Ancient Peruvian Potter's Marks and Their Interpretation through Ethnographic Analogy 36: 460–6.

Dornemann, Rudolph

1988 Tell Hadidi: One Bronze Age Site Among Many in the Tabqa Dam Salvage Area. Bulletin of the American Schools of Oriental Research, 270: 13–42.

Douglas, Mary, and Baron Isherwood

1979 The World of Goods. New York: Basic Books.

Drennan, Richard

1976 A Refinement of Chronological Seriation Using Nonmetric Multi-dimensional Scaling. American Antiquity 41: 290–302.

Evans-Prichard, E. E.

1974 The Nuer. New York: Oxford University Press.

Falconer, Steven

1994 Village Economy and Society in the Jordan Valley: A Study of Bronze Age Rural Complexity. *In* Archaelogical Views from the Countryside, G. Schwartz and S. Falconer, eds., pp. 121–42. Washington, D.C.: Smithsonian Institution Press.

Fielden, Kate

1977 Tell Brak 1976: The Pottery. Iraq 39: 245–56.

Flannery, Kent V.

1968 The Olmec and the Valley of Oaxaca: A Model for Inter-regional Interaction in Formative Times. *In* Dumbarton Oaks Conference on the Olmec, E. P. Benson ed., pp. 79–110. Washington, D.C.: Dumbarton Oaks.

1969 Origins and Ecological Effects of Early Domestication in Iran and the Near East. In The Domestication and Exploitation of Plants and Animals, Peter Ucko, and G. W. Dimbleby, eds., pp. 73–100. Chicago: Aldine.

Frangipane, Marcella, and Alba Palmieri

1988/1989 Aspects of Centralization in the Late Uruk Period in the Mesopotamian Periphey. Origini 14: 539–60.

Fugmann, E.

1958 Hama. Fouilles et Recherches 1931–38, III. Copenhague: National Museet.

Galvin, Kathleen

1987 Forms of Finance and Forms of Production: The Evolution of Specialized Livestock Production in the Ancient Near East. *In* Specialization, Exchange and Complex Societies, E. Brumfiel, and T. Earle, eds., pp. 119–29. Cambridge: Cambridge University Press.

Gell, Alfred

1986 Newcomers to the World of Goods: Consumption among the Muria Gonds. *In* The Social Life of Things, Arjun Apadurai, eds., pp. 110–38. Cambridge: Cambridge University Press.

Grayson, Donald

1979 On the Quantification of Vertebrate Archaeofaunas. Advances in Archaeological Method and Theory 2: 199–237.

1984 Quantitative Zooarchaeology. New York: Academic Press.

Hall, Martin

1987 Archaeology and Modes of Production in Pre-Colonial Southern Africa. Journal of Southern African Studies 14: 1–17.

Hauptmann, Harold

1979 Norsuntepe Kazıları, 1973. Türk Tarih Kurumu Basımevi, Ankara.

1982 Lidar Höyük, 1981. Anatolian Studies 32: 17–18.

1983a Lidar Höyük, 1982. Anatolian Studies 33: 254–256.

1983b Lidar Höyük, 1981. Türk Arkeologi Dergisi 26–2: 93–110.

1984 Lidar Höyük, 1983. Anatolian Studies 34: 226–8.

1993 Vier Jahrtausende Siedlungsgeschichte am mittleren Euphrat. Archëologie in Deutschland. Heft 1: 10–15.

Helms, Mary

1988 Ulysses' Sail. Princeton, N.J.: Princeton University Press.

Henrickson, Elizabeth

1981 Non-Religious Residential Settlement Patterning in the Late Early Dynastic of the Diyala Region. Mesopotamia 16: 43–140.

Hodder, Ian

1982 Symbols in Action: Ethnoarchaeological Studies of Material Culture. Cambridge: Cambridge University Press.

Hole, Frank, Kent Flannery, and James Neely

1969 The Prehistory and Human Ecology of the Deh Luran Plain. Museum of Anthropology, University of Michigan, Memoir I.

Ingraham, M.

1986 The Stratigraphic Sequence. Anatolica 13: 46–53.

Johnson, Allen, and Timothy Earle

1987 The Evolution of Human Societies: From Foraging Group to Agrarian State. Stanford, Calif.: Stanford University Press.

Johnson, Gregory

1973 Local Exchange and Early State Development in Southwestern Iran. Museum of Anthropology, University of Michigan, Anthropological Paper 51.

1982 Organizational Structure and Scalar Stress. *In* Theory and Explanation in Archaeology, Colin Renfrew, Michael Rowlands, and Barbara Abbott Seagraves, eds., pp. 389–421. New York: Academic Press.

1987 The Changing Pattern of Uruk Administration on the Susiana Plain. *In* The Archaeology of Western Iran, Frank Hole, ed., pp. 107–39. Washington, D.C.: Smithsonian Institution Press.

Kendall, D. G.

1971 Seriation from Abundance Matrices. *In* Mathematics in the Archaeological and Historical Sciences, F. R. Hodson, D. G. Kendall, and P. Tâutu, eds., pp. 215–52. Edinburgh: Edinburgh University Press.

Klein, Richard

1976 The Mammalian Fauna of the Klaisies River Mouth Sites, Southern Cape Province, South Africa. South African Archaeological Bulletin 31: 75–98.

Klein, Richard, and Kathryn Cruz-Uribe

1984 The Analysis of Animal Bones from Archaeological Sites. Chicago: University of Chicago Press.

Kopytoff, Igor

1986 The Cultural Biography of Things: Commoditization as Process. *In* The Social Life of Things, Arjun Apadurai, ed., pp. 64–91. Cambridge: Cambridge University Press.

Kramer, Carol

1982 Village Ethnoarchaaology: Rural Iran in Archaeological Perspective. New York: Academic Press.

1985 Ceramic Ethnoarchaeology. Annual Review of Anthropology 14: 77–102.

Kruskal, Joseph B., and Myron Wish

1978 Multidimensional scaling. Quantitative Applications in the Social Sciences, 11. Beverly Hills, Calif.: Sage Publications.

Kühne, Hartmut

1976 Die Keramik vom Tell Chuēra und Ihre Beziehungen zu Funden aus Syrien-Palästina, der Türkei und dem Iraq. Berlin: Gebr. Mann Verlag.

Kurtz, Linda

1985 The Early Bronze Age Lithics of Gritille Höyük, Southeastern Turkey. Senior thesis, Anthropology Department, Bryn Mawr College.

Kussinger, Sonja

1988 Tierknochenfunde vom Lidar Höyük in Südostanatolien (Grabungen 1979–86). Munich: Universität München.

Lees, Susan, and Daniel Bates

1974 The Origins of Specialized Nomadic Pastoralism: A Systematic Model. American Antiquity 39: 187–93.

Longacre, William, Kenneth L. Kvamme, and Masashi Kobayashi

1988 Southwestern Pottery Standardization: An Ethnoarchaeological View from the Phillipines. The Kiva 53(2): 101–12.

Lloyd, Seton

1978 The Archaeology of Mesopotamia: From the Old Stone Age to the Persian Conquest. London: Thames and Hudson.

MacDonald, Mary

1986 The Chipped Stone Sequence. Anatolica 13: 60–6.

Marcus, Joyce

1973 The Iconography of Power among the Classic Maya. World Archaeology 5: 83–94.

1983 On the Nature of the Mesoamerican City. *In* Prehistoric Settlement Patterns: Essays in Honor of Gordon R. Willey, E. Z. Vogt, and R. M. Leventhal, eds., pp. 195–242. Albuqerque and Cambridge, MA: University of New Mexico Press and Peabody Museum.

Marfoe, Leon

1982 Kurban Höyük Excavations, 1981. Ankara: Kazı Sonuçları Toplantısı IV: 95–120.

1990a Introduction. *In* Town and Country in Southeast Anatolia, Vol. II, G. Algaze, ed., pp. 1-20. Chicago: Oriental Institute Publications.

1990b Area F. *In* Town and Country in Southeast Anatolia, Vol. II, G. Algaze, ed., pp. 169–184. Chicago: Oriental Institute Publications.

1990c An Overview of the Horizontal Exposures. *In* Town and Country in Southeast Anatolia, Vol. II, G. Algaze ed., pp. 185–209. Chicago: Oriental Institute Publications.

Marfoe, L., and G. Algaze

1990 Kurban Höyök and Its Wider Context: An Outline of Settlement History. *In* Town and Country in Southeast Anatolia, Vol. I, G. Algaze, ed., pp. 421–32. Chicago: Oriental Institute Publications.

Marfoe, L., and M. Evins

1990 Area Co1. *In* Town and Country in Southeast Anatolia, Vol. 1 (ch. 2), G. Algaze ed., pp. 119–69. Chicago: Oriental Institute Publications.

Marfoe, L., and M. L. Ingraham

1990 Area A. *In* Town and Country in Southeast Anatolia, Vol. 1 (ch. 1), G. Algaze, ed., pp. 23–118. Chicago: Oriental Institute Publications.

Marquardt, William H.

1978 Advances in Archaeological Seriation. Advances in Archaeological Method and Theory I: 257–313.

Matney, T., and G. Algaze

1995 Urban Development at Mid-Late Early Bronze Age Titris Höyük in Southeastern Anatolia. BASOR 299/300: 33–52.

Matthiae, Paolo

1978 The Excavations at Tell Mardikh-Ebla and Their Historical Value. Annali di Ebla: 18–45.

1979 Ebla in the Period of the Amorite Dynasties and the Dynasty of Akkad: Recent Archaeological Discoveries at Tell Mardikh. MANE 1(16). Malibu, Calif.: Undena Press.

1981 Ebla: An Empire Rediscovered. Garden City, N.J.: Doubleday.

Mazzoni, Stefania

1985 Elements of the Ceramic Culture of Early Syrian Ebla in Comparison with Syro-Palestinian EB IV. Bulletin of the American Schools of Oriental Research 257: 1–17.

McCracken, Grant

1988 Culture and Consumption. Bloomington: Indiana University Press.

Meadow, Richard

1978 Effects of Context on the Interpretation of Faunal Remains: A Case Study. *In* Approaches to Faunal Analysis in the Middle East, R. H. Meadow and M. A. Zeder, eds., Peabody Museum Bulletin 2: 15–21.

Meijer, D. J. W.

1977 The Excavations at Tell Selenkahiye. *In* Le Moyen Euphrate: Zone de Contacts et d'Echanges, J. Cl. Margueron ed., Strasbourg, France: Université des Sciences Humaines de Strasbourg 5: 117–26.

Michalowski, P.

1992 Mari: The View from Ebla. *In* Mari in Retrospect, Gordon Young, ed., pp. 243–8. Winona Lake, Ind.: Eisenbrauns.

Miller, Naomi

1986 Vegetation and Landuse. Anatolica 13: 85–89.

Minc, Leah

n.d. Ceramic Change in the Early Aztec Period: Preliminary Results. Unpublished Manuscript on file at the University of Michigan.

Moortgat, Anton, and Ursula Moortgat-Correns

1975 Tell Chuēra in Nordost-Syrien: Vorläufiger Bericht über die Sechste Gradungskampagne 1973. Berlin: Gebr. Mann Verlag.

Mudar, Karen

1982 Early Dynastic III Animal Utilization in Lagash: A Report on the Fauna of Tell Al-Hiba. Journal of Near Eastern Studies 41: 23–34.

Naroll, R.

1956 A Preliminary Index of Social Development. American Anthropologist 58: 687–715.

Odum, Eugene

1971 Fundamentals of Ecology. Philadelphia: W. B. Saunders.

Orthmann, Winfried

1981 Halawa 1977–79. Bonn: Rudolph Habelt.

1986 The Origins of Tell Chuera. *In* The Origins of Cities in Dry-Farming Syria and Mespotamia in the Third Millennium B.C., Harvey Weiss, ed., pp. 61–70. Guilford, N.J.: Four Quarters.

Özdoğan, Mehmet

1977 Lower Euphrates Basin 1977 Survey. Middle East Technical University Lower Euphrates Project Publications, Series I, 2. Istanbul.

Özgüç, Tahsin

1986 New Observations on the Relationship of Kültepe with Southeast Anatolia and North Syria during the Third Millennium B.C. *In* Ancient Anatolia: Aspects of Change and Cultural Development. Essays in Honor of Machteld J. Mellink, Jeanny Vorys Canby et al., eds., pp. 31–47. Madison: University of Wisconsin Press.

Özten, Aliye
1984 Two Pots Recovered in the Excavations at Samsat Belonging to the Late Chalcolithic Period. Anadolu 20: 267–71.
Palmieri, Alba
1985 Eastern Anatolia and Early Mesopotamian Urbanization. *In* Studi Paletnologia in onore di Salvatore M. Puglisi, Mario Liverani, Alba Palmieri, and Renato Peroni, eds., pp. 191–213. Rome: Università di Roma.
Parsons, James J.
1962 The Acorn-Hog Economy of the Oak Wooklands of Southwestern Spain. The Geographical Review 52: 211–35.
Payne, Sebastian
1973 Kill Off Patterns in Sheep and Goats: The Mandibles from Asvan Kale. Anatolian Studies 23: 281–303.
Peacock, David P. S.
1982 Pottery in the Roman World: An Ethnoarchaeological Approach. London: Longman.
Peebles, Christopher, and Susan Kus
1977 Some Archaeological Correlates of Ranked Societies. American Antiquity 42: 421–47.
Peregrine, Peter
1991 Some Political Aspects of Craft Specialization. World Archaeology 23(1): 1–11.
Pettinato, Giovanni
1981 The Archives of Ebla: An Empire Inscribed in Clay. Garden City, N.J.: Doubleday.
1991 Ebla: A New Look at History. Baltimore: Johns Hopkins Press.
Pinnock, Frances
1984 Trade at Ebla. Bulletin of the Society for Mesopotamian Studies, 7: 9–36.
Pollock, Susan
1983a Style and Information: An Analysis of Susiana Ceramics. Journal of Anthropological Archaeology 2: 354–90.
1983b The Symbolism of Prestige: An Archaeological Example from the Royal Cemetary of Ur. Ph.D. dissertation, University of Michigan. University Microfilms, Ann Arbor.
1985 Chronology of the Royal Cemetery of Ur. Iraq 47: 129–58.
Prag, Kay
1970 The 1959 Deep Sounding at Harran in Turkey. Levant 2: 63–94.
Rappaport, Roy
1968 Pigs for the Ancestors: Rituals in the Ecology of a New Guinea People. New Haven, Conn.: Yale University Press.

Reade, J. E.
1968 Tell Taya (1967): Summary Report. Iraq 30: 234–64.
Redding, Richard
1981a Decision Making in Subsistence Herding of Sheeps and Goats in the Middle East. Ph.D. dissertation, University of Michigan. University Microfilms, Ann Arbor.
1981b The Faunal Remains. *In* An Early Town on the Deh Luran Plain, H. T. Wright, ed., pp. 233–61. Museum of Anthropology, University of Michigan Memoir 13. Ann Arbor.
Redford, Scott
1986 Excavations at Gritille (1982–1984): The Medieval Period. A Preliminary Report. Anatolian Studies 36: 103–36.
Reese, David
1990 Marine and Worked Shells. *In* Town and Country in Southeastern Anatolia, G. Algaze, ed., pp. 410–9. Chicago: Oriental Institute Publications.
Rice, Prudence
1981 Evolution of Specialized Pottery Production: A Trial Model. Current Anthropology 22: 219–40.
1987 Pottery Analysis: A Sourcebook. Chicago: University of Chicago Press.
Rothman, Mitchell S.
1988 Centralization, Administration and Function at Fourth Millennium B.C. Tepe Gawra, Northern Iraq. Ph.D. dissertation, Department of Anthropology, University of Pennsylvania.
Rowlands, Michael
1973 Modes of Exchange and the Incentives for Trade, with Reference to Later European Prehistory. *In* The Explanation of Culture Change: Models in Prehistory, Colin Renfrew, ed., pp. 589–600. London: Gerald Duckworth.
Sahlins, Marshall
1972 Stone Age Economics. New York: Aldine.
Schwartz, Glenn
1988a Excavation at Karatut Mevkii and Perspectives on the Uruk/Jemdet Nasr Expansion. Akkadica 56: 1–41.
1988b A Ceramic Chronology from Tell Leilan Operation I. New Haven, Conn.: Yale University Press.
Schwartz, G., and S. Falconer
1994 Rural Approaches to Social Complexity. *In* Archaeological Views from the Countryside: Village Communities in Early Complex Societies, G. Schwartz and S. Falconer, eds., pp. 1–9. Washington, D.C.: Smithsonian Institution Press.

Scott, Susan

1981 Economic and Organizational Aspects of Deer Procurement During the Late Prehistoric Period. Paper presented at the 38th Annual Meeting of the Southeastern Archaeological Conference, Asheville, North Carolina.

Serdagoğlu, Ümit

1977 Surveys in the Lower Euphrates Basin 1975. Middle East Technical University, Lower Euphrates Project Publications, Series I, no. 1. Ankara, Turkey: Turk Tarih Kurumu Basimevi.

Sheets, Payson

1992 The Ceren Site: A Prehistoric Village Buried by Volcanic Ash in Central America. New York: Holt, Rinehart, and Winston.

Silver, I. A.

1970 The Ageing of Domestic Animals. *In* Science in Archaeology, Don Brothwell and Eric Higgs, eds., pp. 283–302. New York: Praeger.

Sinopoli, Carla

1988 The Organization of Craft Production at Vijayanagara, South India. American Anthropologist 90: 580–97.

1994 Political Choices and Economic Strategies in the Vijayanagara Empire. *In* The Economic Anthropoly of the State, Elizabeth M. Brumfiel, ed., pp. 223–42. Monographs in Economic Anthropology, No. 11. Lanham, Md.: University Press of America.

Stein, Gil J.

1986 A Preliminary Report on Period IV Chipped Stone from Kurban Höyük. Unpublished manuscript on file at University of Virginia.

1987 Regional Economic Integration on Early State Societies: Mid Third Millennium BC Pastoral Production at Gritille, Southeast Turkey. Paleorient 13(2): 101–11.

1988 Pastoral Production in Complex Societies: Mid-Late Third Millennium B.C. and Medieval Faunal Remains from Gritille Hoyuk in the Karababa Basin, Southeast Turkey. Ph.D. dissertation, Department of Anthropology, University of Pennsylvania.

Steponaitis, Vincas

1982 Ceramics, Chronology, and Community Patterns: An Archaeological Study at Moundville. New York: Academic Press.

Thissen, L. C.

1985 The Late Chalcolithic and Early Bronze Age Pottery from Hayaz Höyük. Anatolica 12: 75–130.

Thomas, N.

1991 Entangled Objects: Exchange, Material Culture and Colonialism in the Pacific. Cambridge, Mass.: Harvard University Press.

van der Leeuw, S.

1984 Dust to Dust: A Transformational View of the Ceramic Cycle. *In* The

Many Dimensions of Pottery, S. van der Leeuw and A. C. Prichard, eds., pp. 707–73. Amsterdam: University of Amsterdam.

van Liere, W. J.

1963 Capitals and citadels of Bronze-Iron Age Syria in their relationship to land and water. Les Annales Archaelogiques de Syrie 13: 109–22.

van Loon, Maurits

1979 1974 and 1975 Preliminary Results of the Excavations at Selenkahiye near Meskene, Syria. *In* Excavation Reports from the Tabqa Dam Project-Euphrates Valley, Syria, David Noel Freedman, ed., pp. 97–112. American School of Oriental Research, Cambridge.

Veblen, Thorstein

1934 The Theory of the Leisure Class: An Economic Study of Institutions. New York: The Modern Library.

Verhaaren, Bruce

1986 The Excavations at Kurban Höyük: Cross-Sectional Views. Anatolica 13: 66–76.

Voigt, Mary

1983 Hajji Firuz Tepe, Iran: The Neolithic Settlement. University of Pennsylvania University Museum Monograph, No. 50. Philadelphia: University of Pennsylvania.

Voigt, Mary, and Richard Ellis

1981 Excavations at Gritille, Turkey: 1981. Paleorient 7(2): 87–98.

Watson, Patty Jo

1979 Archaeological Ethnography in Western Iran. Viking Fund Publications in Anthropology, No. 57. Tuscon: University of Arizona Press.

Wattenmaker, P.

1987 The Organization of Production and Consumption in a Complex Society: A Study of a Village Site in Southeast Turkey. MASCA Journal 4: 191–203.

1997 Kazane Höyük, 1995: Excavations of an Early City. Kazı Sonuçları Toplantısı 15(1): 177–92.

Wattenmaker, P., and A. Mısır

1994 Excavations at Kazane Höyük, 1992. Kazı Sonuçları Toplantısı 18(1): 177–92.

Wattenmaker, P., and G. Stein

1986 Early Pastoral Production in Southeast Anatolia: Faunal Remains from Kurban Höyük and Gritille Höyük. Anatolica 13: 90–6.

Weiss, H.

1983 Excavations at Tell Leilan and the Origins of North Mesopotamian Cities in the Third Milennium B.C. Paleorient 9: 39–52.

Weiss, H., et al.

1993 The Genesis and Collapse of Third Millennium North Mesopotamian Civilization. Science 261: 995–1004.

Whallon, Robert

1979 An Archaeological Survey of the Keban Reservoir Area of East-Central Turkey. Memoirs of the Museum of Anthropology, University of Michigan, No. 11. Ann Arbor.

Wilkinson, T. J.

1986 Environmental Change and Local Settlement History. Anatolica 13: 69–76.

1989 Extensive sherd scatters and land-use intensity: Some recent results. Journal of Field Archaeology 16: 31–46.

1990 Town and Country in Southeastern Anatolia, Vol. I. Settlement and Land Use at Kurban Höyük and Other Sites in the Lower Karababa Basin. Chicago: Oriental Institute Press.

1994 Structure and Dynamics of Dry Farming States in Upper Mesopotamia. Current Anthropology 35(5): 483–520.

Winter, Irene

1985 After the Battle is Over: 'The Stele of the Vultures' and the Beginning of Historical Narrative in the Art of the Ancient Near East. *In* Pictoral Narrative in Antiquity and the Middle Ages, H. Kessler, and M. Simpson, eds., pp. 11–32. Washington, D.C.: National Gallery of Art.

Wobst, Martin

1977 Stylistic Behavior and Information Exchange. *In* For the Director: Research Essays in Honor of J. B. Griffin, C. Cleland, ed., pp. 317–42. University of Michigan Museum of Anthropology Anthropological Paper No. 61.

Woolley, C. Leonard

1952 Carchemish III. London: British Museum.

Wright, Henry T. (ed.)

1981 An Early Town on the Deh Luran Plain. Excavations at Tepe Farukhabad. Museum of Anthropology, University of Michigan Memoirs No. 13. Ann Arbor.

Wright, Henry T.

1977 Toward an Explanation of the Origin of the State. *In* Explanation of Prehistoric Change, J. Hill ed., pp. 215–30. Albuquerque: University of New Mexico Press.

Wright, Henry T., and Gregory Johnson

1975 Population, Exchange and Early State Formation in Southwestern Iran. American Anthropologist 77: 267–89.

Wright, Henry T., Naomi Miller, and Richard Redding

1981 Time and Process in an Uruk Rural Center. *In* L'Archeologie de L'Iraq du Debut de l'Epoque Neolithiique à 333 Avant Notre Ere, Marie Therese Barrelet, ed., pp. 265–84. Colloques Internationaux du CNRS, No. 580.

Yakar, Jak

1985 The Later Prehistory of Anatolia: The Late Chalcolithic and the Early Bronze Age. BAR International Series 268 (part ii).

Yananc, Refet, and Mesut Elibüyük

1983 Kanuni Devri Malatya Tahrir Defteri (1560). Ankara, Turkey: Gazi University Press.

Yardımıcı, N.

1990 1989 Yılı Şanlıurfa-Harran Ovası Yüzey Araştırma Sonuçlar Toplantısı 8: 401–18. Ankara, Turkey: T. C. Kültür Bakanliği.

Yener, Aslihan

1990 The Small Finds. *In* Town and Country in Southeastern Anatolia, I: The Stratigraphic Sequence at Kurban Höyük, G. Algaze, ed., pp. 397–419. Chicago: Oriental Institute Publications.

Zeder, Melinda

1985 Urbanism and Animal Exploitation in Southwest Highland Iran, 3400–1500 B.C. Ann Arbor, Mich.: University Microfilms.

1988 Understanding Urban Process through the Study of Specialized Subsistence Economy in the Near East. Journal of Anthropological Archaeology 7: 1–55.

1991 Feeding Cities: Specialized Animal Economy in the Ancient Near East. Washington, D.C.: Smithsonian Institution Press.

Zeuner, Frederick E.

1963 A History of Domesticated Animals. New York: Harper and Row.

INDEX

Note: Page numbers in italics refer to figures and plates.